Tokyo

TRAVEL SKETCHBOOK

Kawaii Culture, Wabi Sabi Design, Female Samurais and Other Obsessions

TUTTLE Publishing

Tokyo | Rutland, Vermont | Singapore

AN
"AMAIA WAS HERE"
PROJECT. JAPAN, 2017

I HAVE NO WORDS
TO DESCRIBE THE
WONDER YOU ARE
ABOUT TO BEHOLD.

Amaia Was Here

In February 2017 I went to Tokyo for a month thanks to the PARADISE AIR organization having awarded me a residency. Part of the project I presented to them, called "Amaia Was Here," consisted in drawing at least one picture a day to create a visual diary of my stay there. I would exhibit these drawings in Japan, as well as in Spain, as a way of building a small bridge between East and West.

When I considered turning "Amaia Was Here" into a publishing project (as in making it a BOOK) I realized I'd need much more material to make it interesting.

This is why you'll see dates on some drawings (those making up "Amaia Was Here") and not on others.

Wabi Sabi

During the time I spent there, I noticed there were two kinds of Japan: two sides of the same coin. The megamodern, supertechnological Japan of neon, fluorescence, Harajuku, Akihabara district, video games... coexists with the Zen Japan of tradition, ceramics, gardens, contact with nature, patience, silence...

Within the latter I found WABI SABI, a term defining the beauty of imperfect things, things that are modest, humble and unconventional.

We don't always have the same level of stability. There are times in life when we're up, and times we feel more lost. In my case, the day I took that flight to Tokyo, February 15th, was one of the latter. As was the entire month, and the one after that, and the one that came after that as well.

The first time I came across the concept of WABI SABI I knew I had found the guiding principle for this book.

In the book with the same title by L. Koren.

TOKYO CITY VIEW
MORI ARTS CENTER

こらづくり会議
会長
堀尾 眞誠

松戸まちづくり会議
千葉県松戸市本町 15-4 ハマトモビル 401
📞 047-364-8832
✉ info@matsudo-artline.com
💻 http://www.matsukai.info

松戸こらづくり会議
副会長
高橋俊夫

松戸まちづくり会議
千葉県松戸市本町 15-4 ハマトモビル 401
📞 080-5090-6840
✉ ttoshi66@ka7.koalanet.ne.jp
💻 http://www.matsukai.info

白河だる

「白河だるま」の起源

　今から約300年前、時の
を習得させ、旧正月14日を
うれています。

DARUMA
instructions

「白河だるま」の特色↓

TOKYO

「るま」の技術
りと言い伝え
ています。)

晁の考による
、びんひげは
い感じが特

願えは必す成就するという縁起
成就した時にもう片方の目を入
い事が特にない場合は両目を入

POO-shaped
gummy

白河だ
佐川だ
〒961-0907
電話 0248-23

Week 1

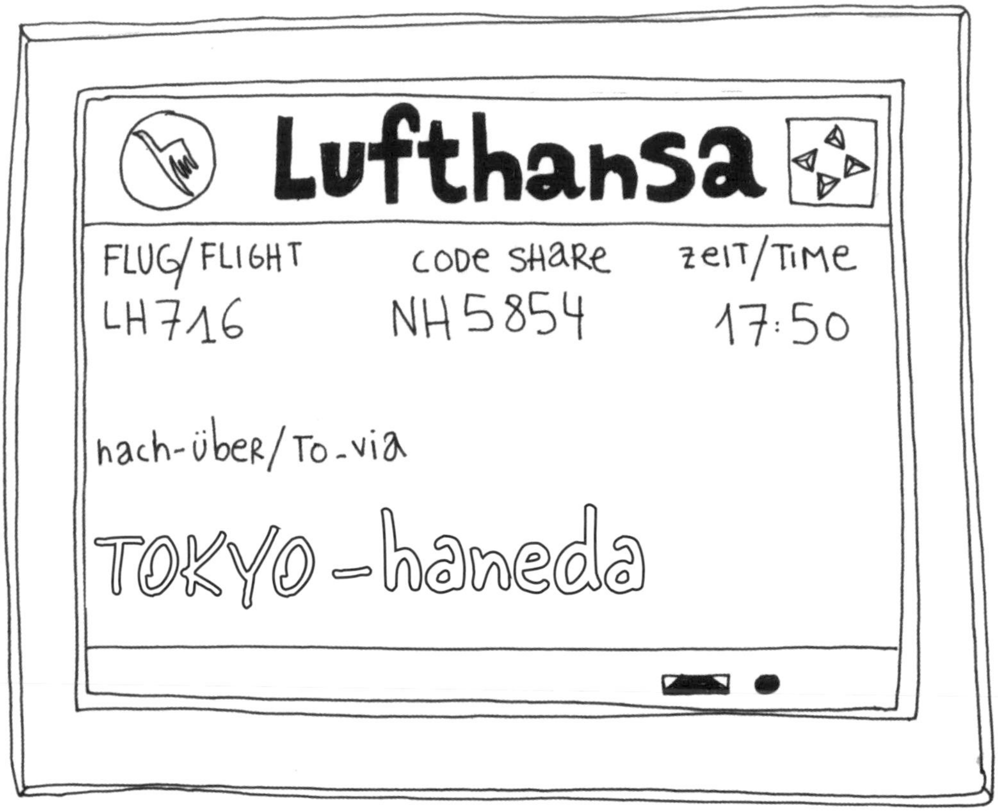
Lufthansa
FLUG/FLIGHT
CODE SHARE
ZEIT/TIME
LH716
NH5854
17:50
nach-über/To-via
TOKYO-haneda

Barcelona – Tokyo flight
with 1 stop in Frankfurt - - - - - - - - ->
12 hours on a plane.

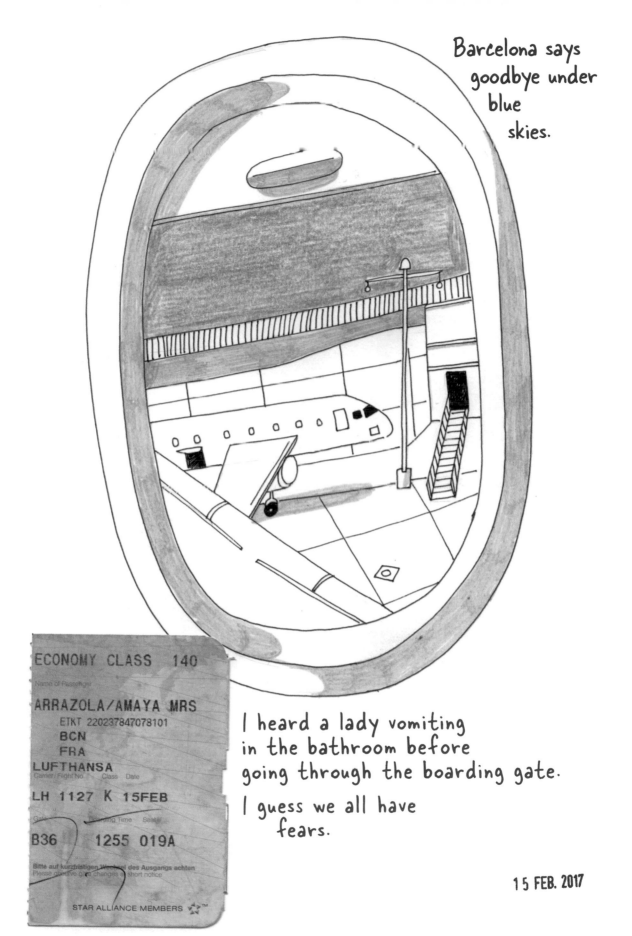

Barcelona says goodbye under blue skies.

ECONOMY CLASS 140
Name of Passenger
ARRAZOLA/AMAYA MRS
    ETKT 220237847078101
        BCN
        FRA
LUFTHANSA
Carrier / Flight No.   Class   Date
LH 1127 K 15FEB
Gate   Boarding Time   Seat
B36   1255 019A
Bitte auf kurzfristigen Wechsel des Ausgangs achten
Please observe gate changes on short notice
STAR ALLIANCE MEMBERS ✱™

I heard a lady vomiting
in the bathroom before
going through the boarding gate.

I guess we all have
        fears.

15 FEB. 2017

46.5 million Spaniards
in 505,370 km^2
or a population of 92.01 per km^2

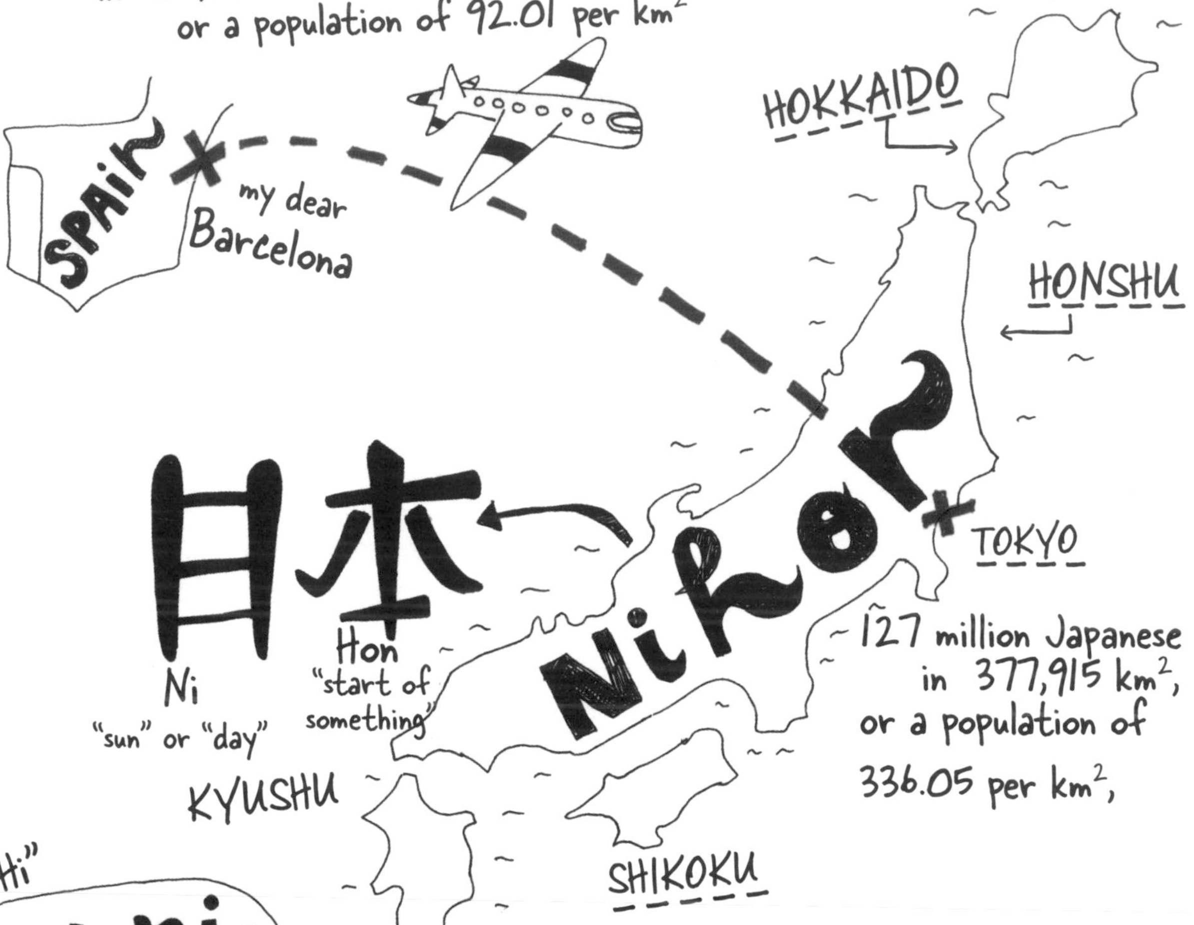
SPAIN
my dear Barcelona
HOKKAIDO
HONSHU
日本
Ni
"sun" or "day"
Hon
"start of something"
Nihon
TOKYO
KYUSHU
SHIKOKU

127 million Japanese
in 377,915 km^2,
or a population of
336.05 per km^2,

"Hi"

konni-chiwa

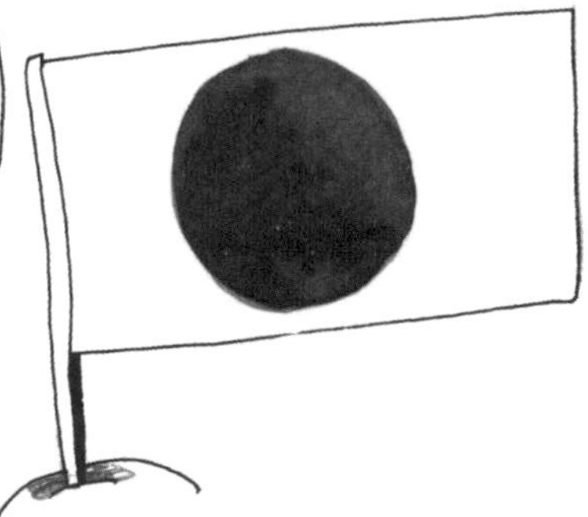

HINOMARU (in Japanese)

Informal "Thanks"

arigato

More formal "Thank you" or "Thank you very much"

ARIGATO GOZAIMASU

The Japanese flag is white with a red circle in the middle. It's a "Sun Disc." The sun is really important in Japan; not for nothing do they call it "Land of the Rising Sun."

(Okay, let me rectify that. The Chinese gave it that name because for them the sun did rise over there.)

Japan's motto is "PEACE and PROGRESS." Very fitting for a country where not bothering your neighbor and working yourself to death are the two pillars of society.

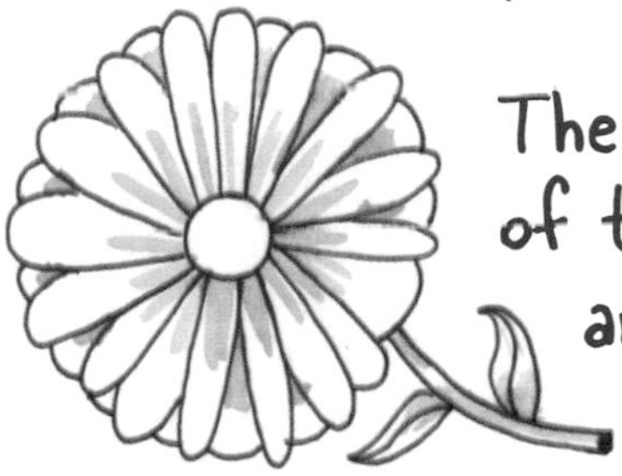

The 16-petal CHRYSANTHEMUM is the symbol of the imperial family, the national coat of arms, and one of the country's oldest symbols.

MOUNT FUJI, the highest peak in all of Japan, is considered a sacred mountain. Traditionally, women weren't allowed to climb to the summit. As an active volcano, it poses little risk. Super touristy.

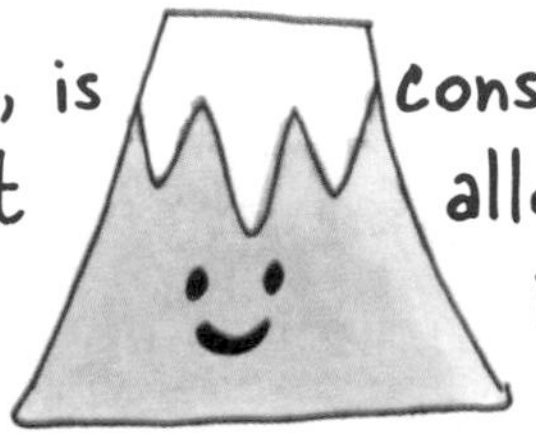

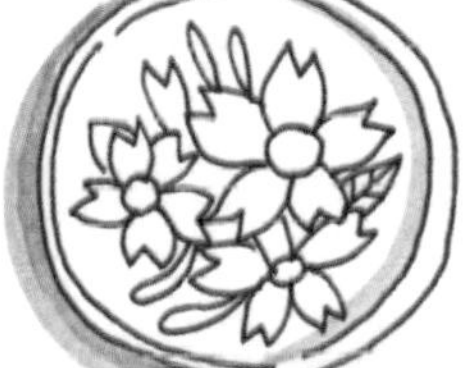

Japan's currency is the YEN. The 100-yen coin has a cherry blossom (another HUGE Japanese symbol) and the 5-yen coin has a little hole in the middle like the old 25-peseta coins.

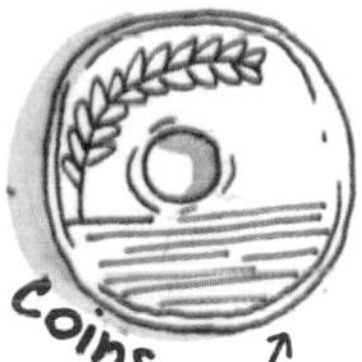

The TEA CEREMONY, a very Japanese ritual that truly represents the character of the country, comes from Zen Buddhism, and is basically this: serving green tea or matcha to guests in accordance with certain rules.

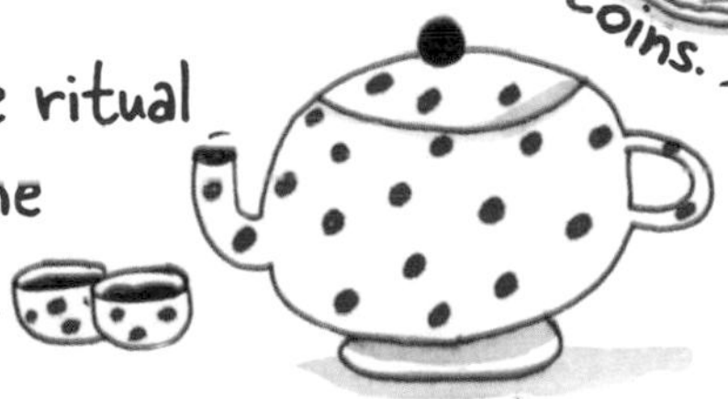

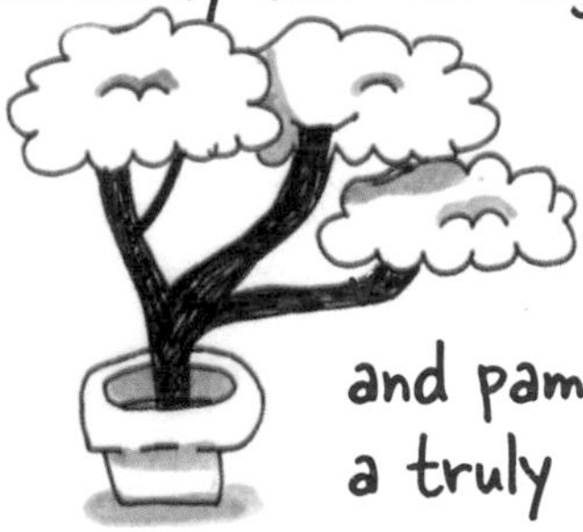

BONSAIS, which I thought were little planted branches, are mini trees that are taken care of and pampered. There are competitions, and caring for them is a truly an art form.

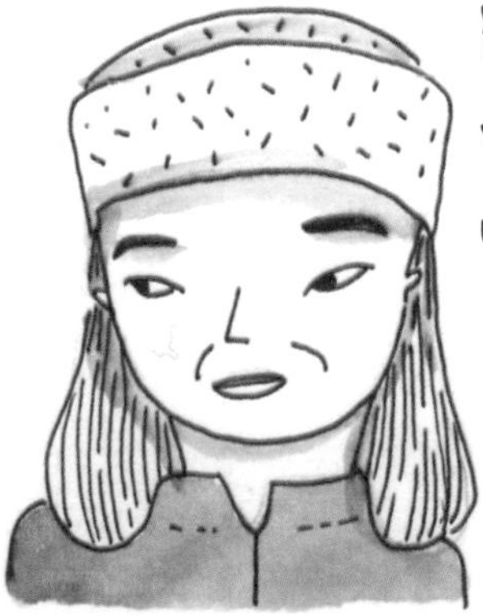

PRINCESS MASAKO was diagnosed in 2003 with severe depression, they say due to being unable to produce a male heir. In Spain they call her the "trapped butterfly." She's had tons of fertility treatments and suffered a miscarriage. With all that pressure, I'd be depressed too ☹

The buildings in Tokyo seem to be made of piles of small cages. Cages where people live alongside their dreams, their lives, their stories...

Buildings that are like concrete and glass giants.

My housing, courtesy of the residency awarded me, is in <u>Matsudo</u>, Chiba Prefecture. This enormous bedroom community has a population of almost 500,000.

Tokyo

Matsudo

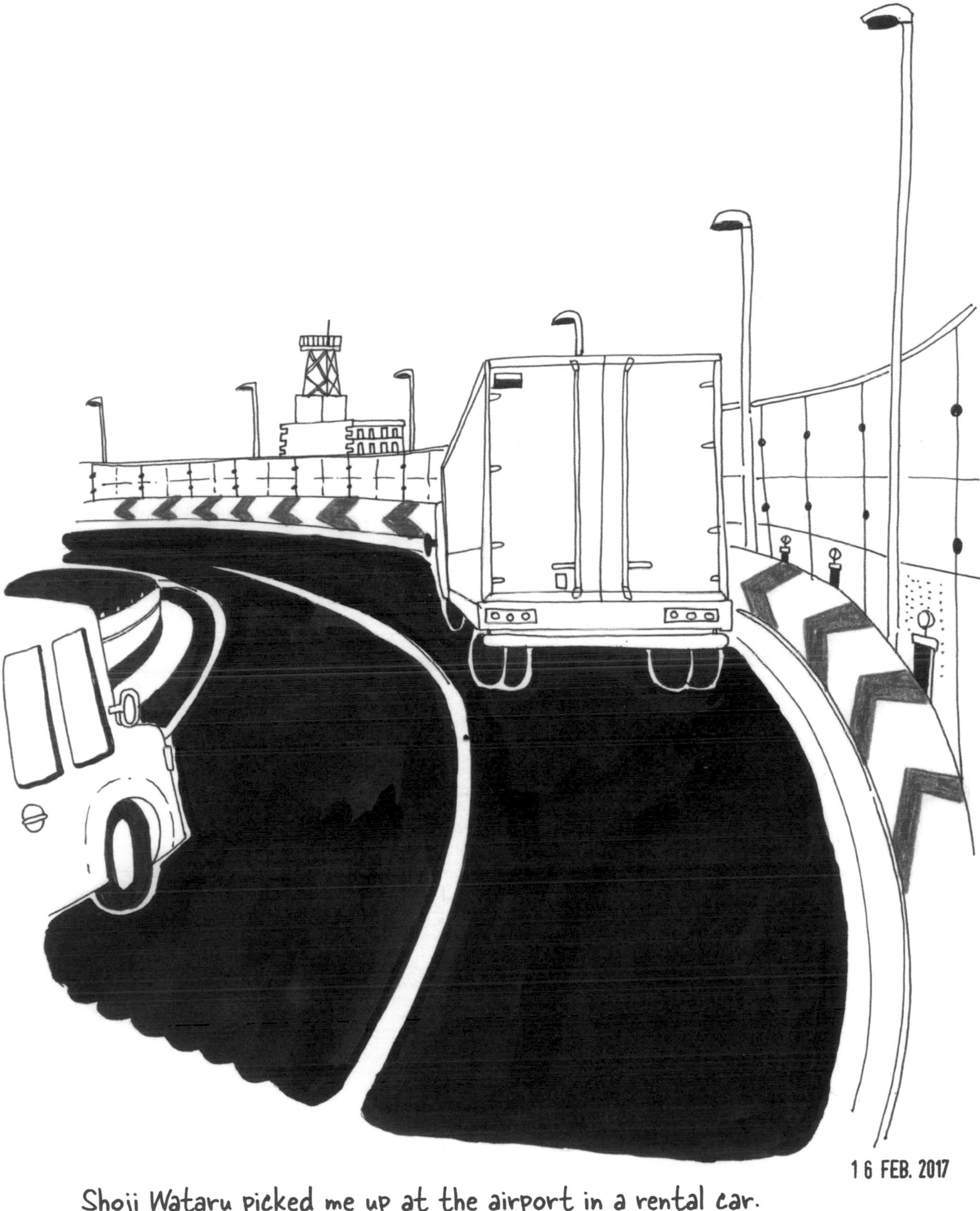

16 FEB. 2017

Shoji Wataru picked me up at the airport in a rental car.

Residency Manager.

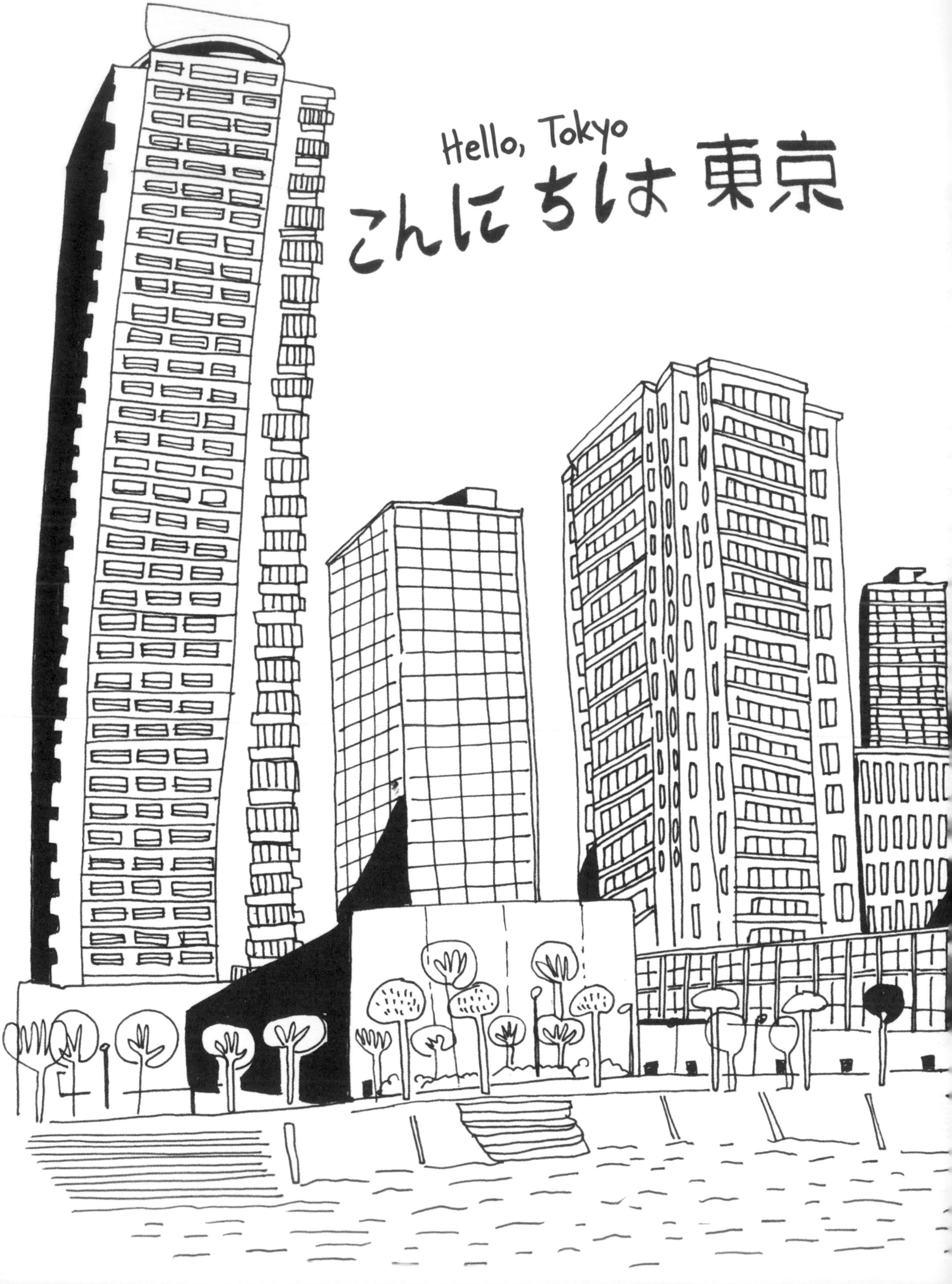
Hello, Tokyo
こんにちは 東京

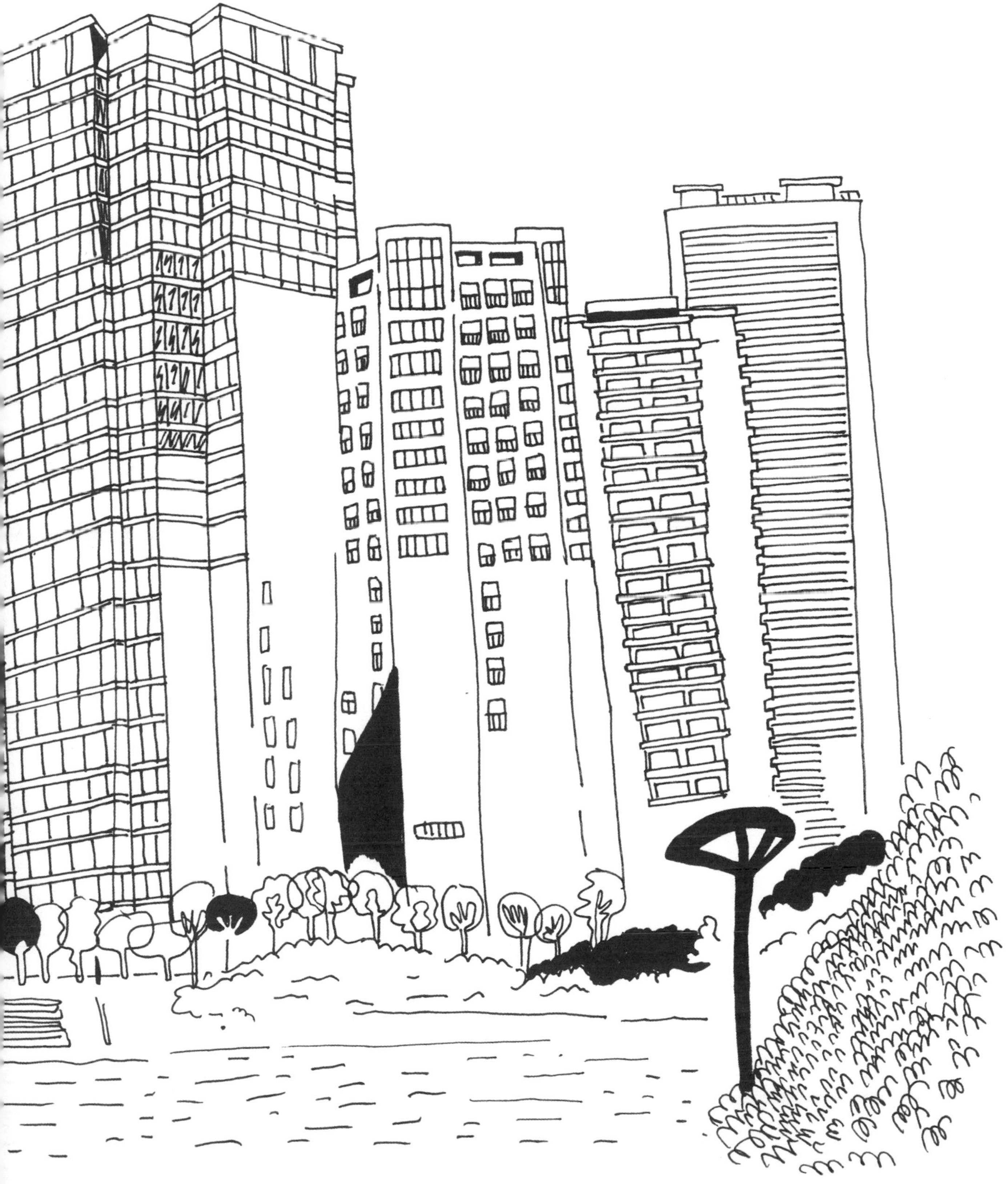

I arrive at PARADISE AIR in Matsudo.

Following an ancient tradition in this city, housing is exchanged for artwork.

Shoji and Junpei take in artists who in turn leave something they've done for Matsudo.

That would be me.

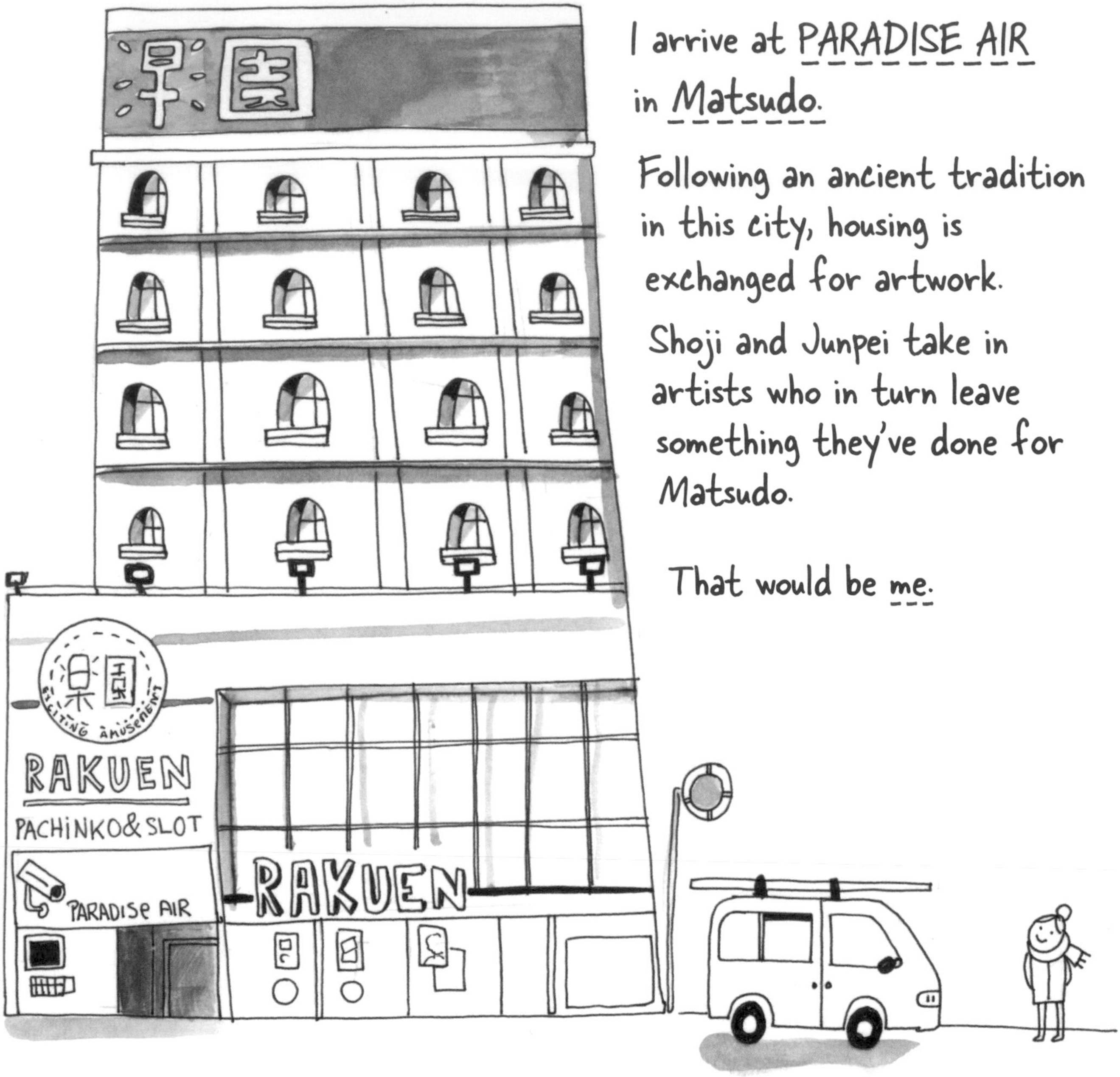
EXCITING AMUSEMENT
RAKUEN
PACHINKO&SLOT
PARADISE AIR
RAKUEN

The Residence is an old LOVE HOTEL (differentiated from business hotels in that couples use them to have sexual intercourse). The whole project is sponsored by a pachinko company (a crazy Japanese fad, a game of chance I don't understand that is played in places that test the limits of your senses of hearing, sight and smell).

ALL NOISE. ALL LIGHTS.

WELCOME TO JAPAN!!!...

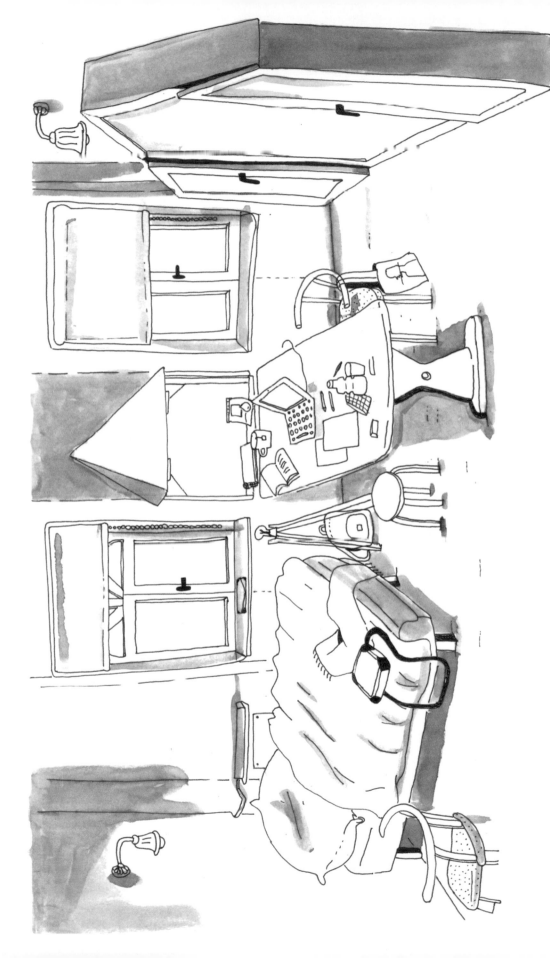

And this is my room...

17 FEB. 2017

These little demons are pachinko mascots,
and the residency is called PARADISE AIR ...

My room is on the 4th floor. On floor 2/3 there's a door that
connects to the pachinko parlor. When I walk by it I can hear the
noise from hundreds of slot machines filtering through the crack.
The floor is orange from the cigarette smoke that gets through.
It's like the door to hell.

18 FEB. 2017

The units of time used in Japan are **eras**, or **nengō**. One era lasts as long as its emperor who, when he dies or abdicated, takes the name of the era. So Emperor Akihito, when he stepped down in 2019, became Emperor Heisei.

Major PERIODS and ERAS

HEIAN PERIOD (794–1192)

This was the classical Japan of the arts, and the peak of the imperial court. "Heian" means PEACE and TRANQUILITY.

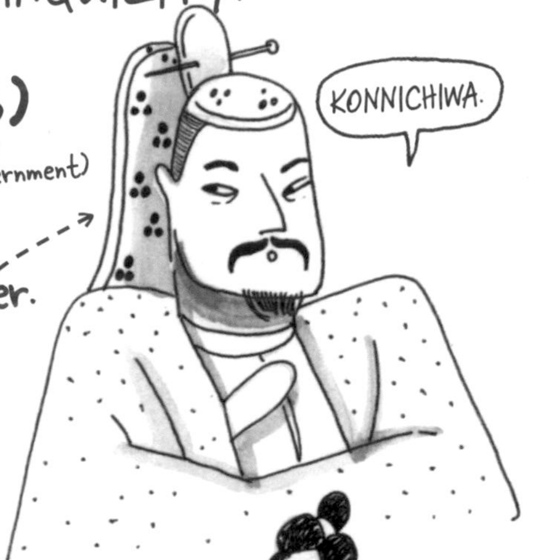
KONNICHIWA.

KAMAKURA PERIOD (1192–1333)

The figure of the emperor disappears, the samurais arrive and the first shogunate (military government) is installed. Minamoto no Yoritomo was the founder.

SENGOKU PERIOD (1468–1568)

Marked by war.

EDO PERIOD (1603–1867)

This is the longest era. The shogun continues to command until the emperor is reinstated.

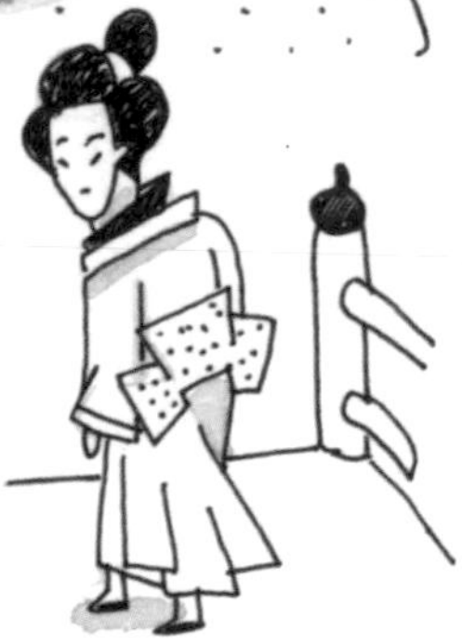

MEIJI ERA (1868–1912)

The emperor returns. This is the birth of the "modern Japan" we know.

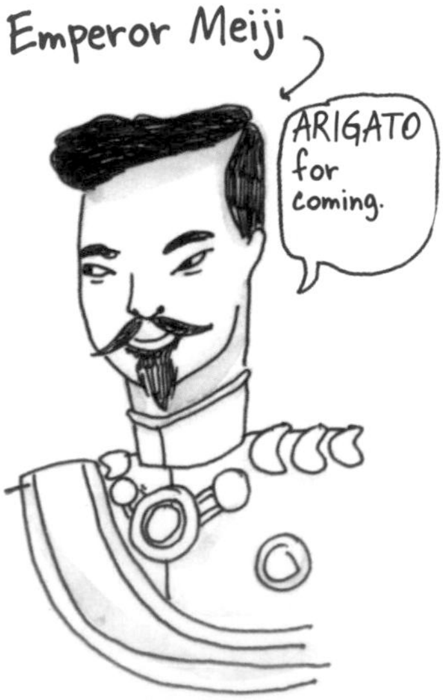
Emperor Meiji
ARIGATO for coming.

TAISHŌ ERA (1912–1926)

SHŌWA ERA (1926–1989)

HEISEI ERA (1989–2019)

REIWA ERA TODAY!

In Japan the era comes first, then the year within the era. So in the Japanese calendar, the year 2017 is Heisei 29.
I was born in 1984, so I'm from Shōwa 59.
(It feels strange to think I'm from another era...)

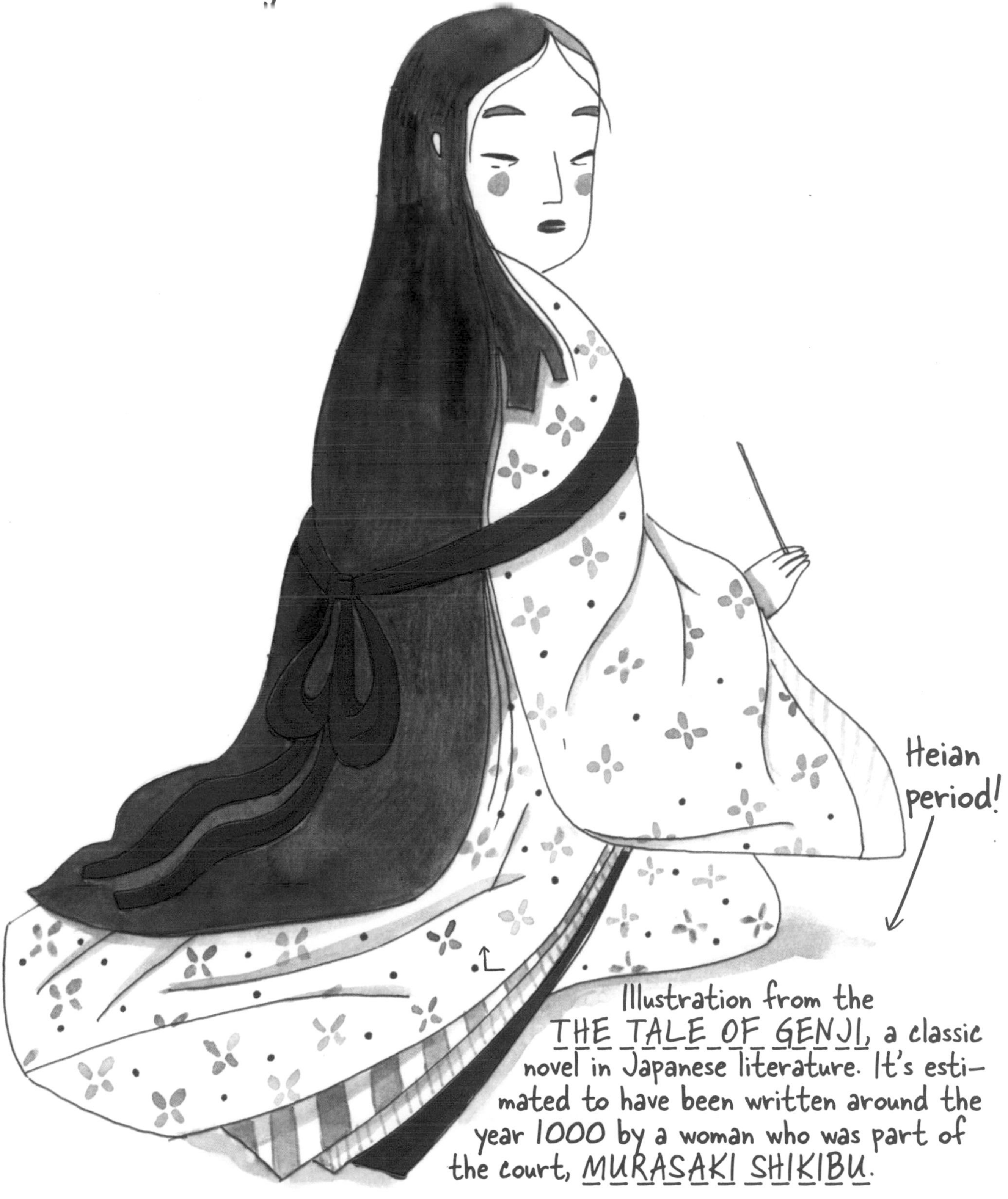
Heian period!

Illustration from the THE TALE OF GENJI, a classic novel in Japanese literature. It's estimated to have been written around the year 1000 by a woman who was part of the court, MURASAKI SHIKIBU.

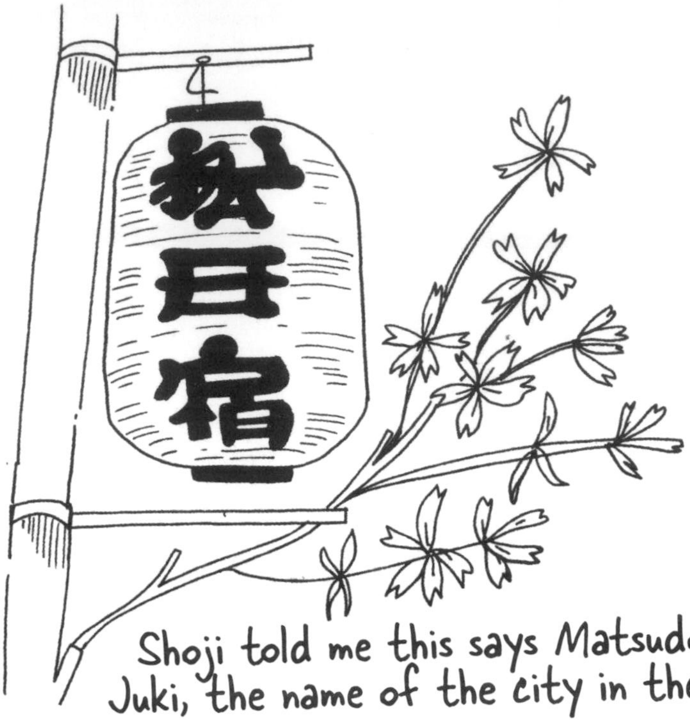
松戸宿

Shoji told me this says Matsudo Juki, the name of the city in the Edo period.

Dragon fountain in the Matsudo temple.

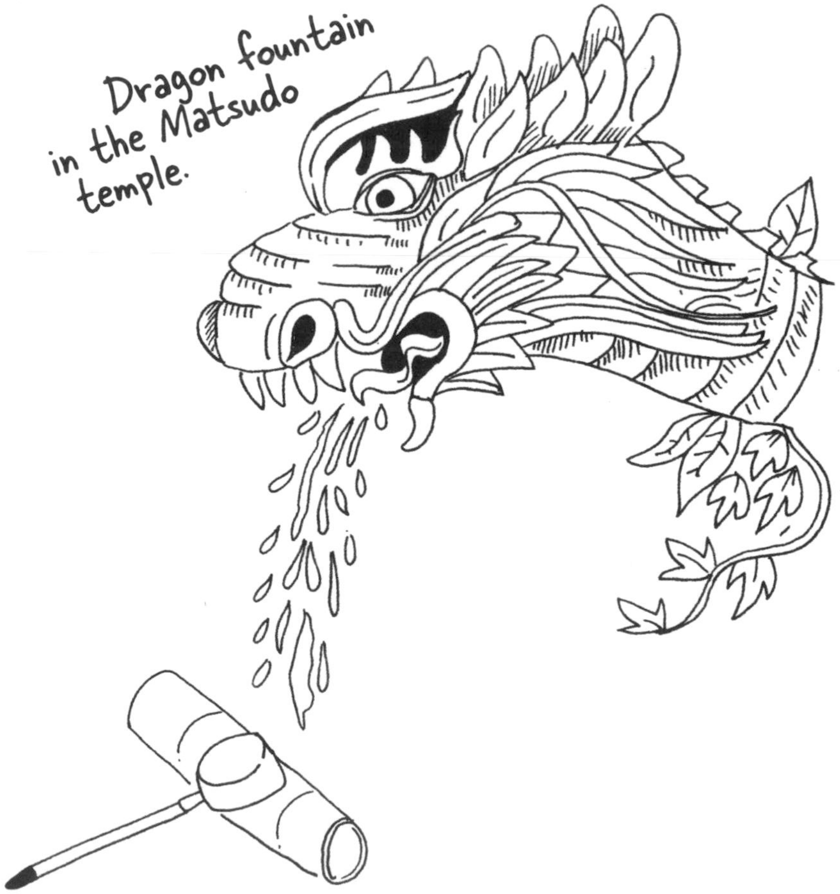

Killer jetlag. You don't sleep at night and you're a zombie by day.

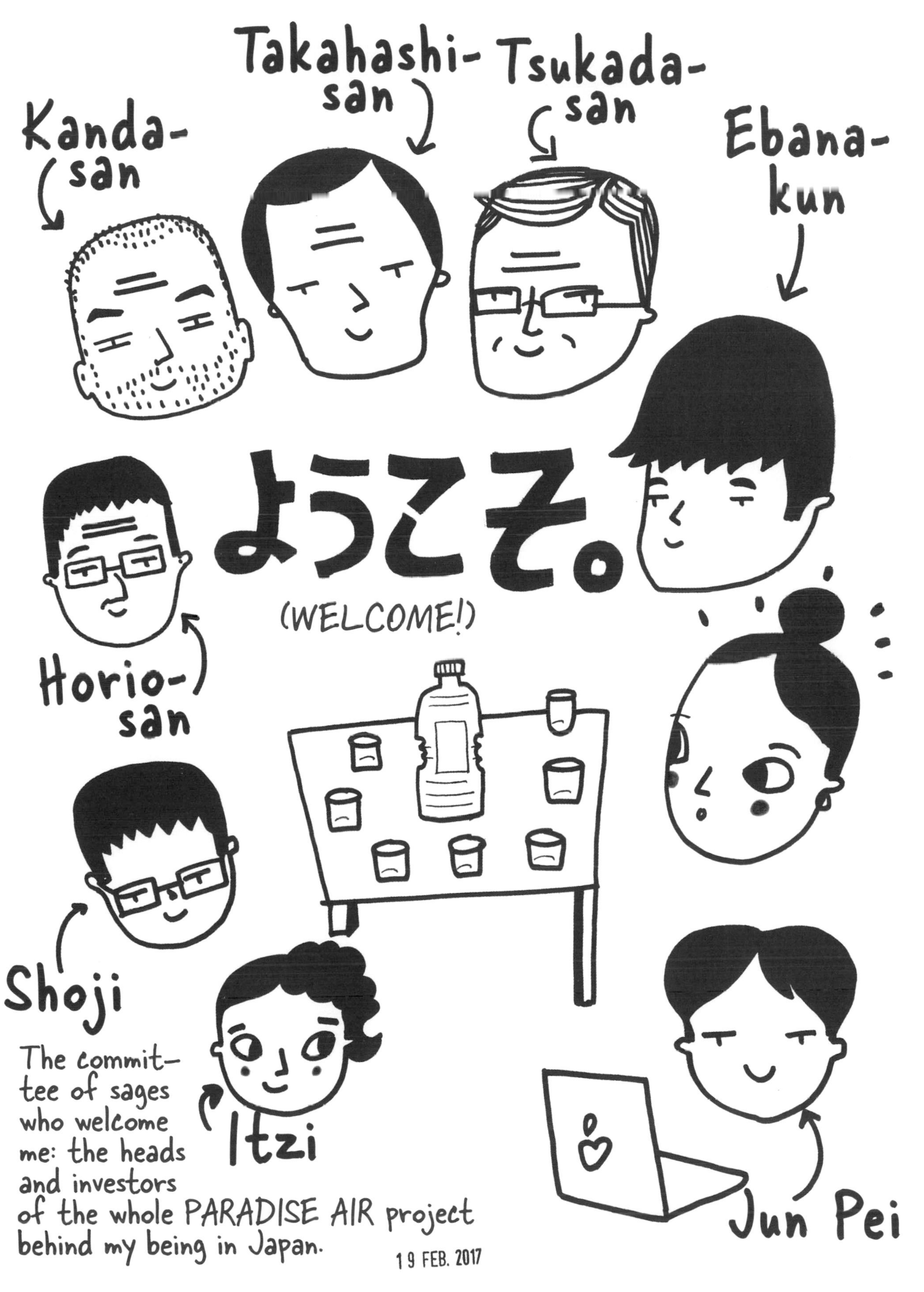
Takahashi-san
Tsukada-san
Kanda-san
Ebana-kun
ようこそ。
(WELCOME!)
Horio-san
Shoji
Itzi
Jun Pei
The committee of sages who welcome me: the heads and investors of the whole PARADISE AIR project behind my being in Japan.
19 FEB. 2017

Here's a secret:
 I bought myself a daruma. It's
about 5 inches (12 cm) high.
I drew in its pupil and told myself
that the day this book comes out,
the day I see it published, I'll draw
the other one.

Since then I've had it with me,
 patiently watching me.

DARUMA

Daruma dolls are figurines with no arms or legs. They're based on Bodhidharma, a fellow who, according to legend, meditated in a cave so long that his limbs fell off. The thing is, you buy them with no eyes. You make a wish or set yourself a challenge, then you draw in a pupil. When you get your wish, you make another one, then you draw in the other pupil.

...🌀   🌀...

You put it where you can see it to remember you have this goal to reach.

It's a symbolic representation of OPTIMISM, PERSISTENCE and DETERMINATION.

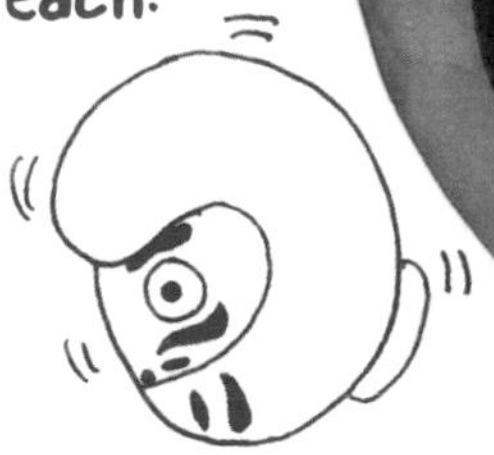

...

It's a great idea, because the egg shape rights itself whenever it falls over. That's why it tends

NANAKOROBI YAOKI

"fall 7 times, GET UP 8."

to come with this phrase.

Shoji took me to a Daiso: a superstore where everything costs 100¥ / 200¥ / 300¥. I bought this Mount Fujis plate. Very Japan. The little ball there is a mochi. I thought it was adorable, but I didn't like it at all when I tried it.

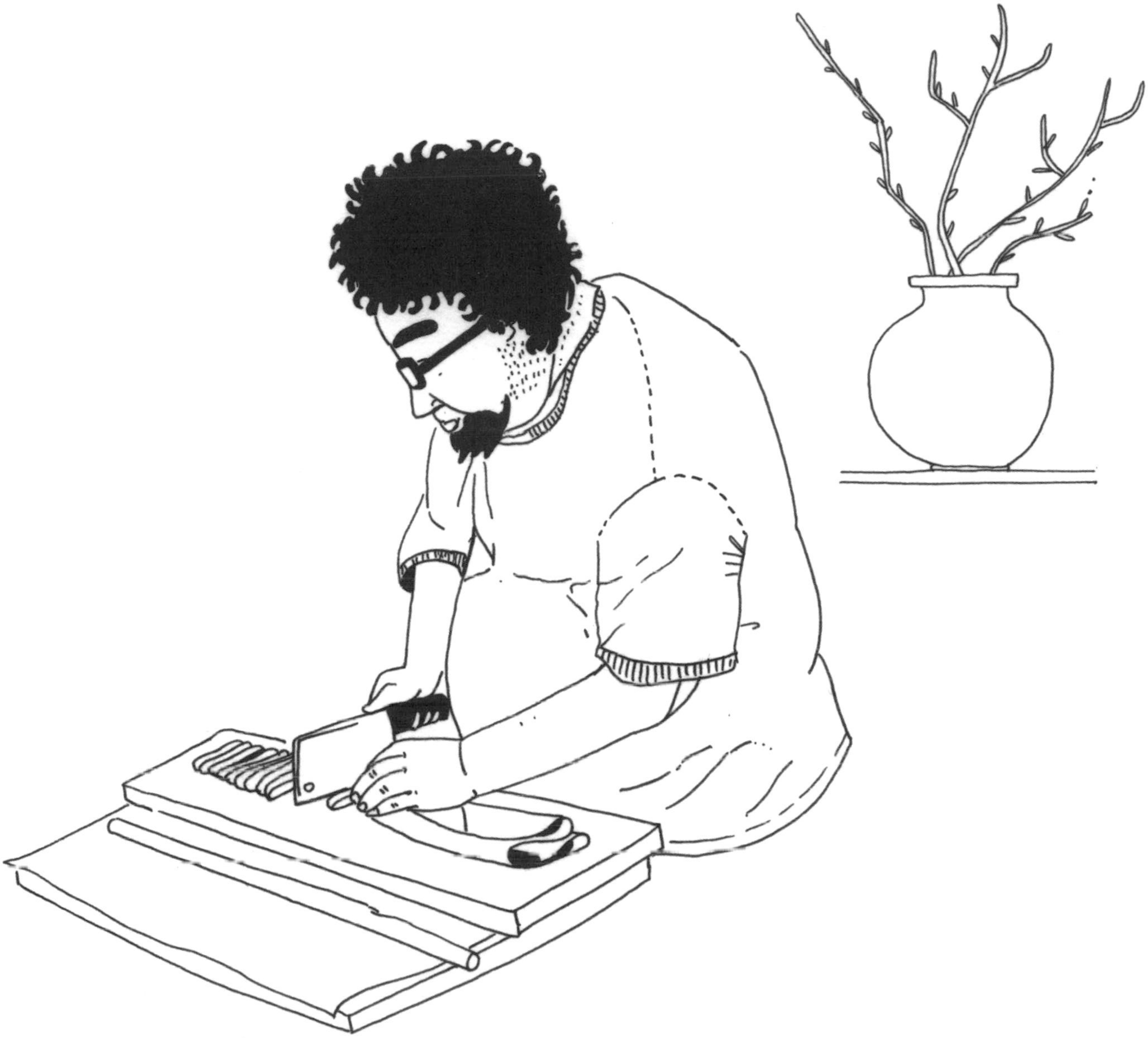

A guy makes ramen noodles by hand.

2 1 FEB. 2017

Izakaya are Japanese pubs. You can ask for things to drink and to eat. Some are more Western, while others have traditional Japanese furnishings, with tatami mats, low tables and that kind of thing. These are typical after-work spots.

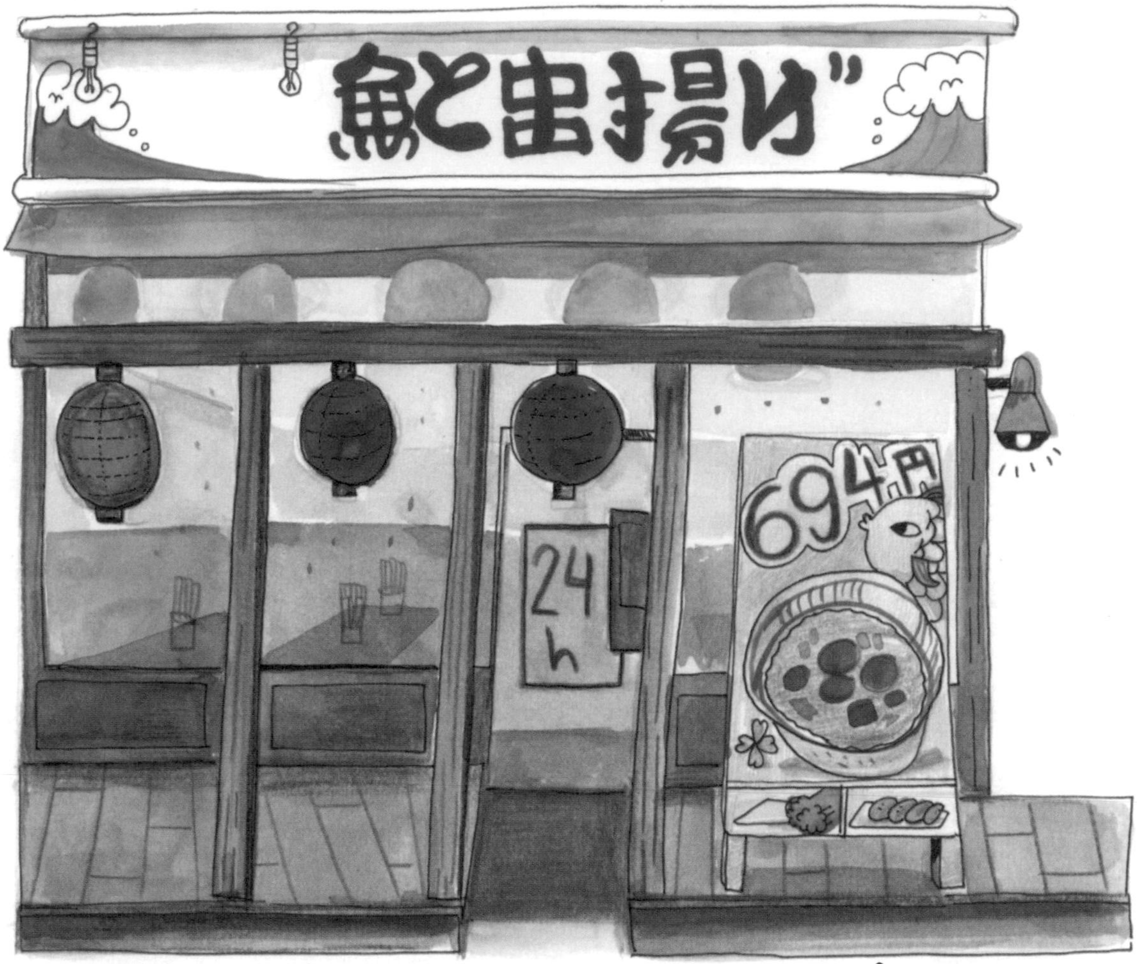

魚と串揚げ
24 h
694円

I like it because they serve a lot of small dishes. They date back to the EDO period, when sake was sold by the liter and they began offering meals to people who drank in front of the store.

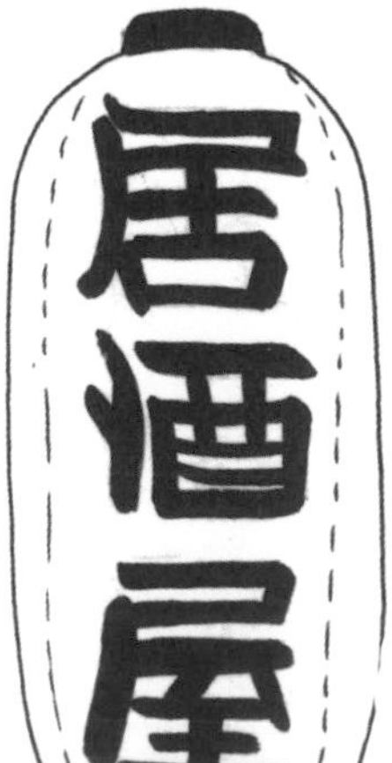

居酒屋

Red AKA CHŌCHIN lantern, a sign for this kind of bar.

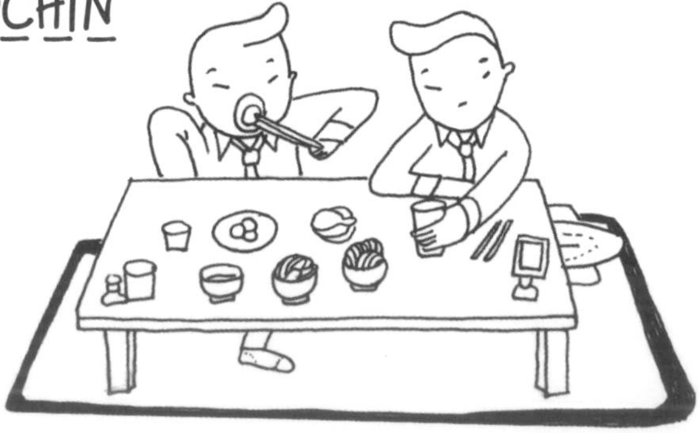

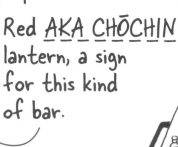

Ramen restaurants are all over the place. Some are better than others. There are usually lines, but they move quickly because people order, sit, eat, slurp and leave.

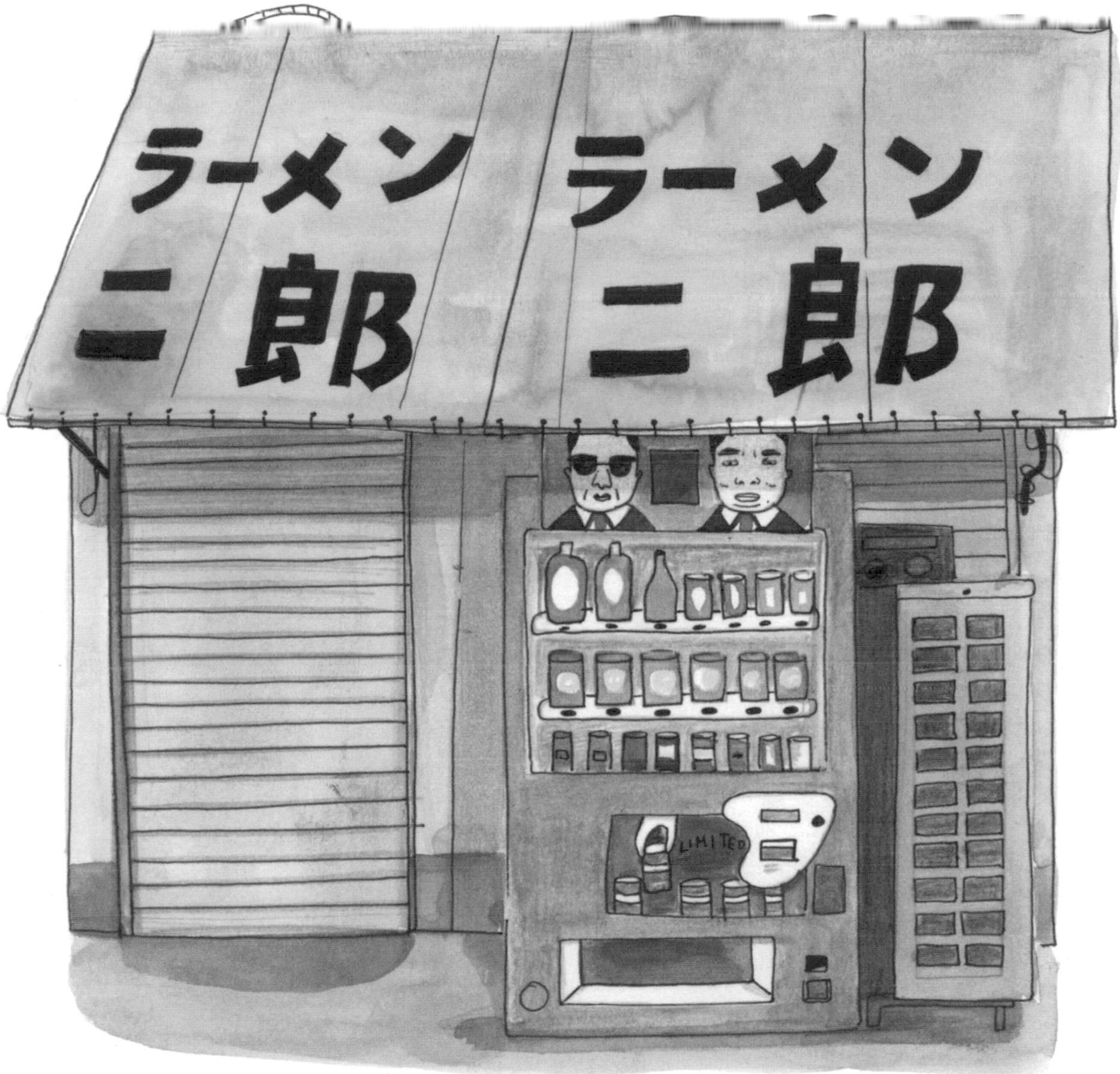
ラーメン ラーメン
二郎 二郎
LIMITED

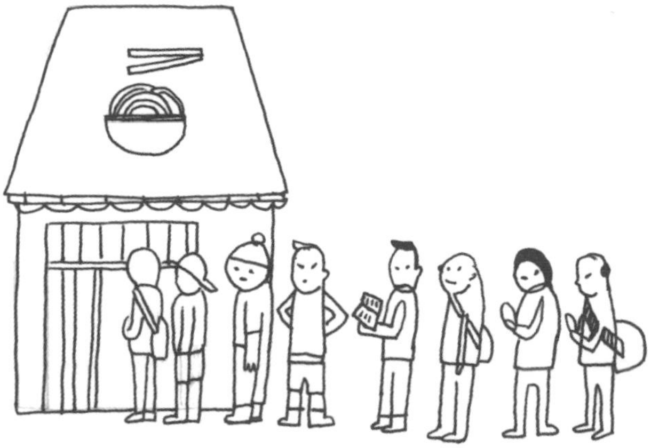

I've discovered that the number of people in line is directly proportional to how good the ramen is.

When I got to Japan I had the idea that I would be eating sushi and maki all day. I thought the Nippon diet was basically raw fish, but... no! They eat every-thing. A lot of rice, that's true, in different styles, like **ONIGIRI** or **SUSHI**, which is bite-size finger food. Then there are other hot dishes, like the famous **RAMEN**. A broth that tends to be fish- or miso- or meat-based with Chinese-style wheat noodles topped with little things: egg, veggies...

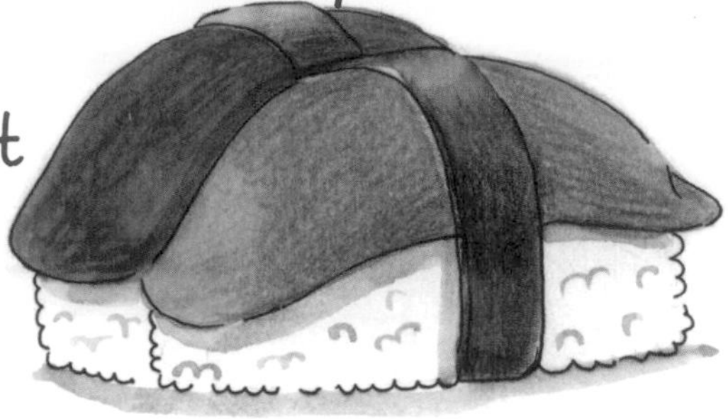

TONKATSU is breaded pork eaten by itself or with rice.

Although we don't consider it polite to <u>SLURP</u>, ramen has to be eaten that way in order to capture ALL the flavor.

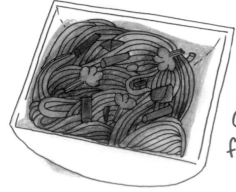

YAKISOBA is a plate of noodles, usu-ally wheat. They're fried and eaten dry (unlike ramen). The special flavor comes from yakisoba sauce.

BENTO is a serving of take-out more than a meal in itself. It's a typical lunch for the working class. Usually with rice, meat or fish, and a side of vegetables. It's like a Japanese lunchbox. Japanese people almost always prepare their bento at home, but you can also buy it packaged.

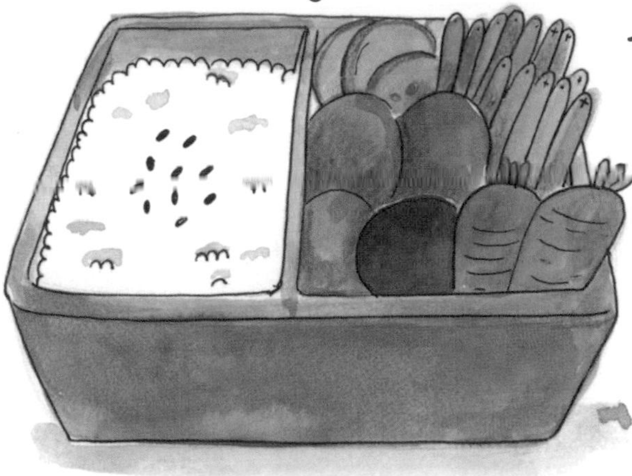

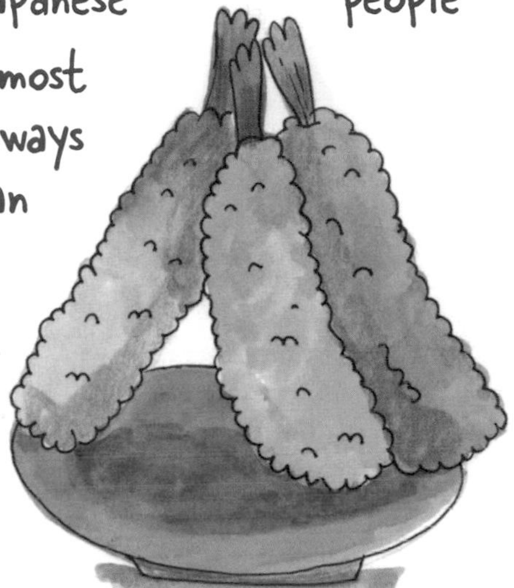

TEMPURA is batter-fried vegetables or seafood. The origin is Portuguese, from the time when missionaries didn't eat meat because it was Lent. It quickly became popular throughout the country.

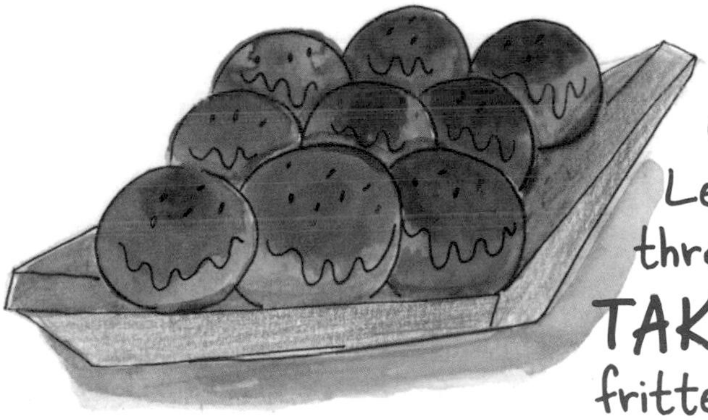

TAKOYAKI is a kind of wheat fritter filled with octopus. For eating in the street.

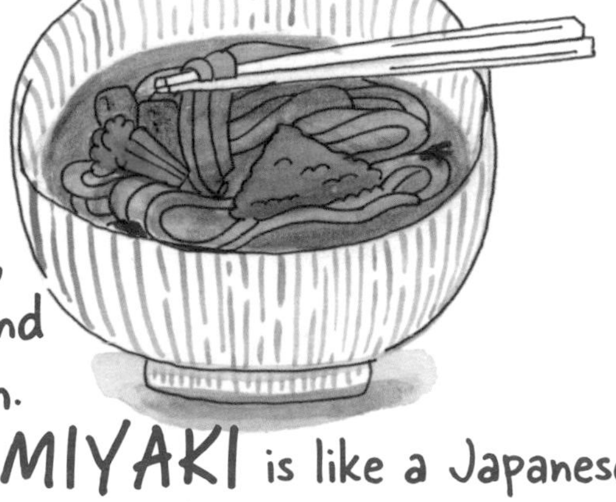

UDON is a fat wheat-flour noodle served in dashi, soy sauce and mirin broth.

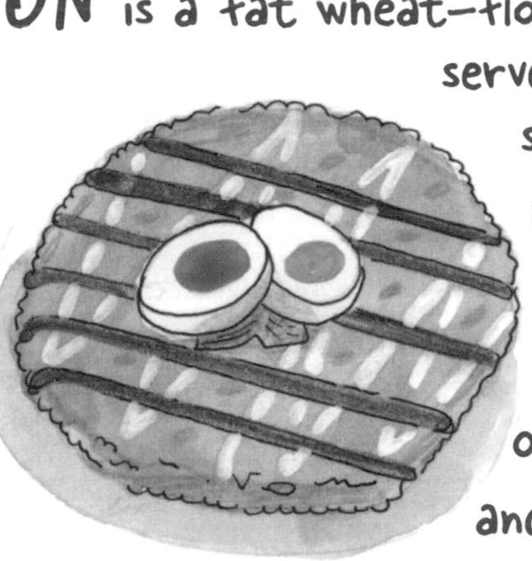

OKONOMIYAKI is like a Japanese omelet with a ton of veggies and meat or fish. The key is the okonomiyaki sauce and Japanese mayonnaise.

In Japan, thanks to Kawaii culture and its cuteness aesthetic, there are coffee shops where they serve you matcha tea with a Hello Kitty in floating foam.

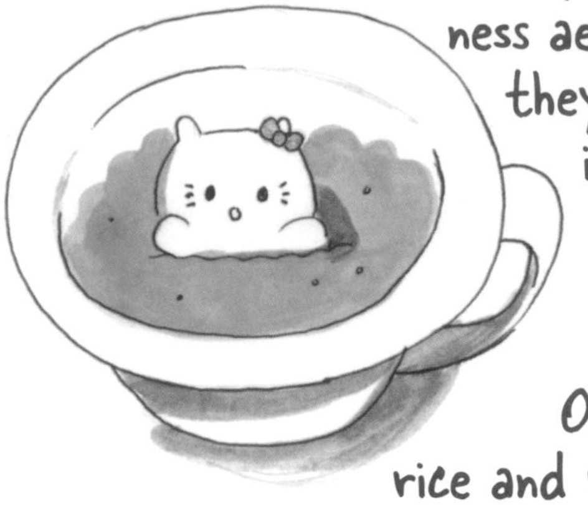

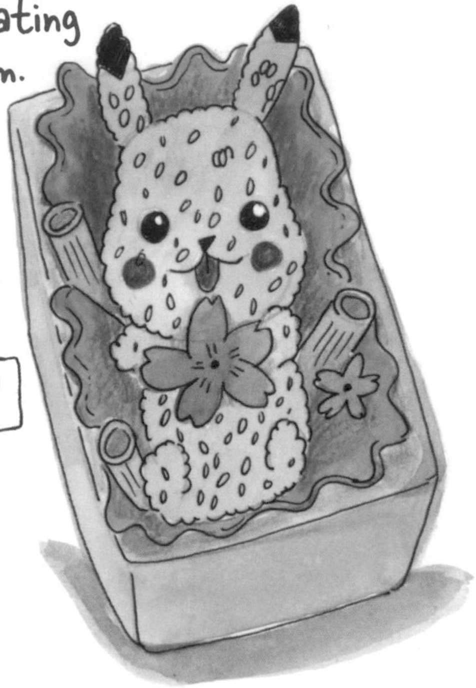

Or rice and pasta bento with a smiley Pikachu to greet you.

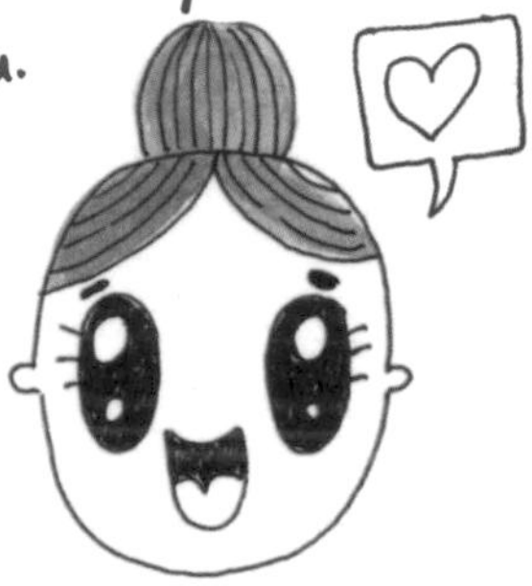

In the spring, some snack bars get out the special SAKURA:

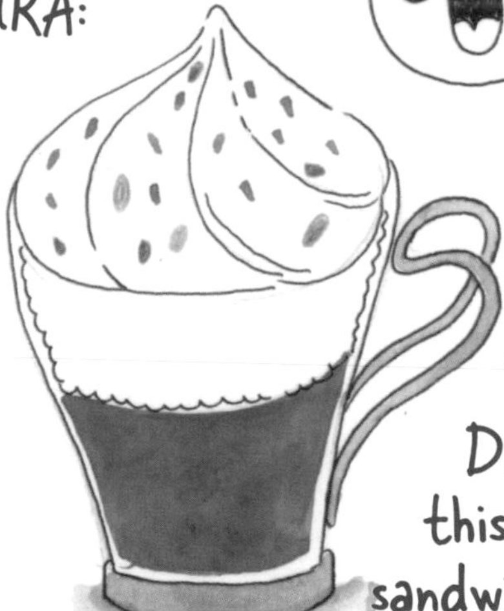

A PINK coffee (call it coffee, call it whatever) whose color makes reference to the cherry blossom season. The "oddest" thing I've ever seen was in a Daiei supermarket: this spaghetti sandwich with corn and tomato sauce.

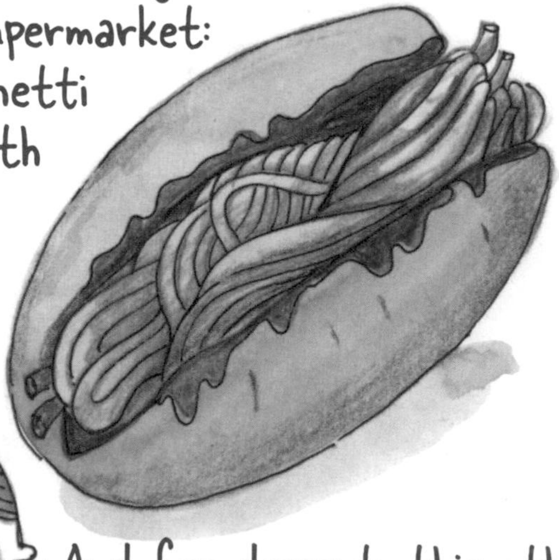

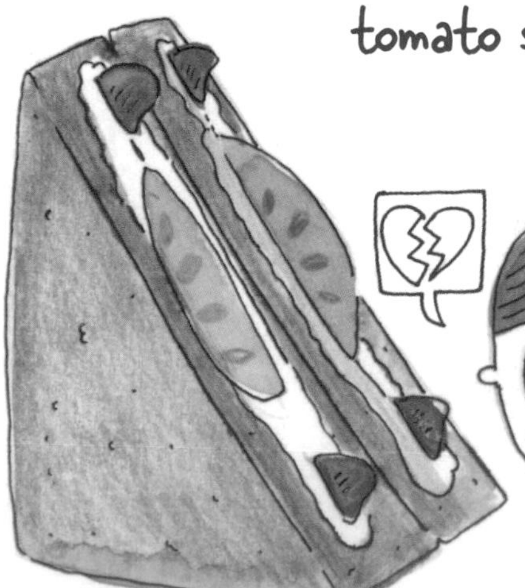

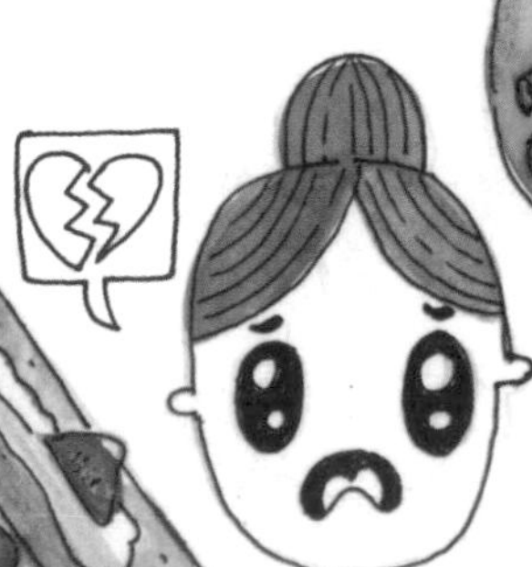

And for dessert, this other sandwich filled with cheese, kiwi and orange.
(Boo-ya.)

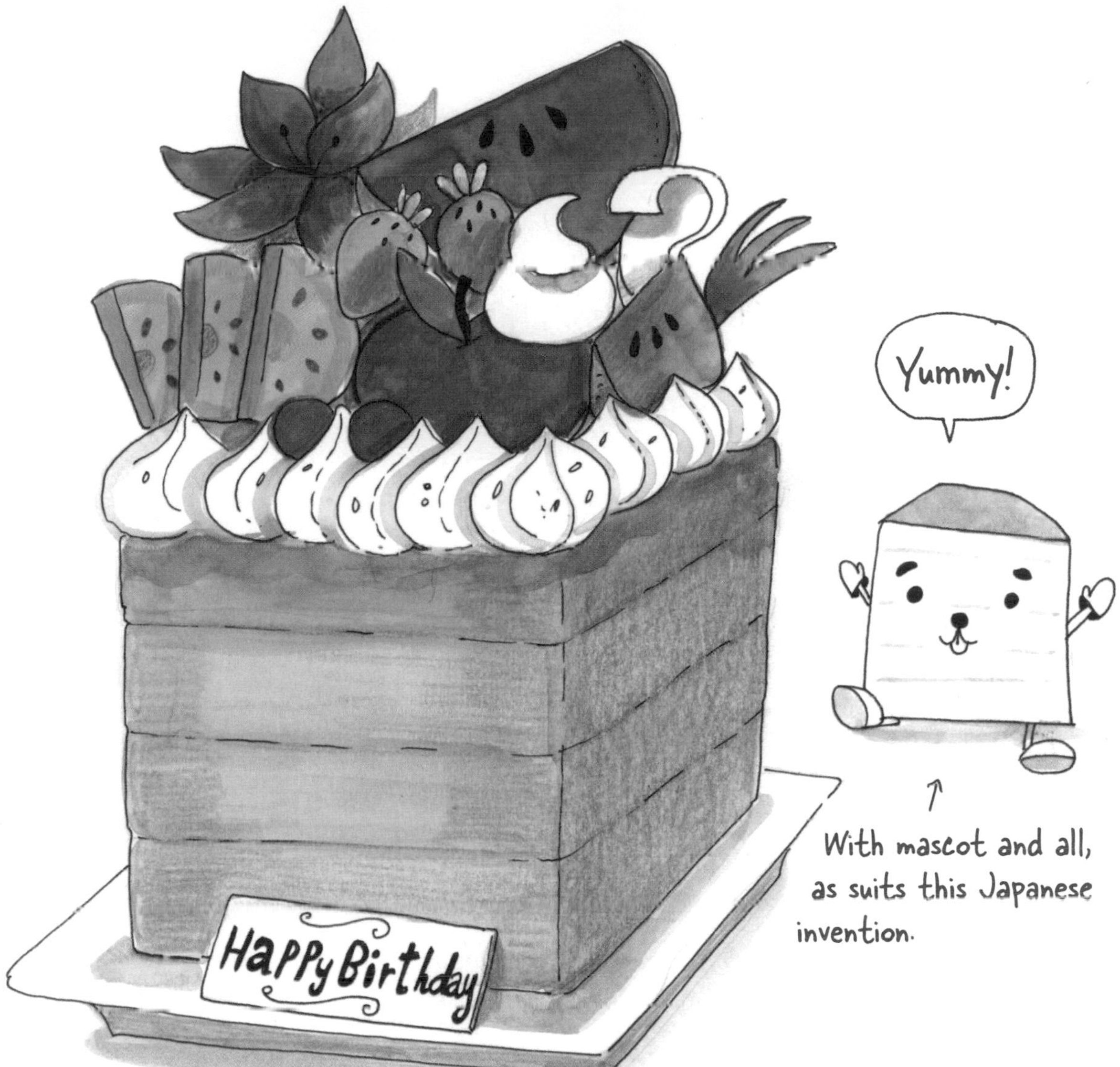
Happy Birthday
Yummy!
With mascot and all, as suits this Japanese invention.

Taking the cake is this sliced bread cake I saw in a shop window in Shibuya.

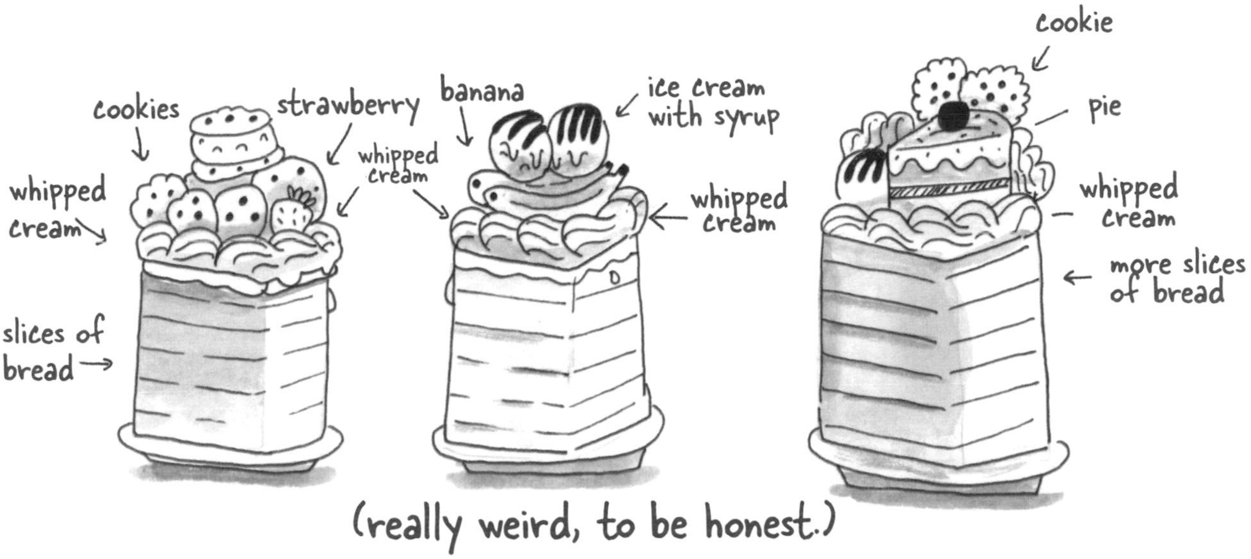
cookies
strawberry
whipped cream
whipped cream
slices of bread
banana
ice cream with syrup
whipped cream
cookie
pie
whipped cream
more slices of bread

(really weird, to be honest.)

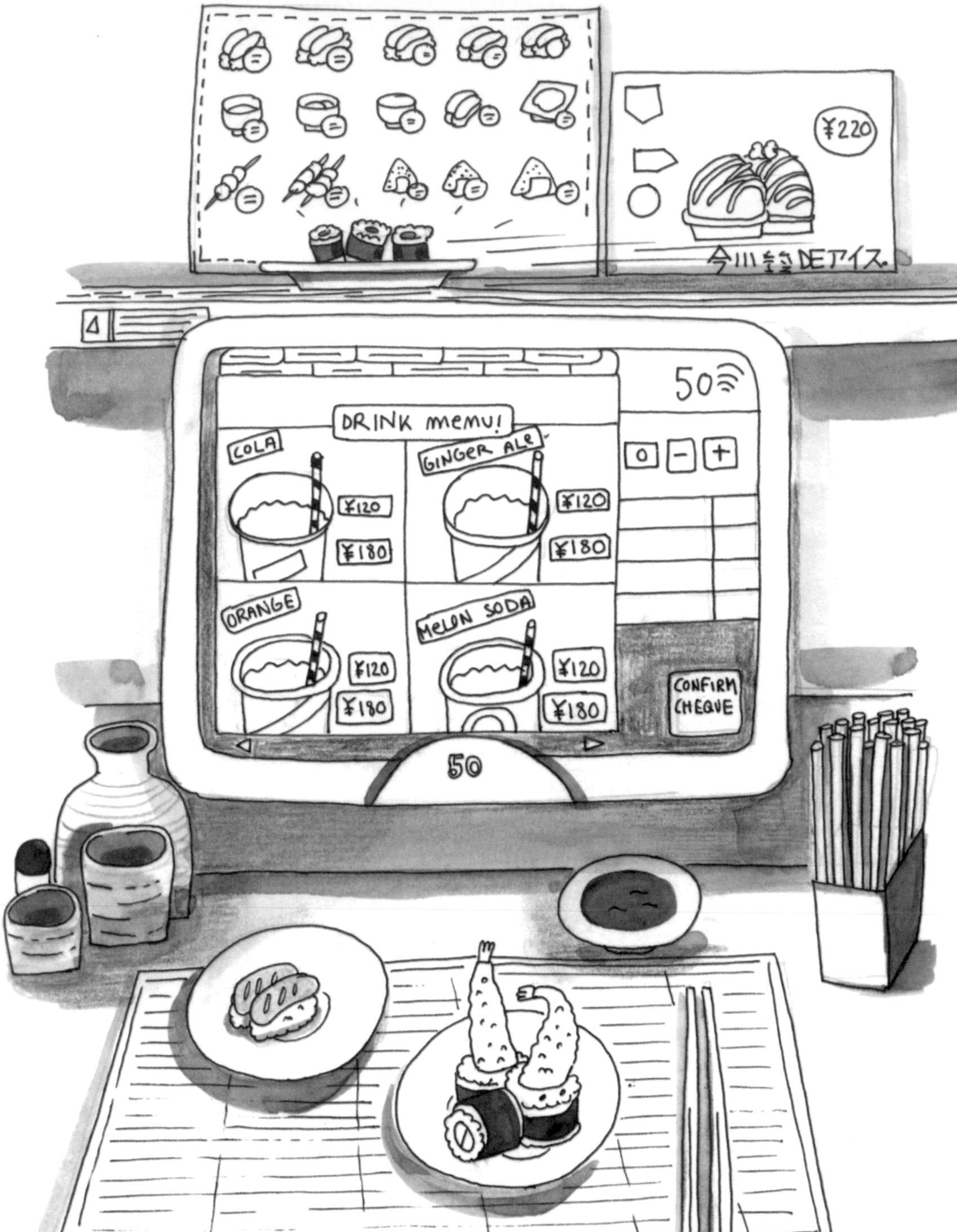
¥220
DRINK memu!
COLA
GINGER ALE
¥120
¥180
¥120
¥180
ORANGE
MELON SODA
¥120
¥180
¥120
¥180
50
CONFIRM CHEQUE
50

(They say only men prepare sushi because they have colder hands than women.)

I was in a restaurant in Shibuya where you sit in front of a screen, select what you want, and the food arrives on a kind of conveyor belt right to your seat. You deal with no one.

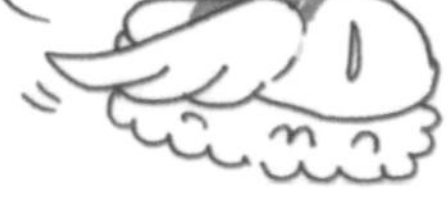

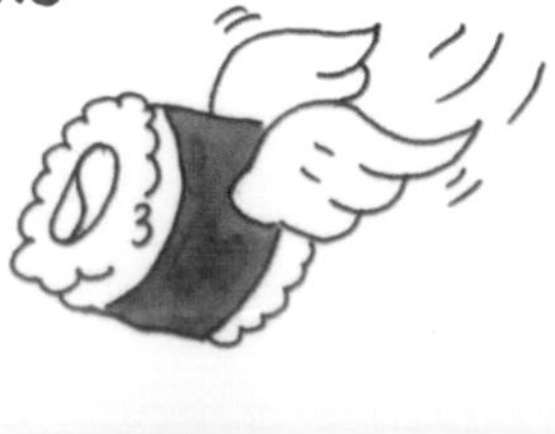

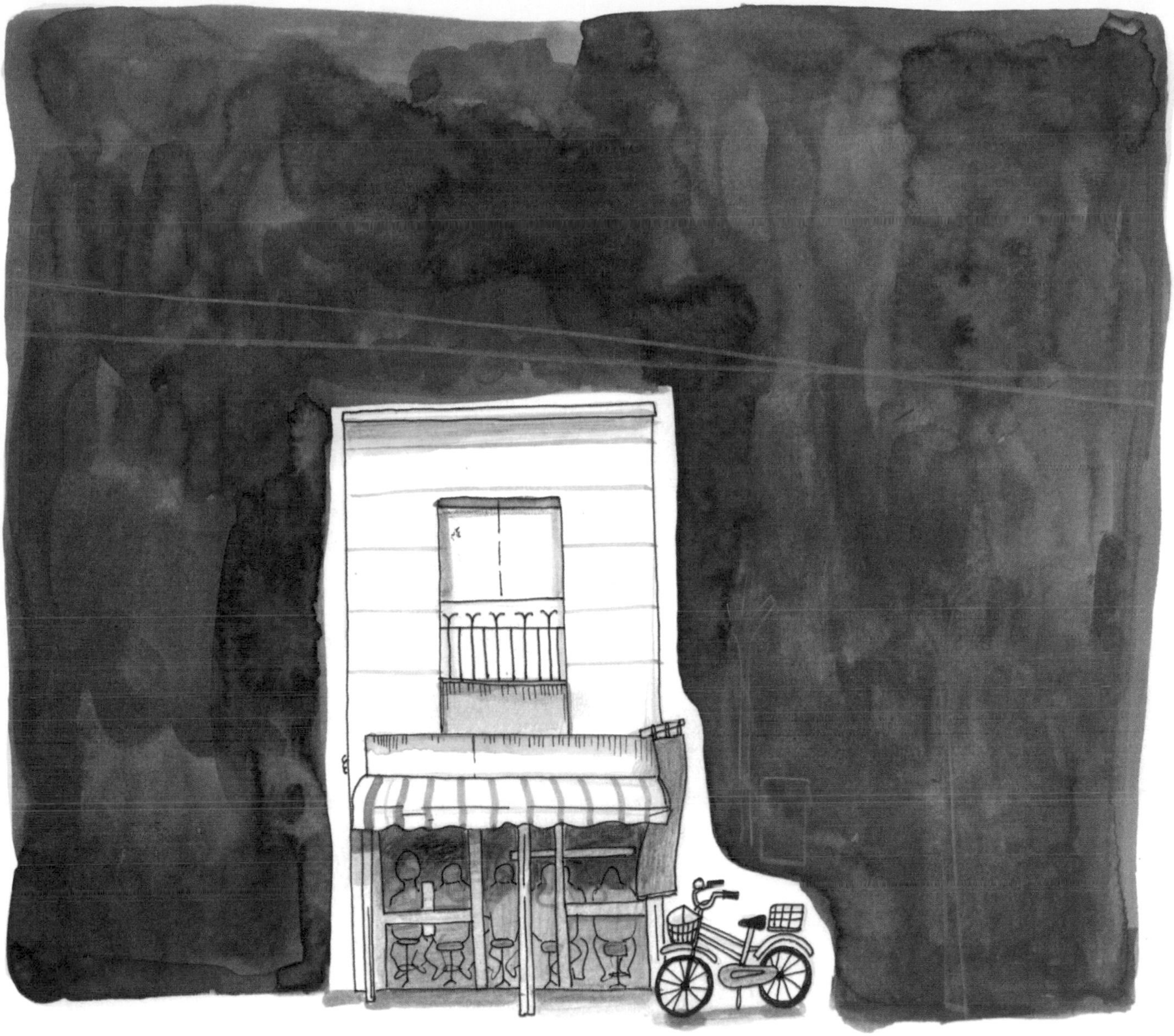

An izakaya that seats only five people. All in ten square meters.
A bar and five drinkers. There are times I see someone waiting
for a place to free up so they can sit.

Lunch with Takahashi-san
← - - - - -

Workshop for about 100 children in a Japanese school.

I made this mini dictionary so I could communicate with them.

BONITO ♥ = iiNE
♥

CAT = NEKO ねこ

DOG = iNU いぬ

FiSH = OSAKANA さかな

BOY = OTOKONOKO おとこのこ

GIRL = ONNANOKO おんなのこ

RABBIT = USAGI うさぎ

YOKU DEKI. MASHITA

HAJIME
A
J

GOOD WORK!

Week 2

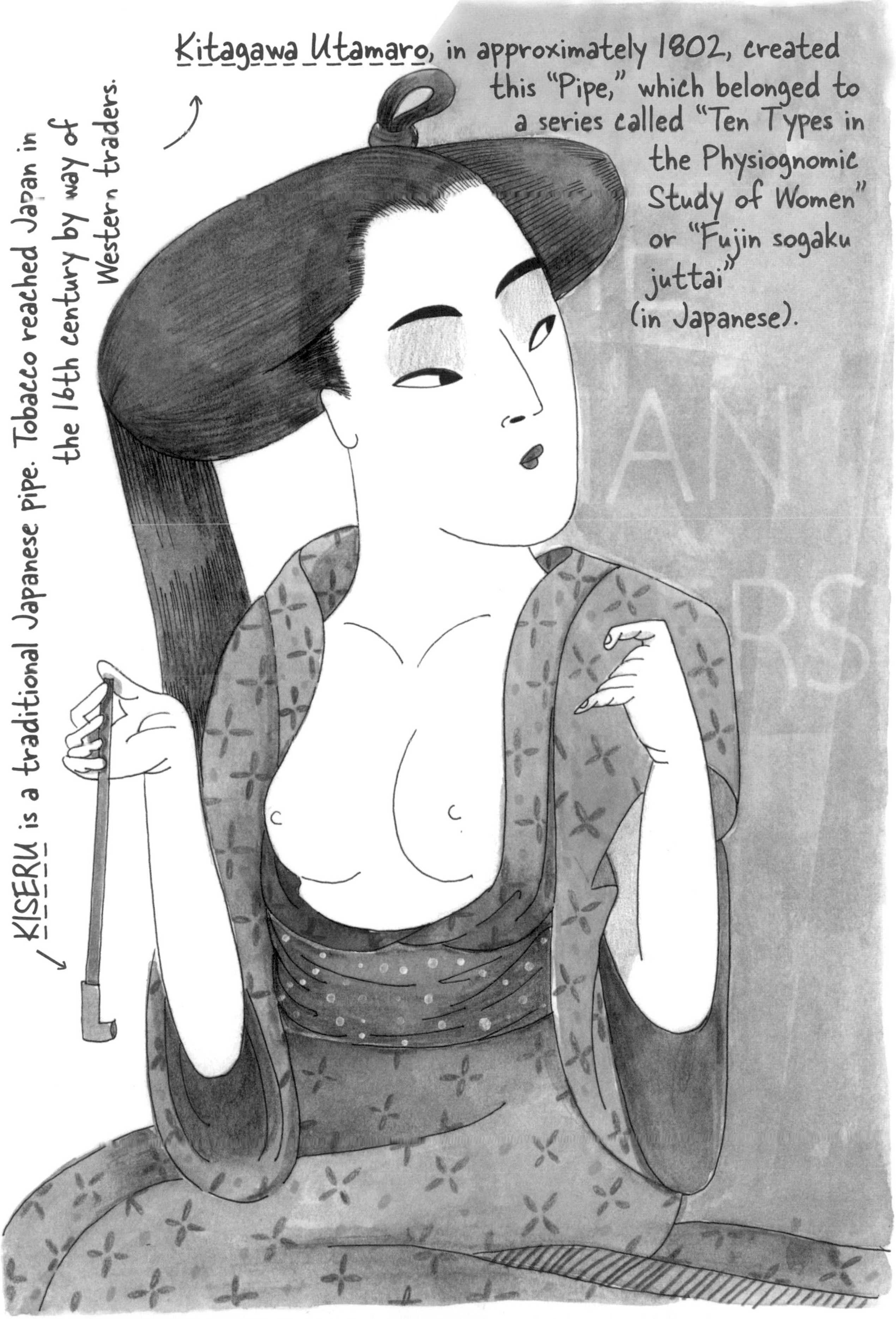
Kitagawa Utamaro, in approximately 1802, created this "Pipe," which belonged to a series called "Ten Types in the Physiognomic Study of Women" or "Fujin sogaku juttai" (in Japanese).
KISERU is a traditional Japanese pipe. Tobacco reached Japan in the 16th century by way of Western traders.

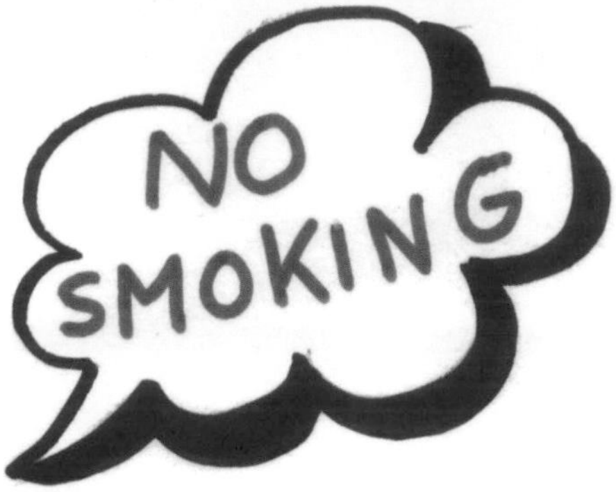
NO SMOKING

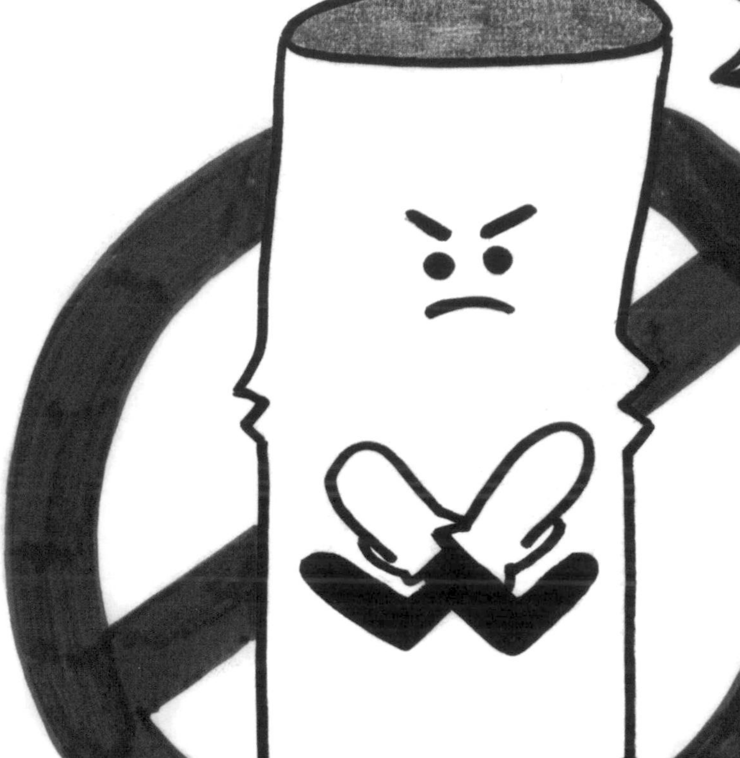

I've always been surprised by how graphically "infantilized" the Japanese are. There is no single NO SMOKING sign, but there are 20,000 cigarettes painted all over the city. This one, with its little hands in its pockets, is my favorite.

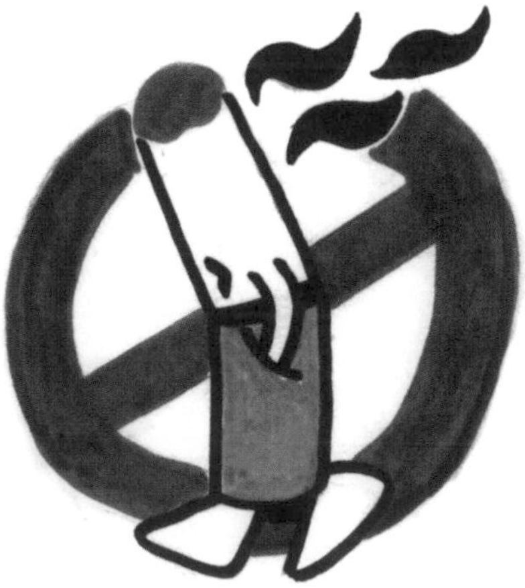

22 FEB. 2017

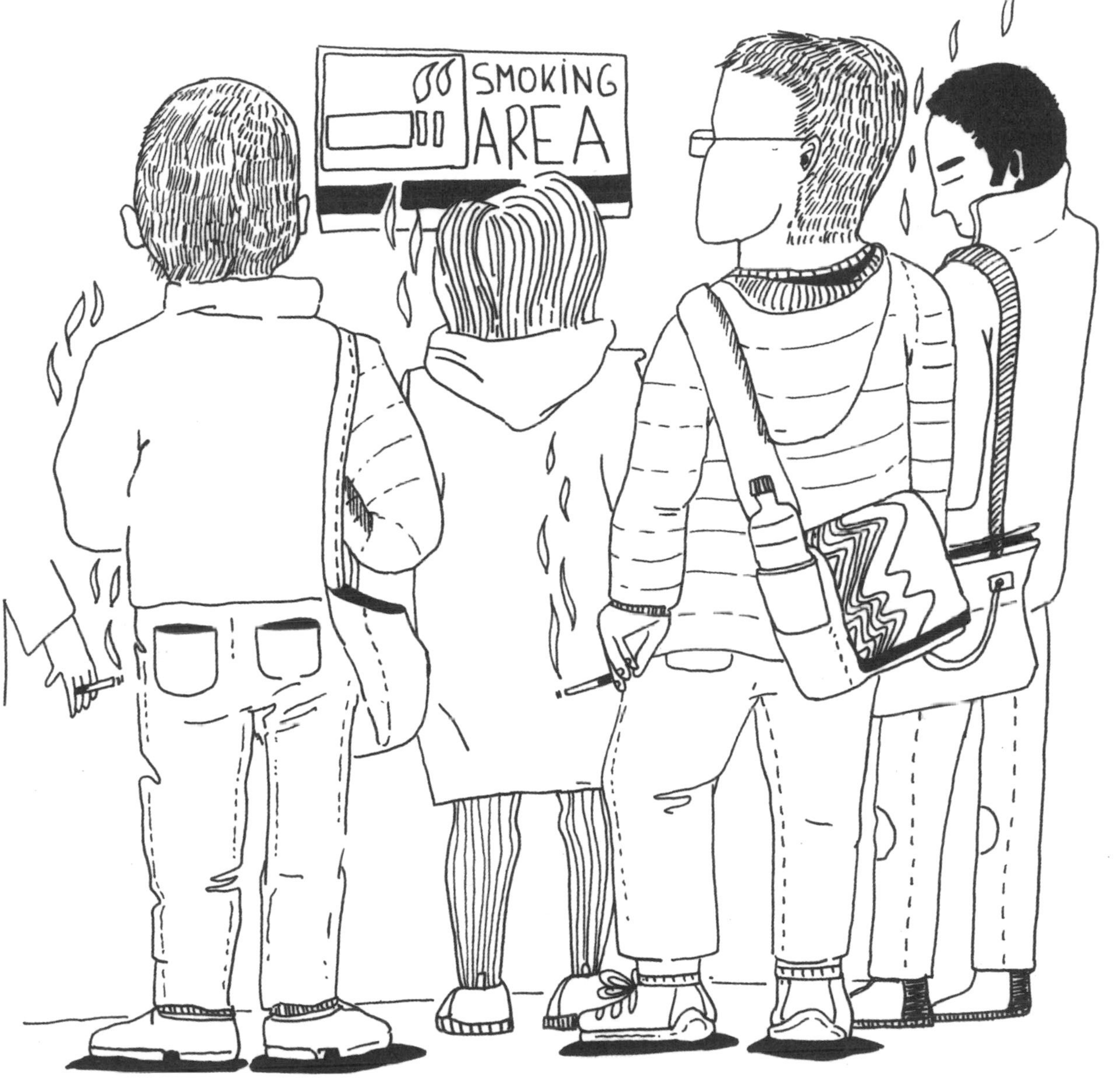
SMOKING
AREA

Despite the fact that the Japanese are FAIRLY HEAVY smokers, you can't smoke in Japan outside the designated areas in the street. So this means you sometimes encounter groups of smokers all looking in the same direction, all crowded together, yet each immersed in a solitude all their own.

22 FEB. 2017

Sign in a tobacco-lover restaurant.

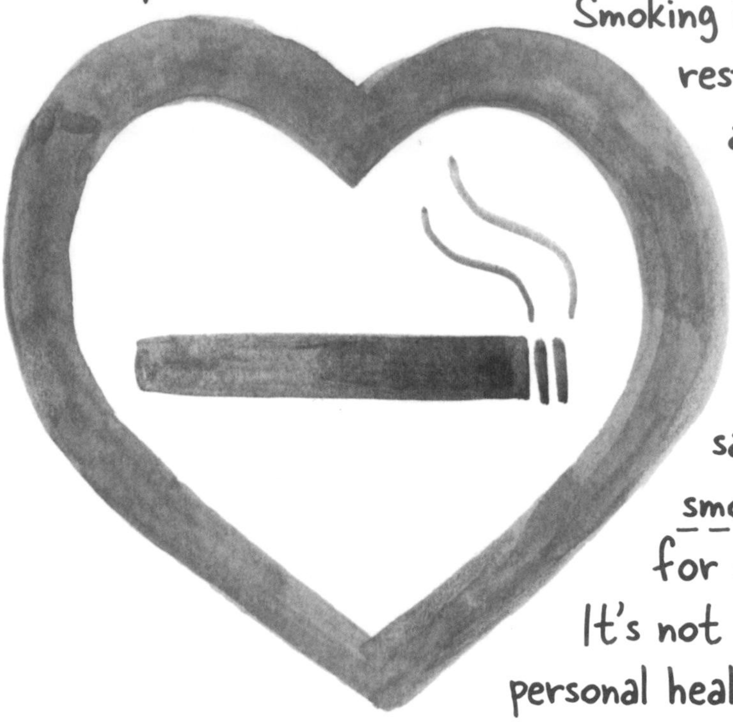

Smoking is allowed in almost all restaurants and bars. There are places where no-smoking areas coexist with smoking areas, but in general they're pretty permissive. As I've already said, where they DON'T smoke is outdoors, except for specially designated areas. It's not so much a question of personal health as it is a question of not bothering others with the smoke, not burning other people's clothing, not having children breathe in the smoke... And above all, NOT POLLUTING.

Tokyo has ALMOST NO TRASH CANS. If a cigarette butt ends up in the street, it's everyone's problem. Ashtrays were installed in designated areas, and that was that. Once again, the collective and their well-being prevail over individuals (and their vices).

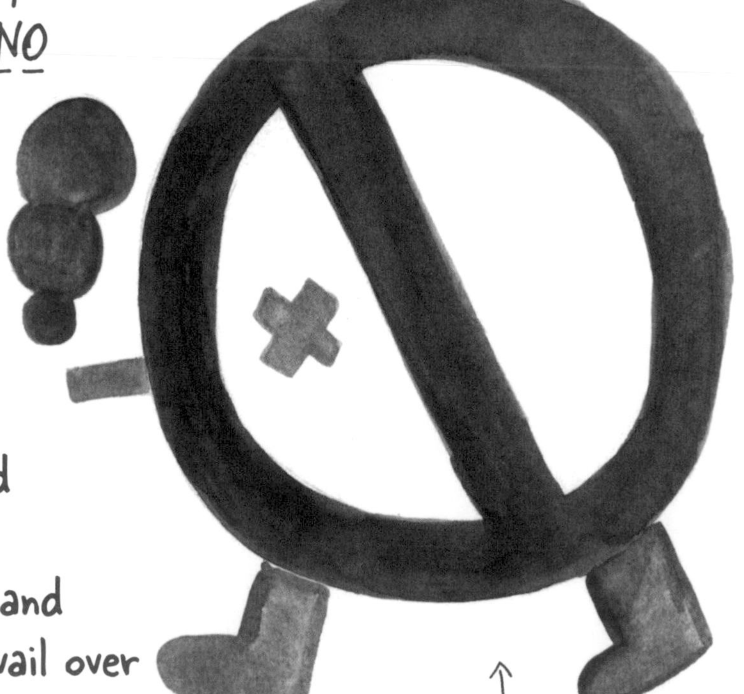

Sign painted on the streets of Tokyo.

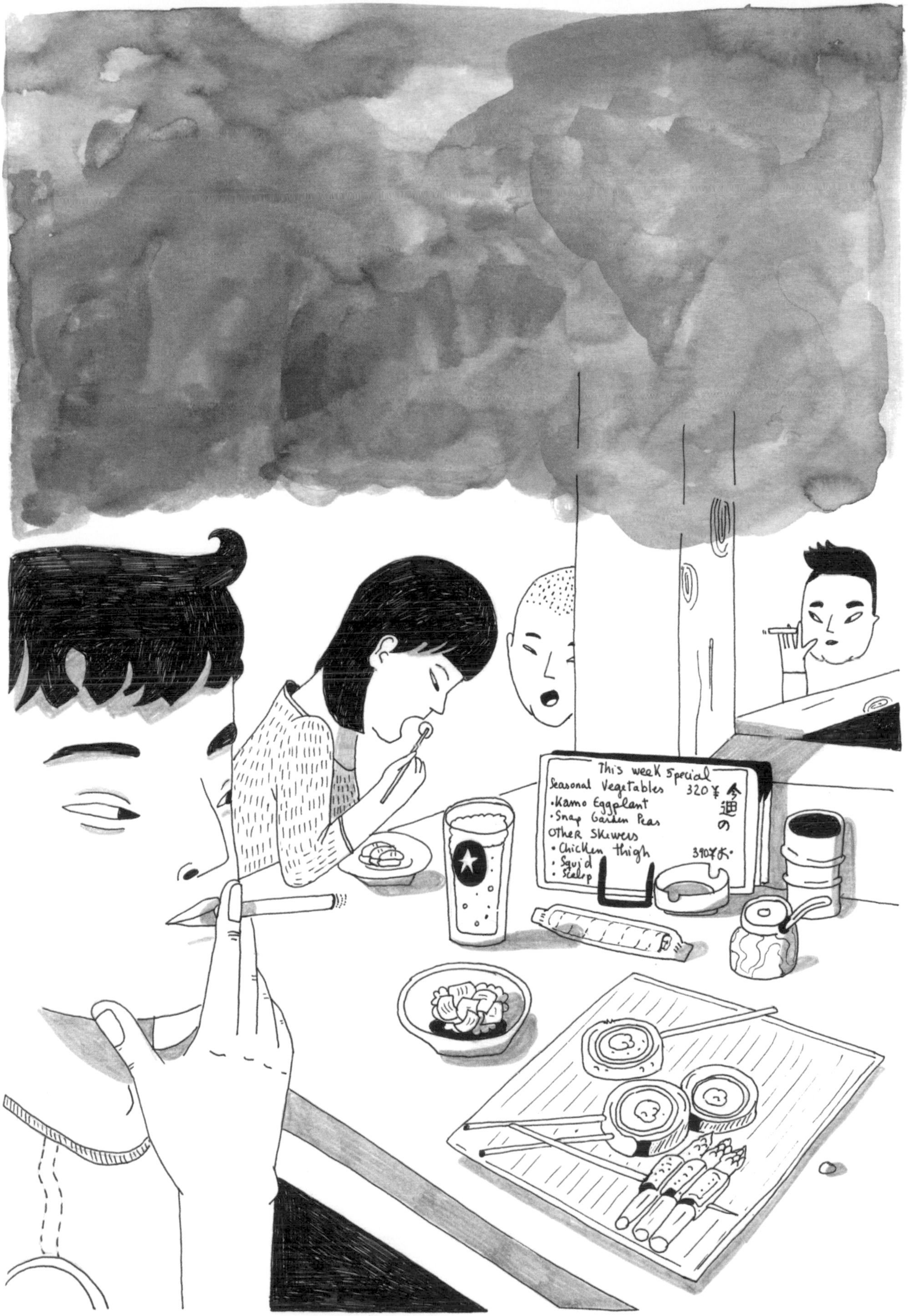
This week Special
Seasonal Vegetables 320¥
今週の
•Kamo Eggplant
•Snap Garden Peas
OtheR Skiwers
•Chicken thigh 390¥
•Squid
•Scalop

(Pond in Ueno Park.) –––––––––––––→

The living image of the Japanese mentality:
 living and working in tall, gray buildings, and
having fun in colorful, duck–shaped
 pedal boats.

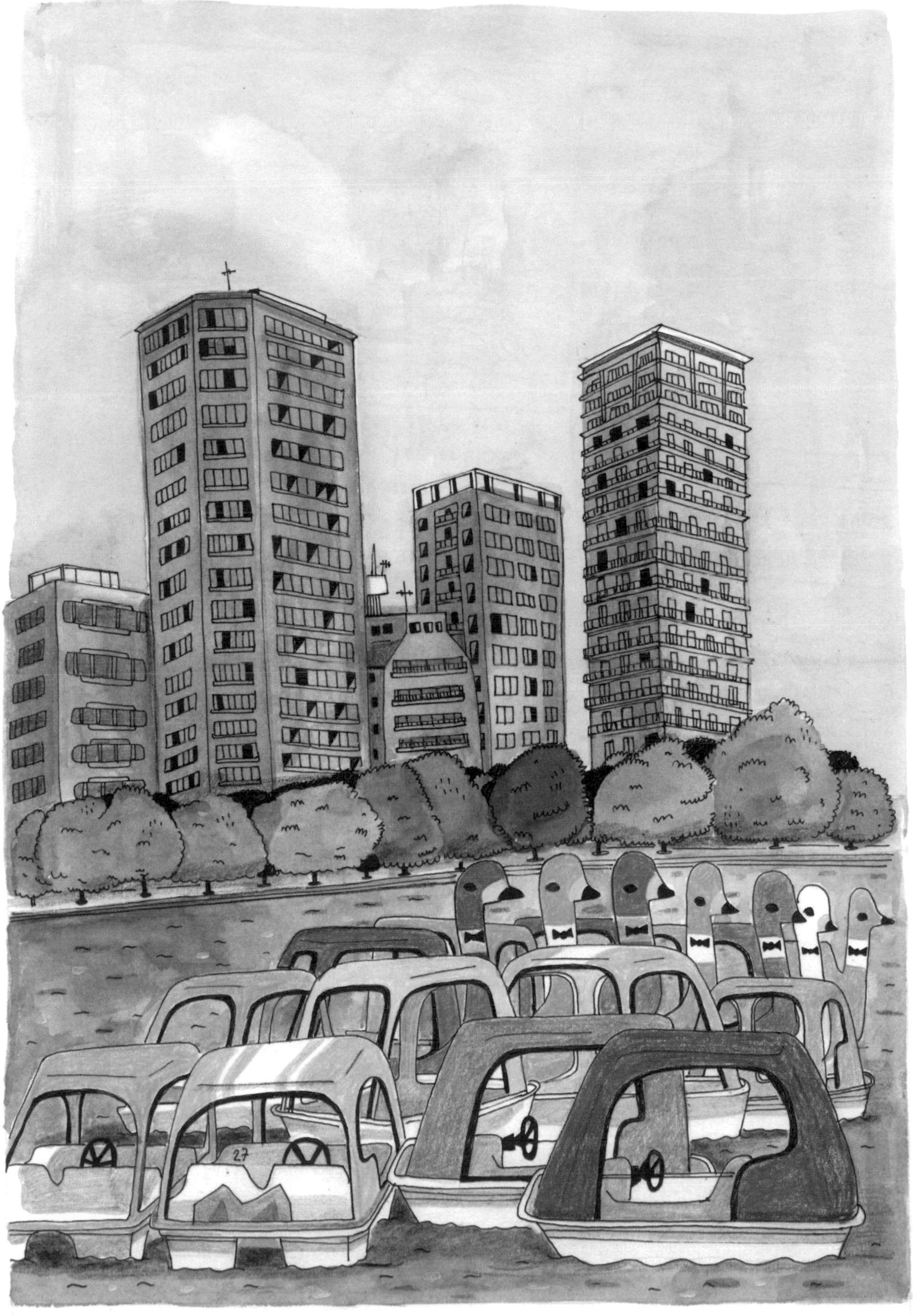
27

Poster I saw in the
Kinshichō station.
It has to do with a literary competition
or something. ------------→

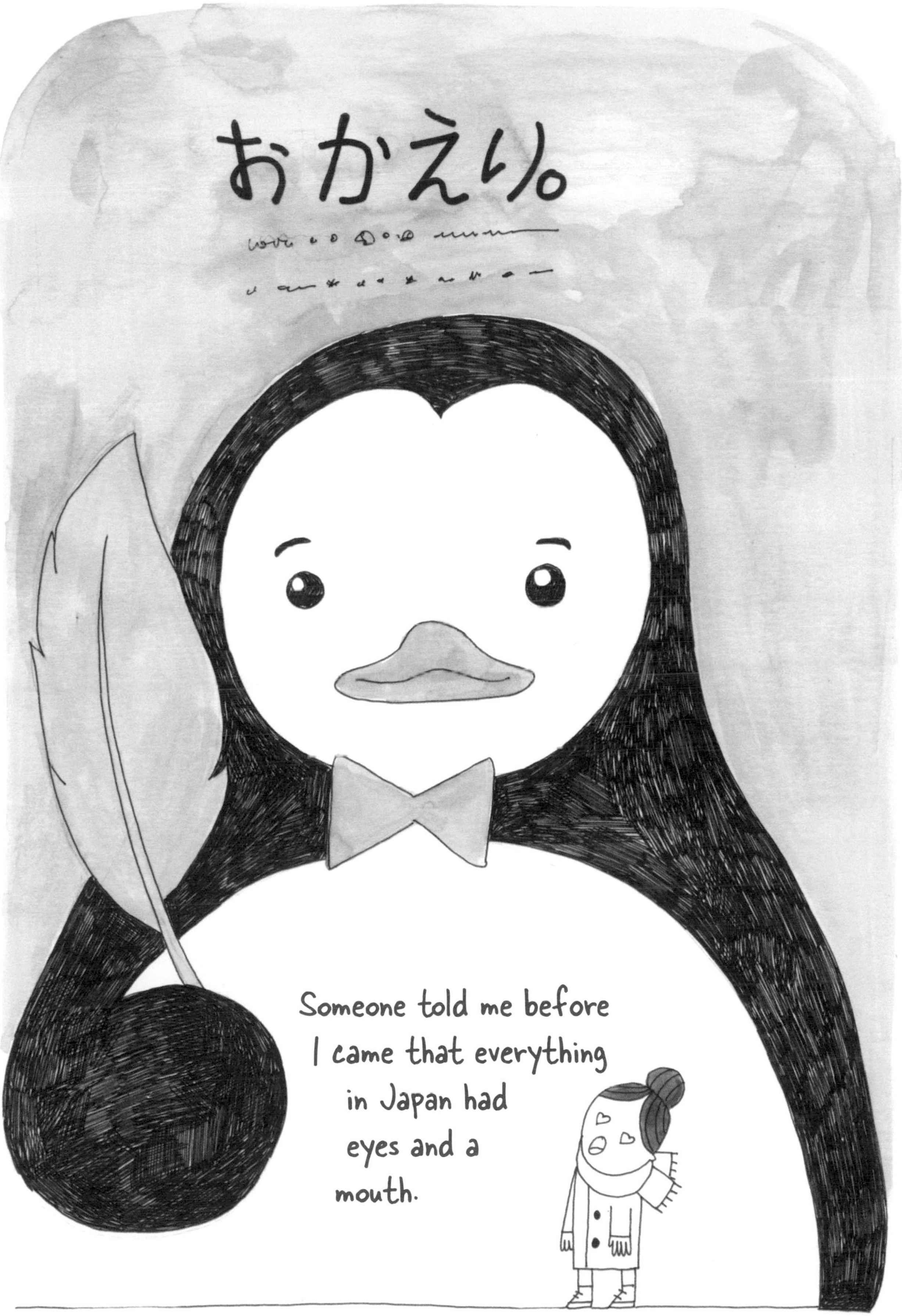
おかえり。
Someone told me before I came that everything in Japan had eyes and a mouth.

Construction site signage near Ueno Park.

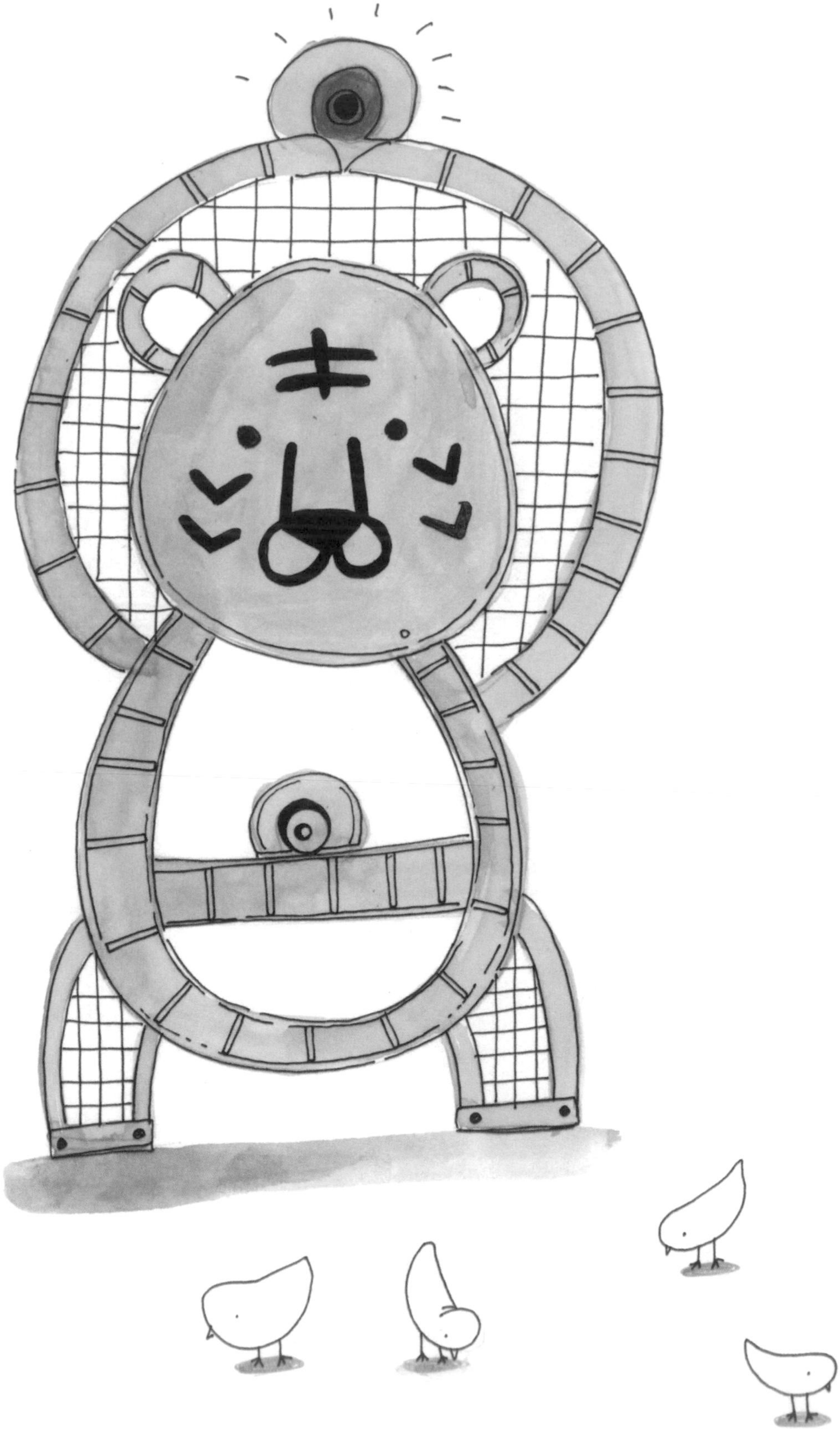

A postal service mail box in front of the zoo.

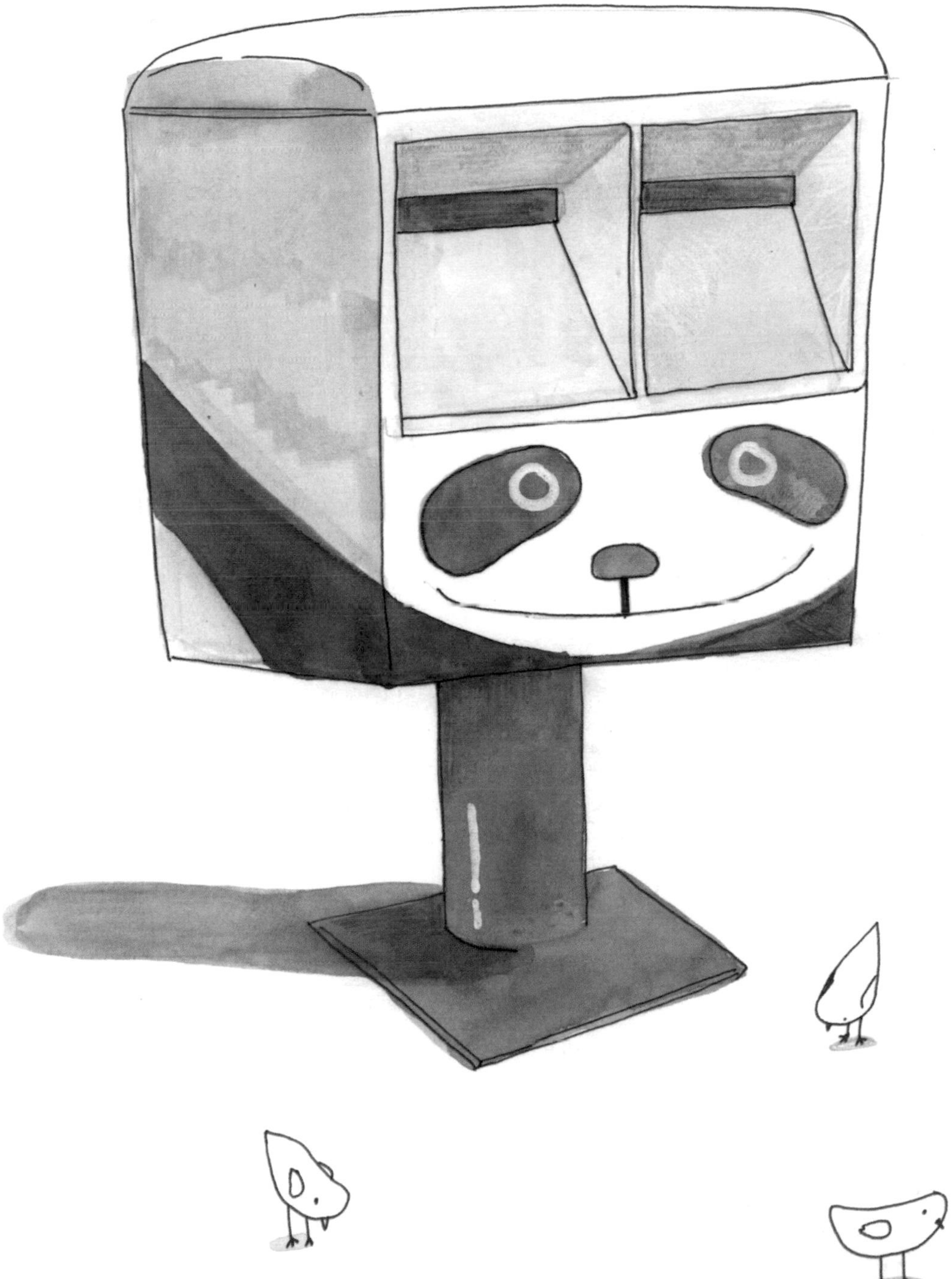

Kawaii

- The term kawaii is fundamental to Japanese culture. Beginning about thirty years ago, this aesthetic trend has now become more of a sociological phenomenon. Kawaii is adorable, cute. It's huggable, chubby, pastel tones can also be an attitude: a high-pitched woman's voice, or awkward, infantilized behavior.

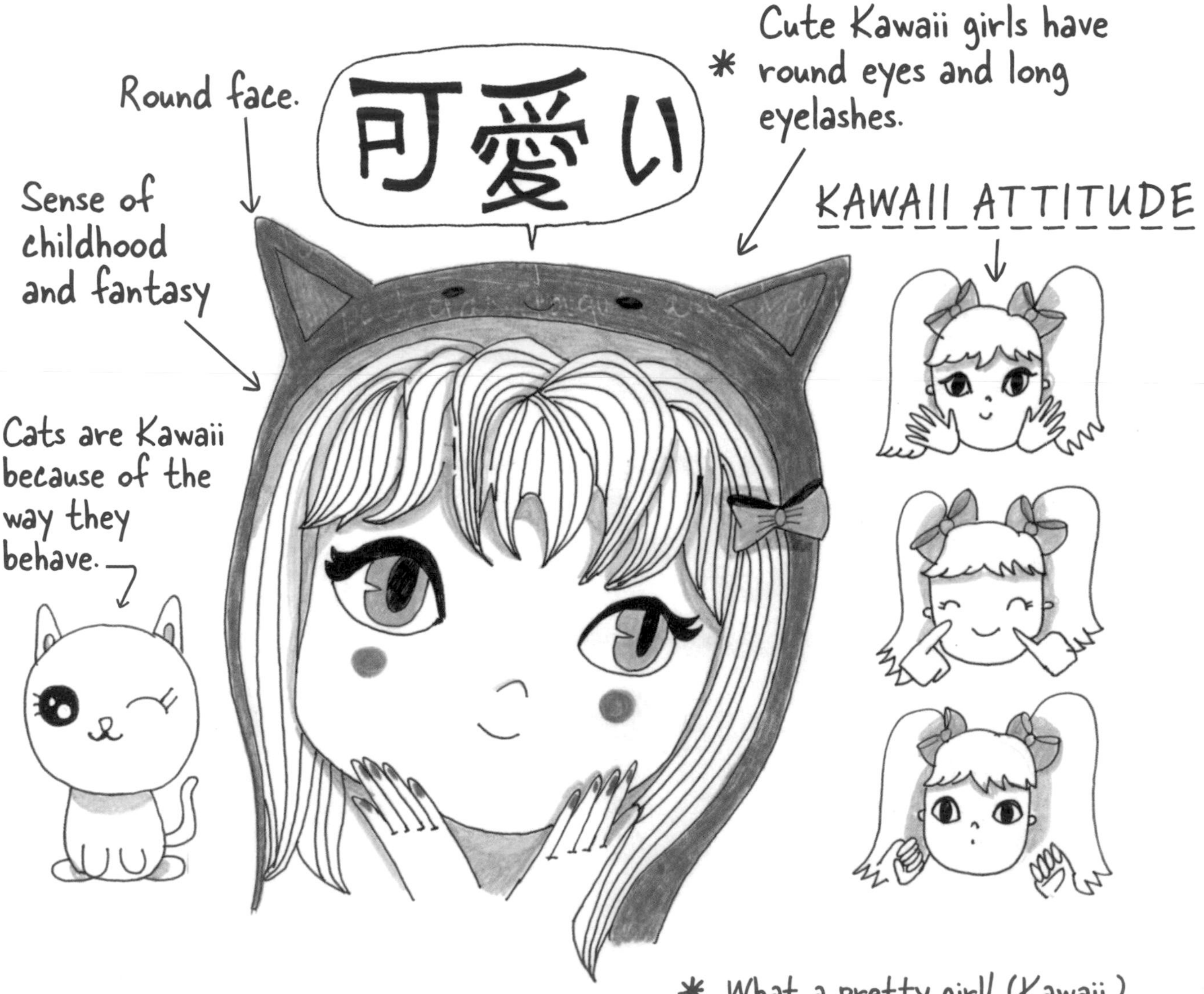
Cute Kawaii girls have round eyes and long eyelashes.
*
Round face.
可愛い
Sense of childhood and fantasy
KAWAII ATTITUDE
Cats are Kawaii because of the way they behave.

* What a pretty girl! (Kawaii.)

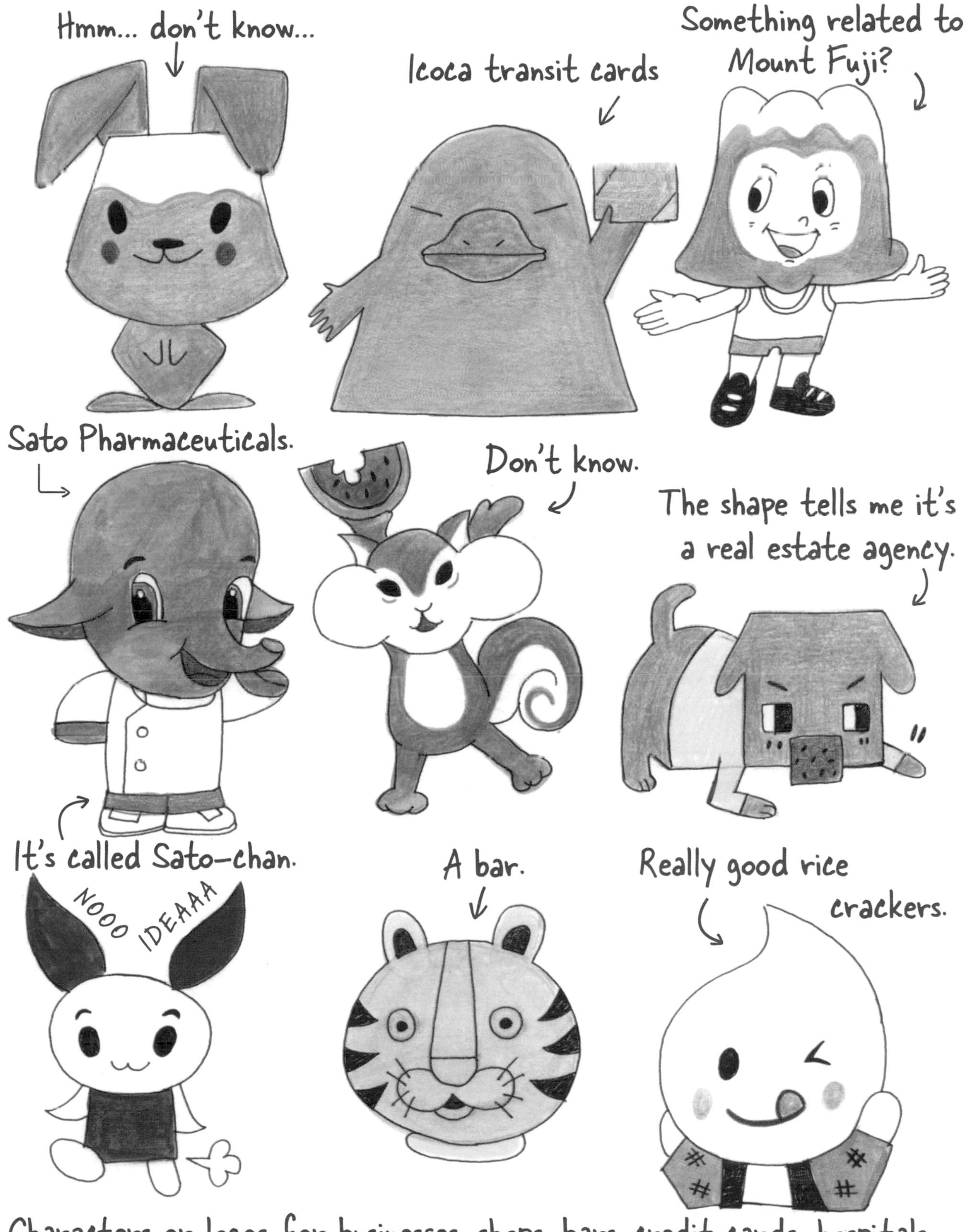
Hmm... don't know...
Icoca transit cards
Something related to Mount Fuji?
Sato Pharmaceuticals.
Don't know.
The shape tells me it's a real estate agency.
It's called Sato-chan.
NOOO IDEAAA
A bar.
Really good rice crackers.

Characters or logos for businesses, shops, bars, credit cards, hospitals... It's jarring to have such a contradictory association between official agencies, cities, armies, airports and smiley little dolls.

This is me in kawaii mode.

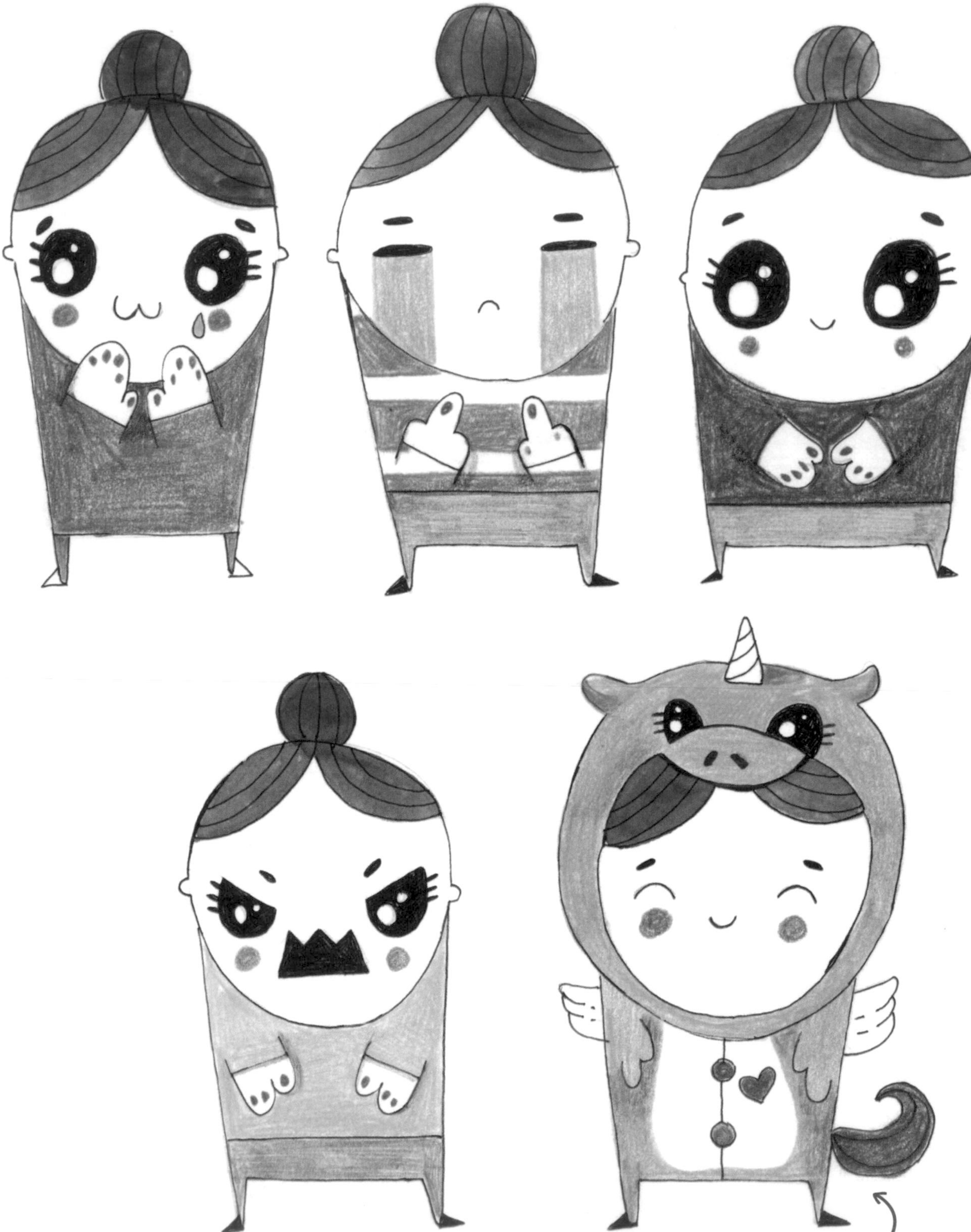

More kawaii than ever.

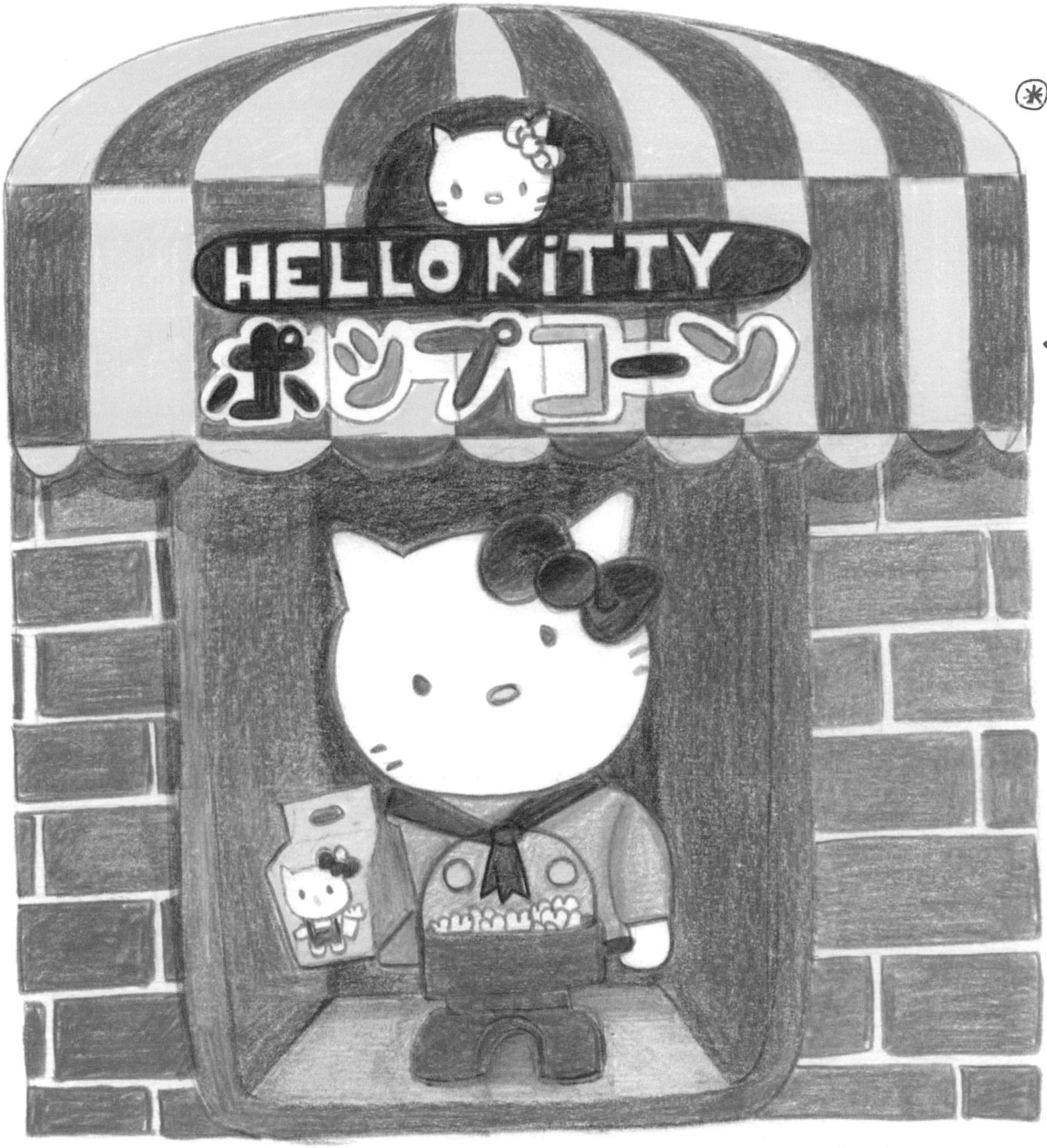
HELLO KiTTY
ポンプコーン

The Beyoncé of kawaii is Hello Kitty.

The kawaii movement came about as a kind of "rebellion" against the establishment.
An army of rebellion against responsibilities, growing up, work, RULES.
This immaturity turned fashion began as something subversive, a kind of CUTENESS REVOLUTION.

⊛ Popcorn popper in the Hello Kitty shop in Shinjuku.

Today I saw a man walking a cat
as if it were a dog.

2 3 FEB. 2017

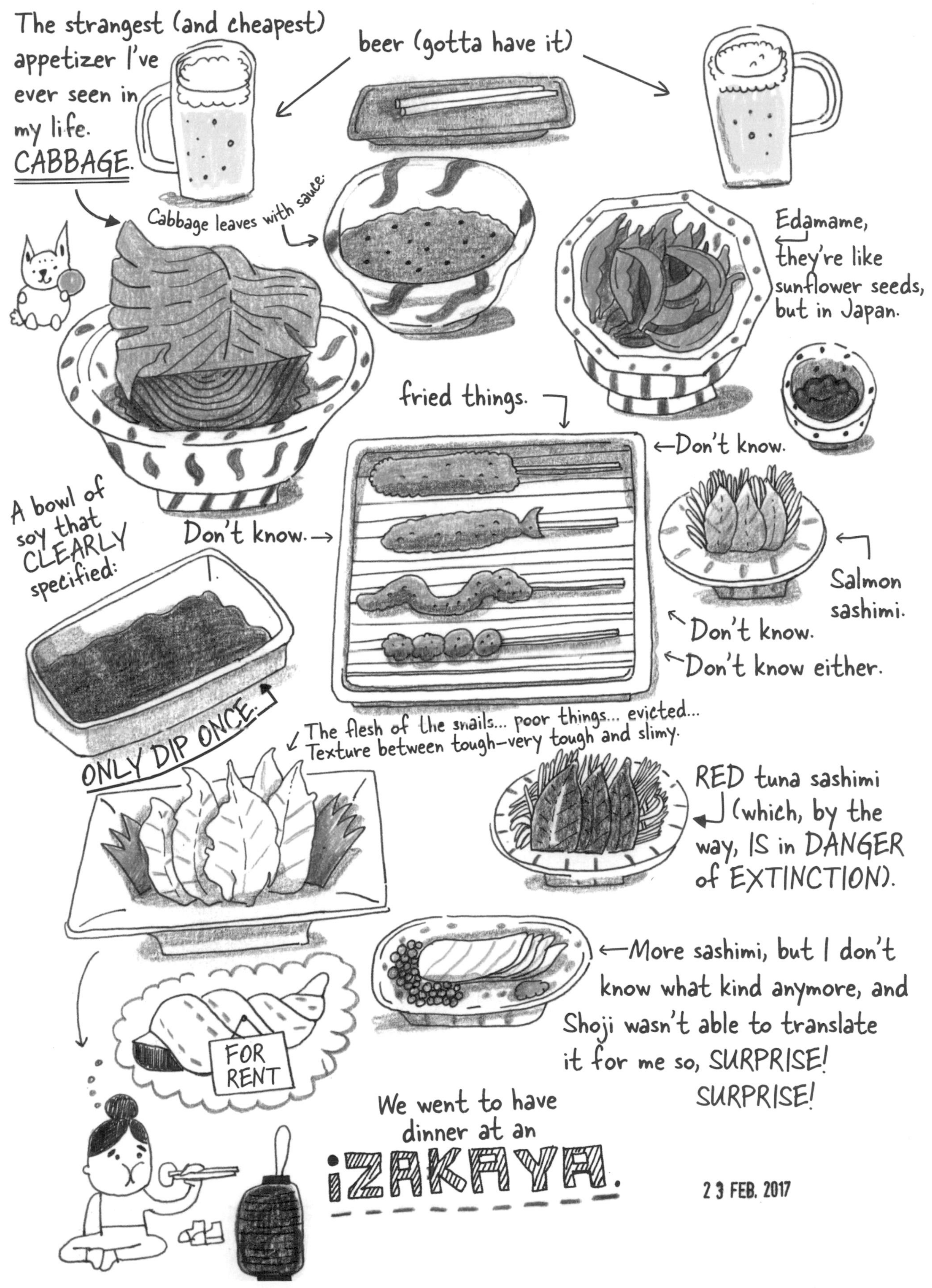

The strangest (and cheapest) appetizer I've ever seen in my life. CABBAGE.
beer (gotta have it)
Cabbage leaves with sauce.
Edamame, they're like sunflower seeds, but in Japan.
fried things.
Don't know.
Don't know.
Salmon sashimi.
Don't know.
Don't know either.
A bowl of soy that CLEARLY specified:
ONLY DIP ONCE.
The flesh of the snails... poor things... evicted...
Texture between tough—very tough and slimy.
RED tuna sashimi (which, by the way, IS in DANGER of EXTINCTION).
More sashimi, but I don't know what kind anymore, and Shoji wasn't able to translate it for me so, SURPRISE! SURPRISE!
FOR RENT
We went to have dinner at an
iZAKAYA.
23 FEB. 2017

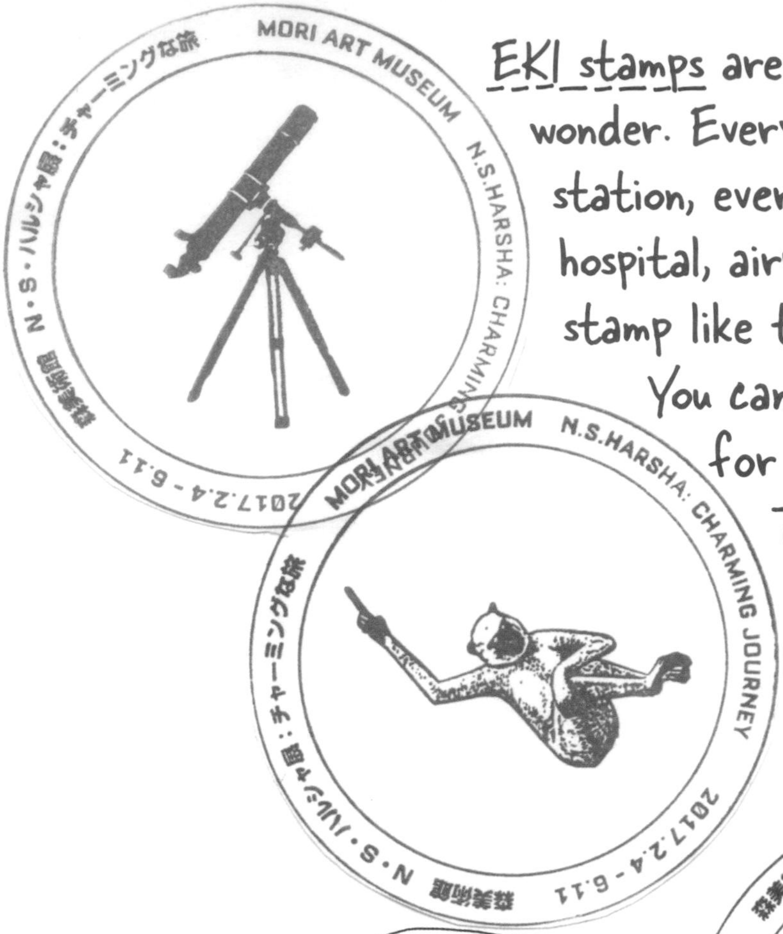
MORI ART MUSEUM
N.S.HARSHA: CHARMING JOURNEY
森美術館 N・S・ハルシャ展：チャーミングな旅
2017.2.4 - 6.11

EKI stamps are another Japanese wonder. Every subway and train station, every school, town hall, hospital, airport, museum... has a stamp like this.

You can buy a special album for collecting them.

These are from the N. S. Harsha exhibit at the Mori Art Museum.

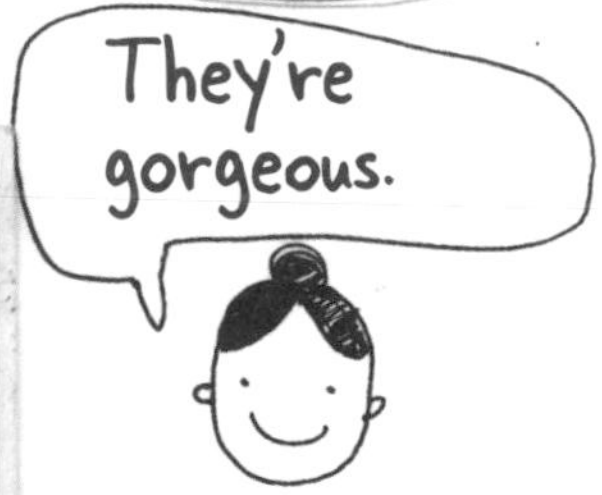
They're gorgeous.

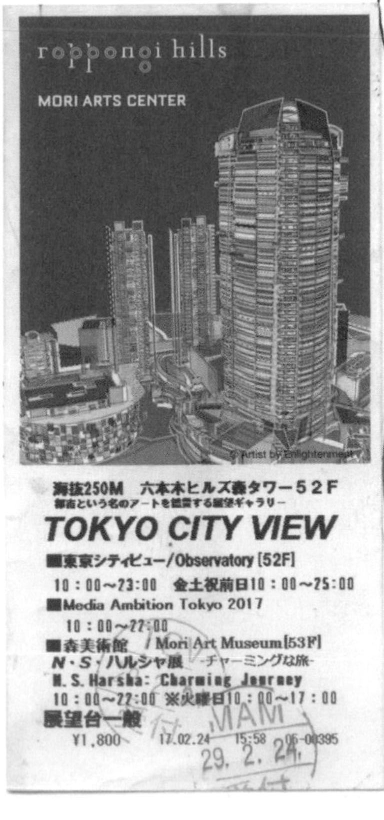

roppongi hills
MORI ARTS CENTER

© Artist by Enlightenment

海抜250M 六本木ヒルズ森タワー52F
都市という名のアートを鑑賞する展望ギャラリー

TOKYO CITY VIEW

■東京シティビュー/Observatory [52F]
10：00〜23：00 金土祝前日10：00〜25：00
■Media Ambition Tokyo 2017
10：00〜22：00
■森美術館 / Mori Art Museum [53F]
N・S・ハルシャ展 -チャーミングな旅-
N. S. Harsha: Charming Journey
10：00〜22：00 ※火曜日10：00〜17：00
展望台一般
¥1,800 17.02.24 15:58 06-00395
MAM 29. 2. 24.

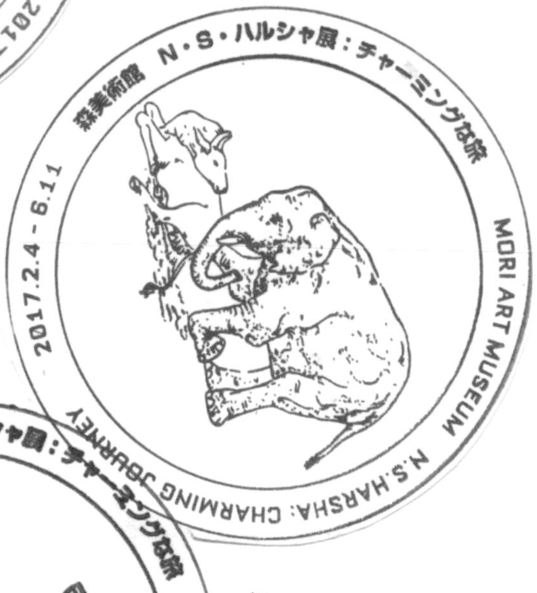
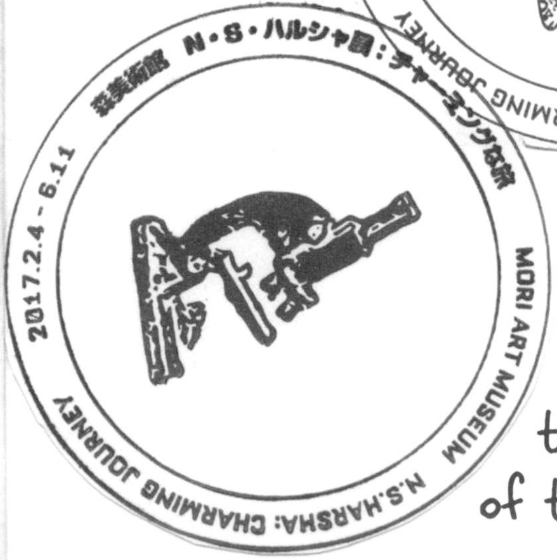
森美術館 N・S・ハルシャ展：チャーミングな旅
MORI ART MUSEUM
N.S.HARSHA: CHARMING JOURNEY
2017.2.4 - 6.11

(I have my own eki stamp; you can see it on the first page of this book.)

24 FEB. 2017

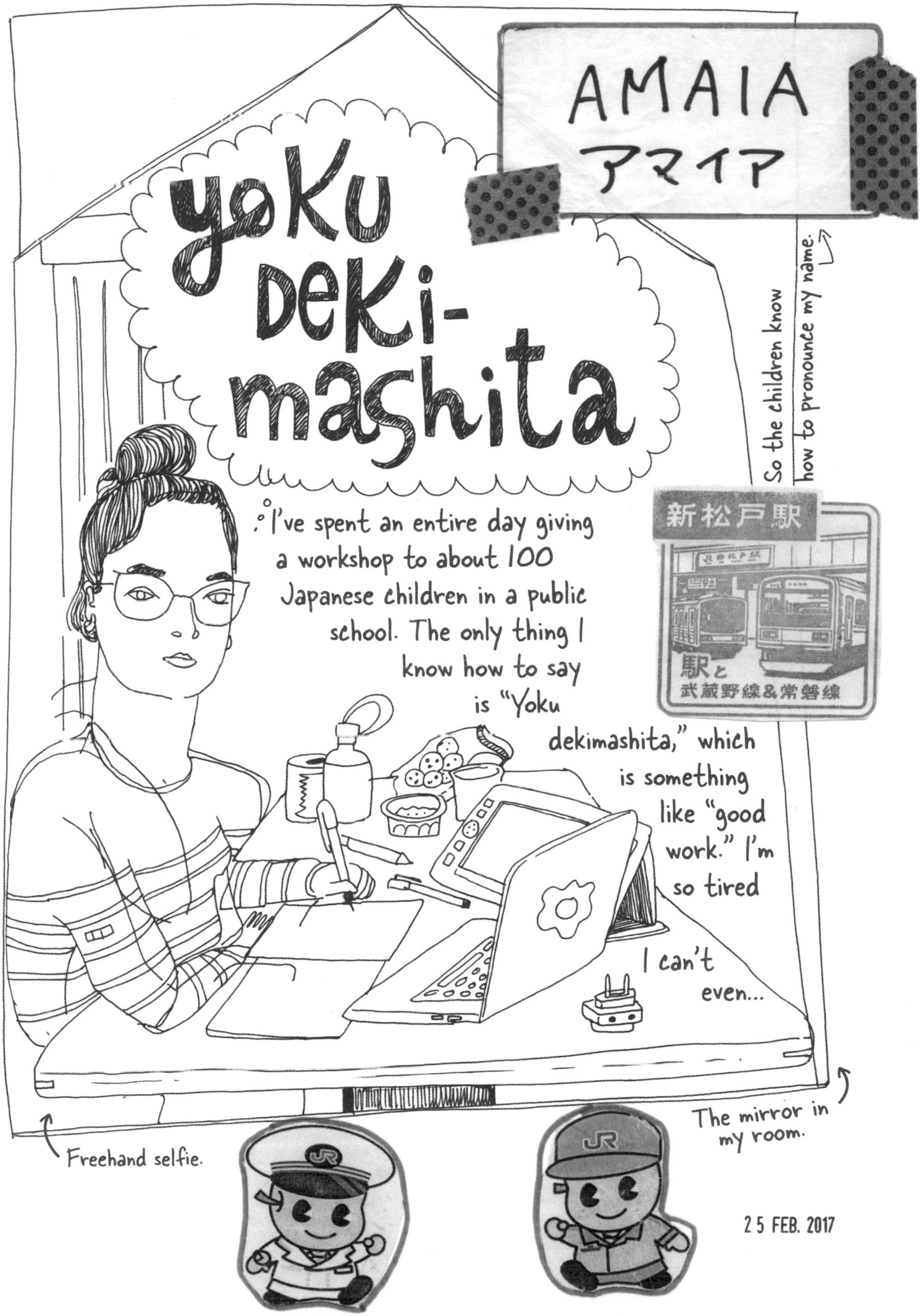

AMAIA
アマイア
So the children know how to pronounce my name.
yoku deki-mashita
I've spent an entire day giving a workshop to about 100 Japanese children in a public school. The only thing I know how to say is "Yoku dekimashita," which is something like "good work." I'm so tired
I can't even...
新松戸駅
駅と
武蔵野線&常磐線
Freehand selfie.
The mirror in my room.
JR
JR
25 FEB. 2017

I discovered Sou Fujimoto
thanks to my
sister Idoia.   — — — — — — — — — →
This building is in
Itabashi, east of Tokyo.

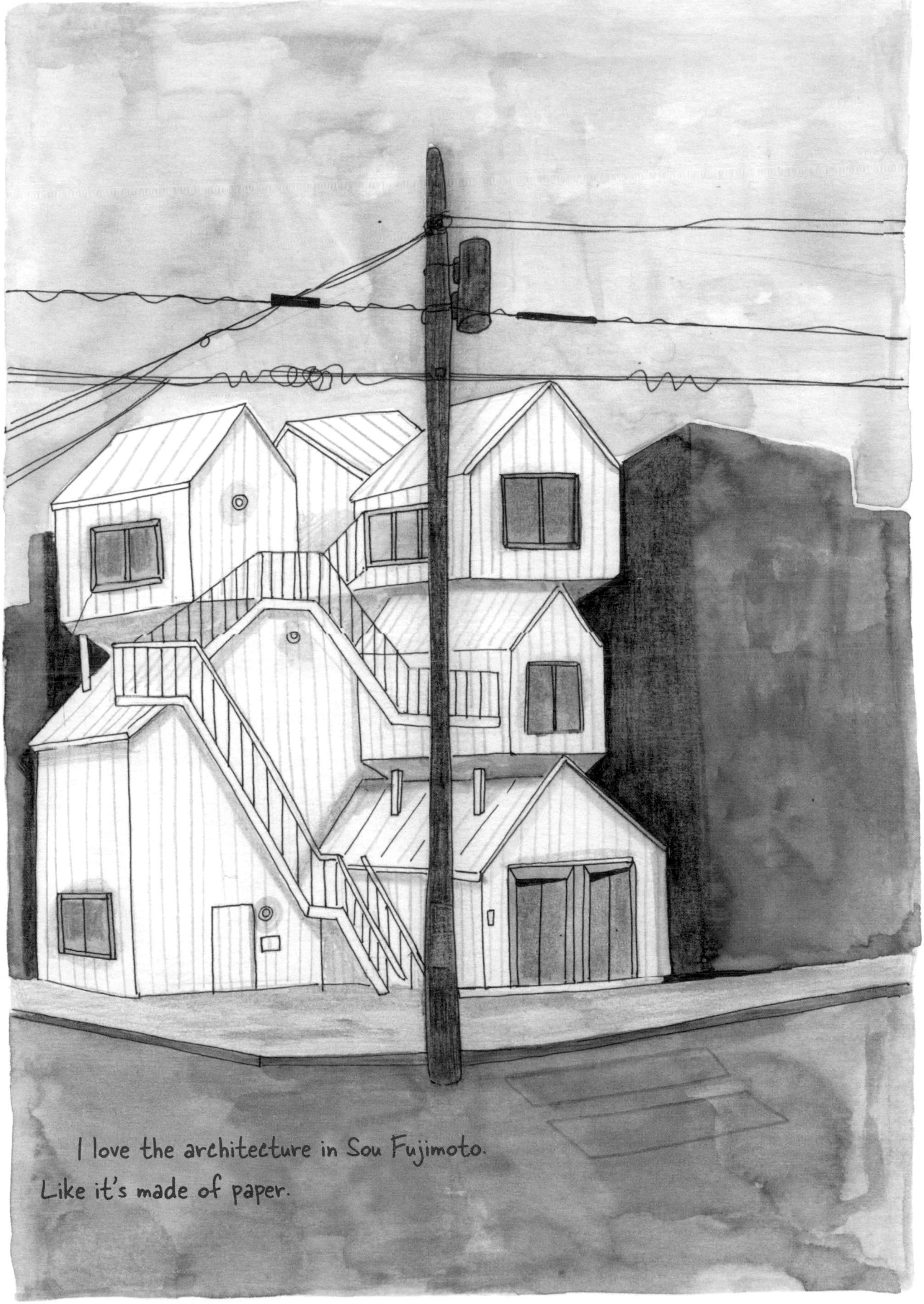
I love the architecture in Sou Fujimoto.
Like it's made of paper.

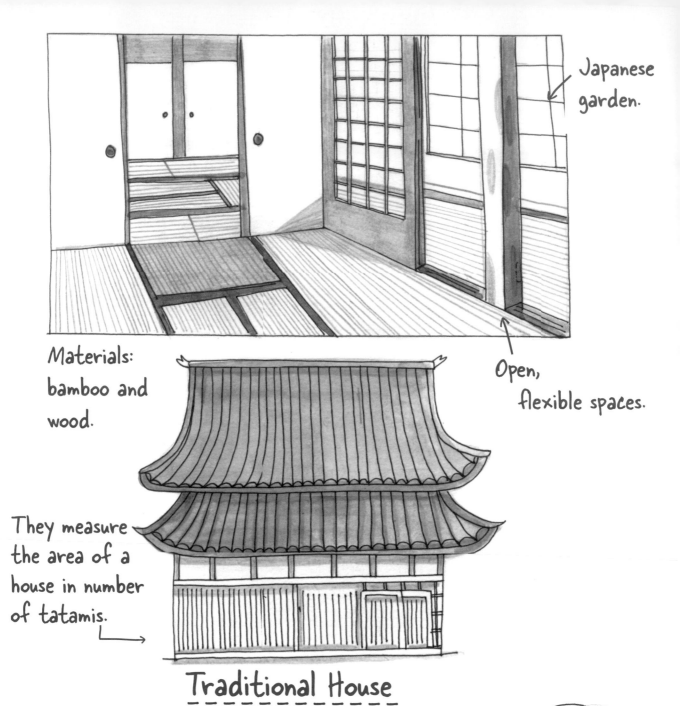

Japanese garden.

Materials: bamboo and wood.

Open, flexible spaces.

They measure the area of a house in number of tatamis.

Traditional House

Open spaces where no room has any specific, designated function, except for the bathroom, washroom, kitchen and genkan. The furniture is portable and the walls moveable so air circulates and there's no mold.

A small space in the entryway where they leave shoes.

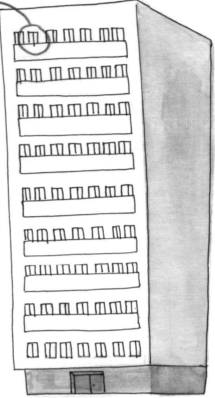

KYOSHO JUTAKU

Designer micro houses are increasingly fashionable.

Where do they sleep?

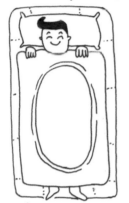

In futons they roll up and store.

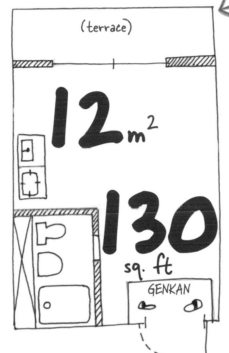

(terrace)

12 m²

130 sq. ft

GENKAN

Gigantic buildings full of hundreds of apartments that are about 110 square feet (10 m²).

Such small houses in a country where consumption is everything? Where do they put things?

Modern Houses or Mansions

There is no space in Tokyo. The country is small in size, and its population is enormous. This means homes are tiny: the city has taken up all the domestic space.

336 people/← km².

Example of a maximum reduction of habitable space.

NAKAGIN CAPSULE TOWER (1972)

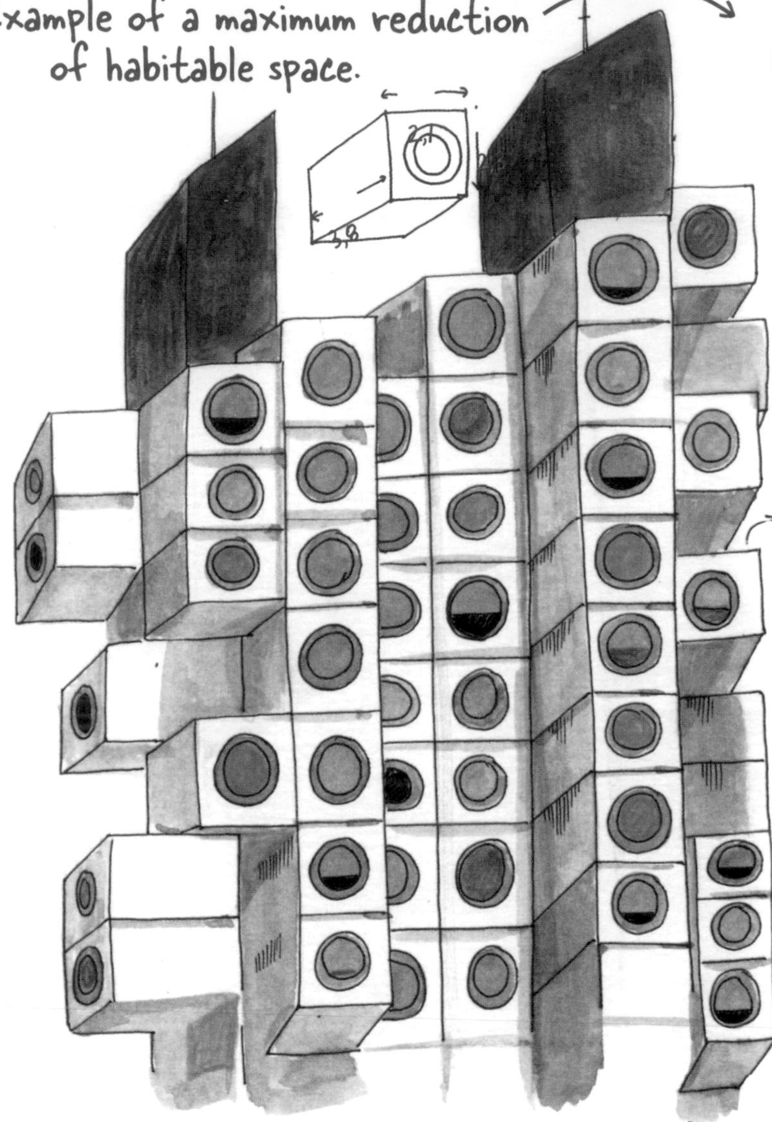

The first example of capsule architecture in the world.

It was conceived for single salarymen.

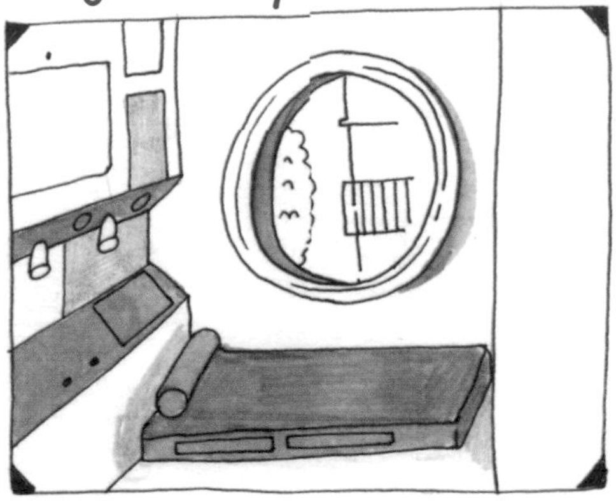

The residents wanted it demolished, but many experts said

NO WAY.

This high-rise is the mother of the famous capsule hotels.

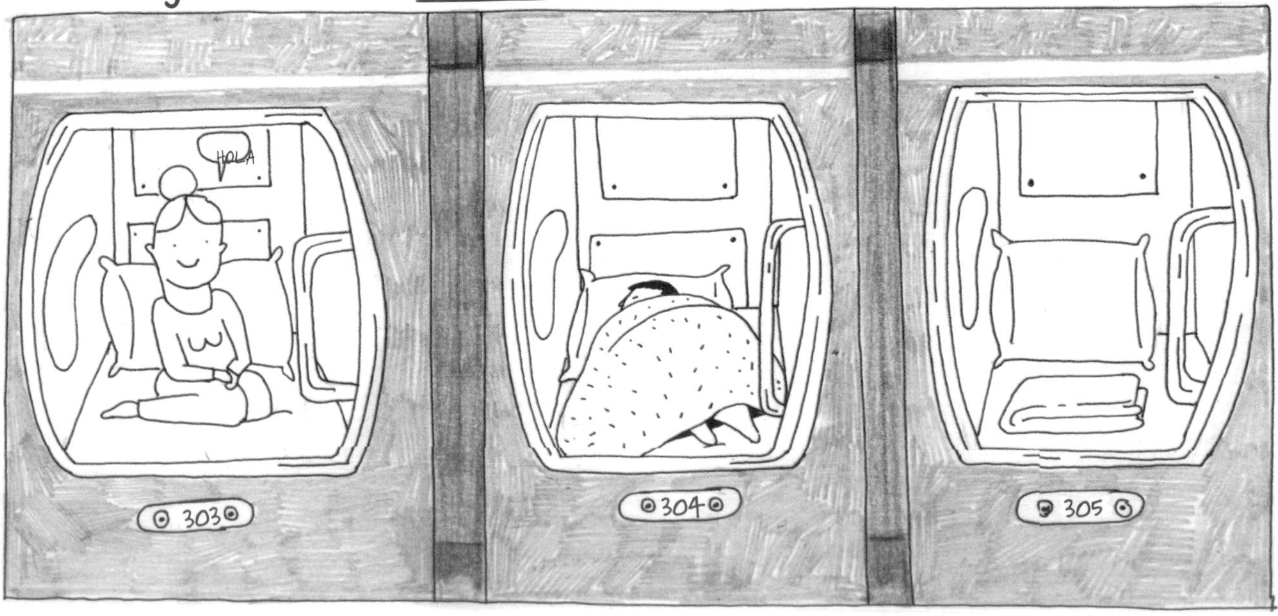
HOLA
303
304
305

Built between 1919 and 1923.

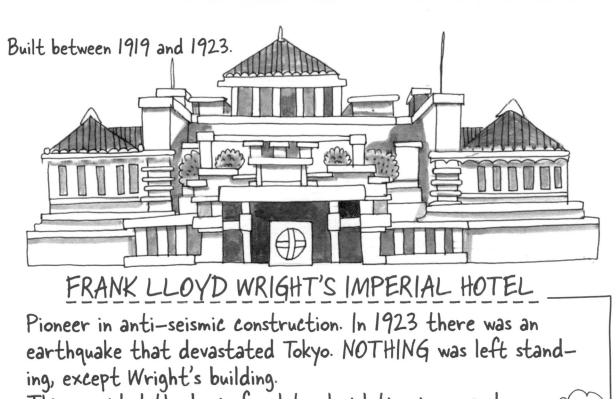

FRANK LLOYD WRIGHT'S IMPERIAL HOTEL

Pioneer in anti-seismic construction. In 1923 there was an earthquake that devastated Tokyo. NOTHING was left standing, except Wright's building.
This provided the basis for later legislation in regard to buildings and seismic movements.

mmm...

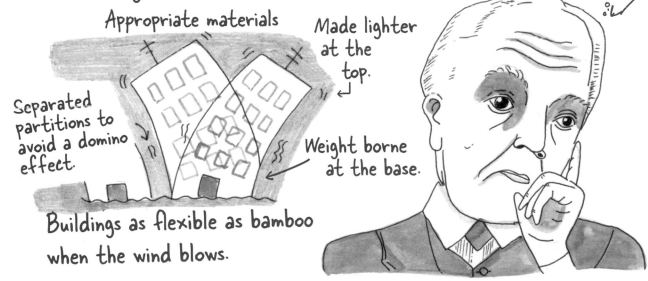

Appropriate materials

Made lighter at the top. ←

Separated partitions to avoid a domino effect.

Weight borne at the base.

Buildings as flexible as bamboo when the wind blows.

Despite the measures taken to fight the effects of earthquakes, Japan isn't obsessed with the permanence of buildings. It seems to me that they understand they have finite life cycles (being born, living, dying) just like any being within nature.

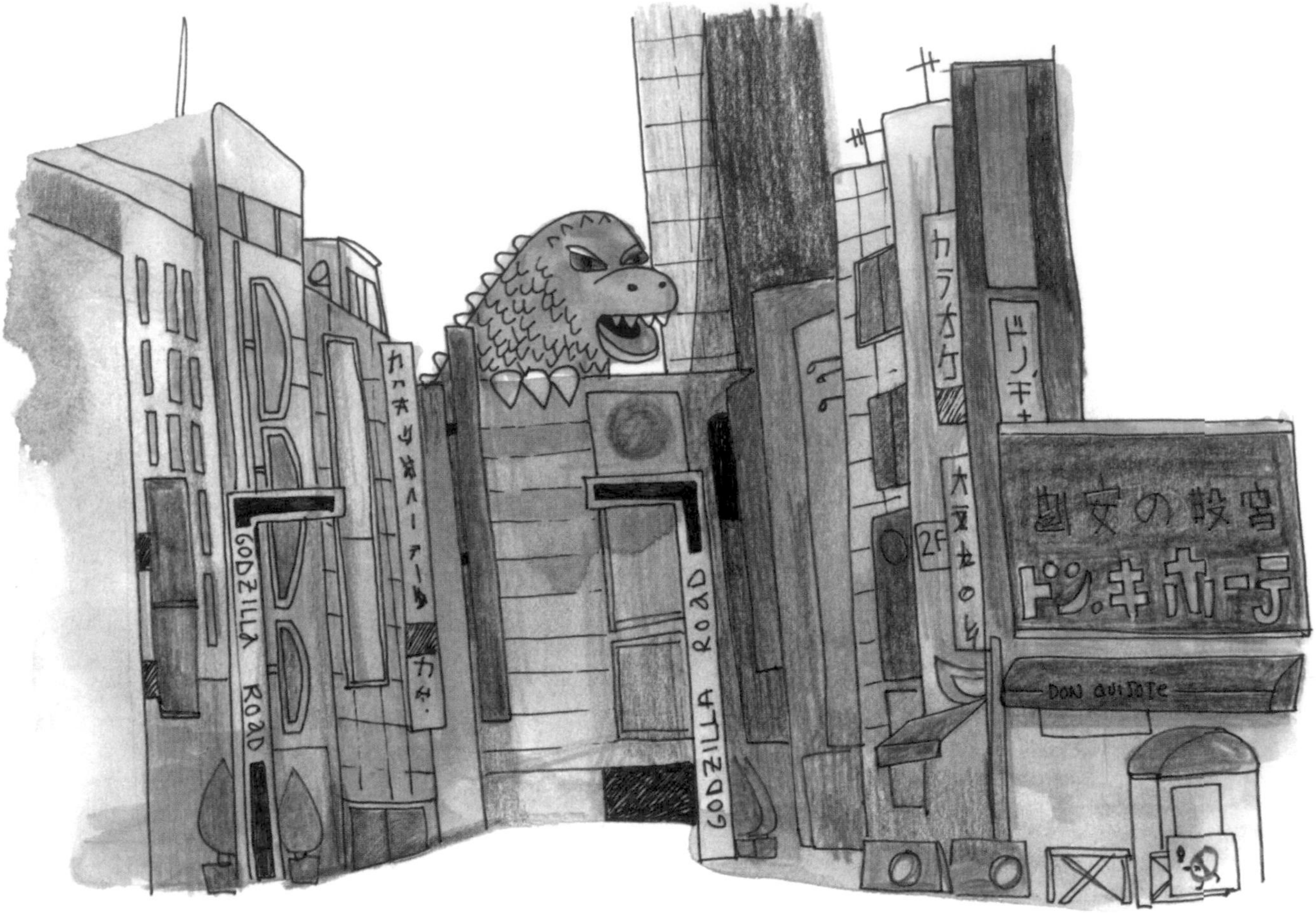
GODZILLA ROAD
GODZILLA ROAD
2F

"Godzilla Road" in Shinjuku.

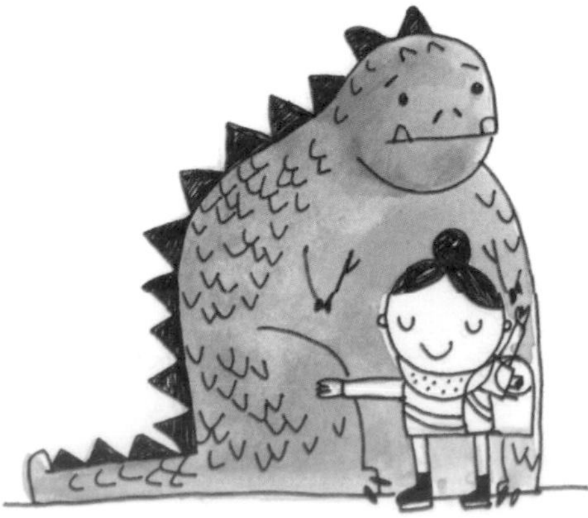

Mutant dinosaur that shows up in Tokyo because of some nuclear commotion.

Shibuya Crossing is used by a million people every day. One of the most populated places, where the least amount of people live.

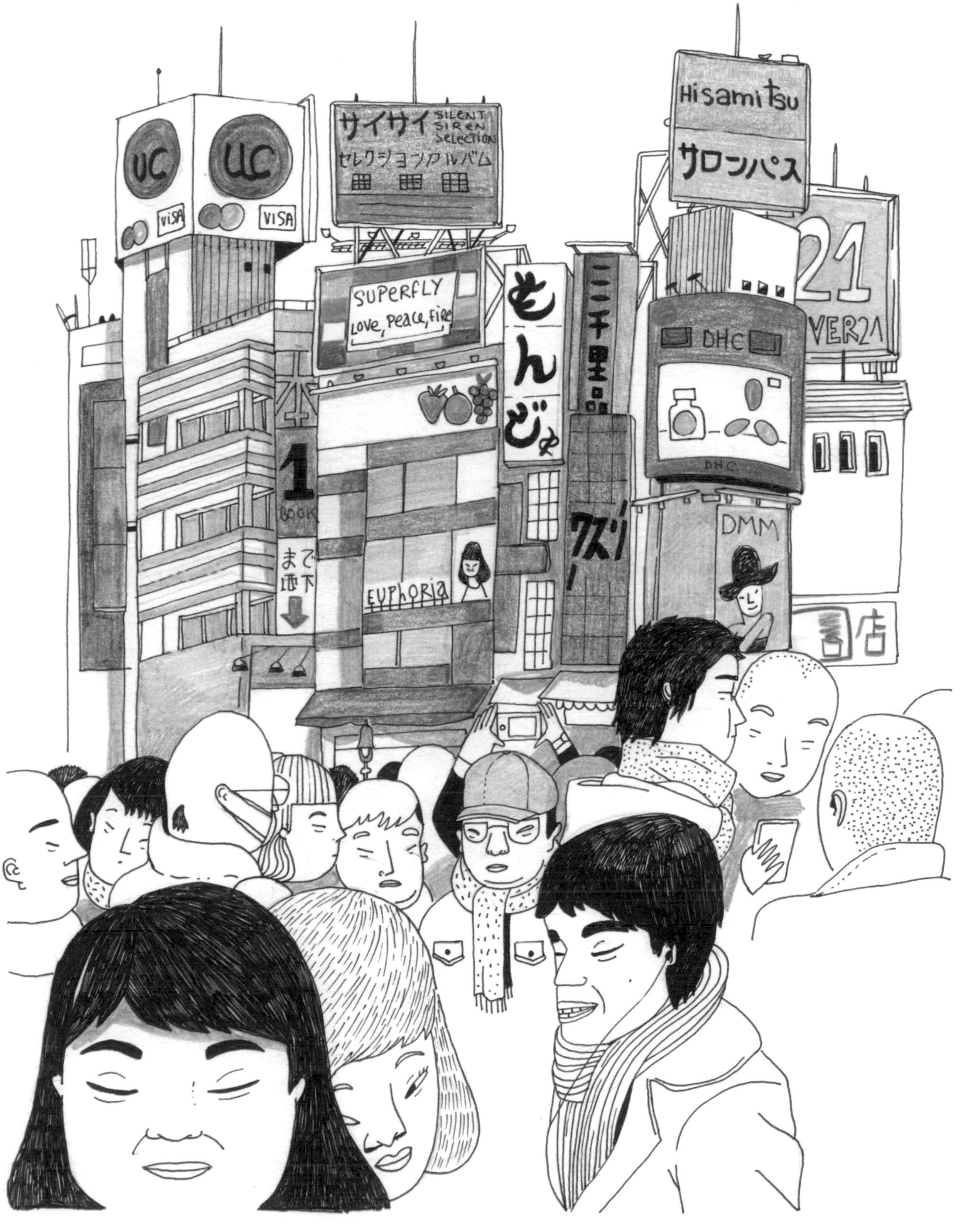
UC
VISA
サイサイ SILENT SIREN SELECTION
セレクションアルバム
Hisamitsu
サロンパス
21
VER21
SUPERFLY
Love, Peace, Fire
もんじゃ
DHC
DMM
1
BOOK
EUPhoRia

Typical brand of Japanese beer → **Asahi**

Beer Hall

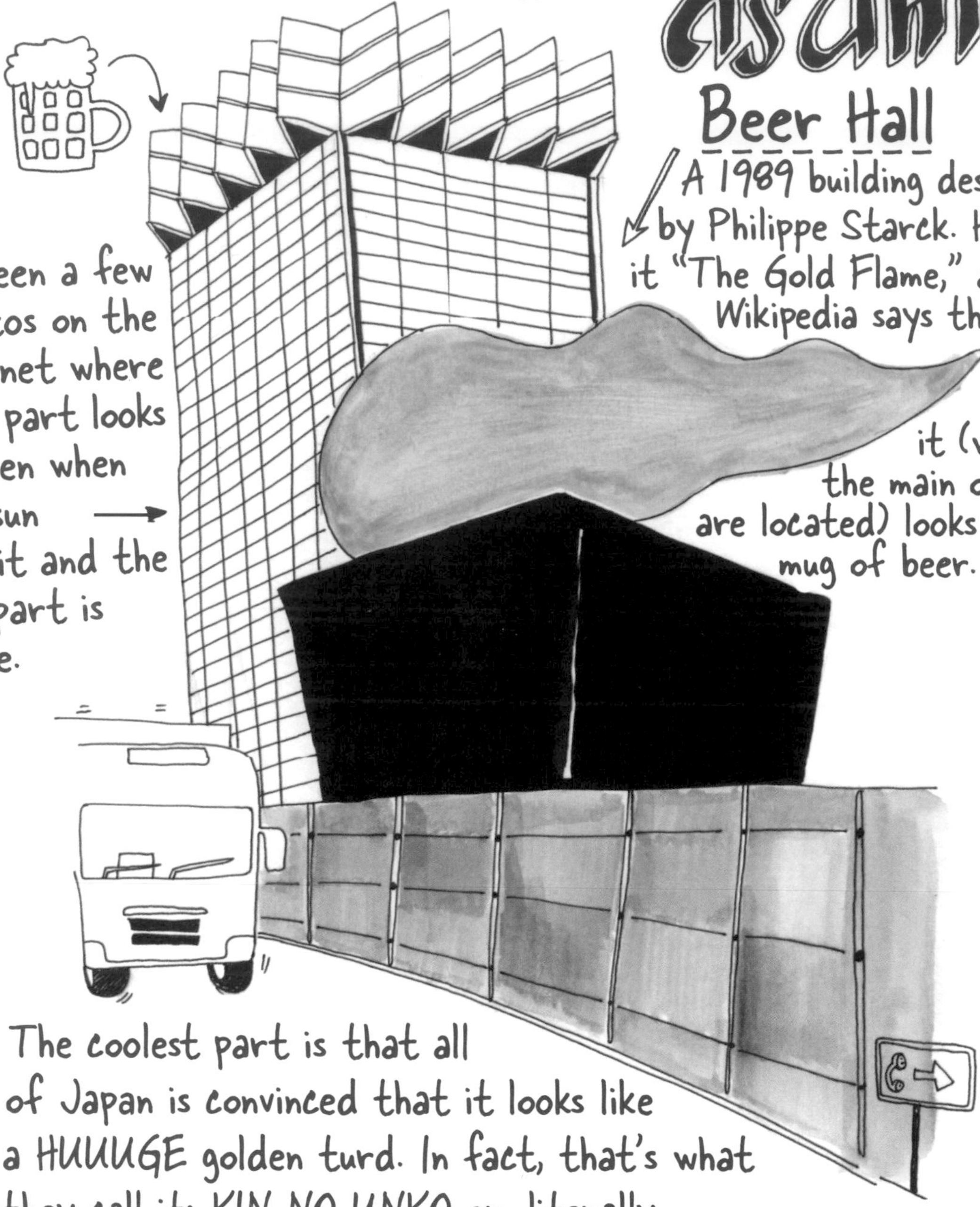

I've seen a few photos on the Internet where this part looks golden when the sun → hits it and the top part is white.

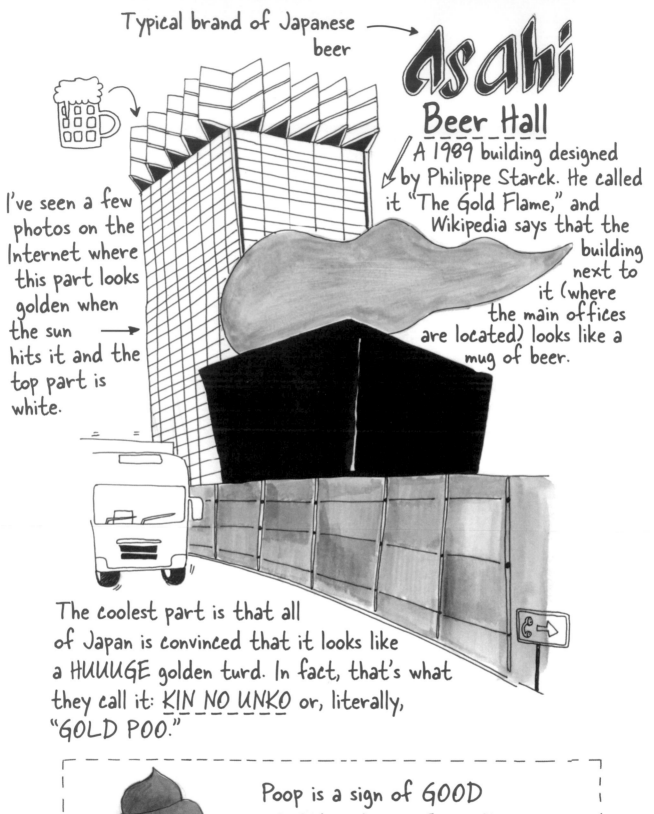

A 1989 building designed by Philippe Starck. He called it "The Gold Flame," and Wikipedia says that the building next to it (where the main offices are located) looks like a mug of beer.

The coolest part is that all of Japan is convinced that it looks like a HUUUGE golden turd. In fact, that's what they call it: KIN NO UNKO or, literally, "GOLD POO."

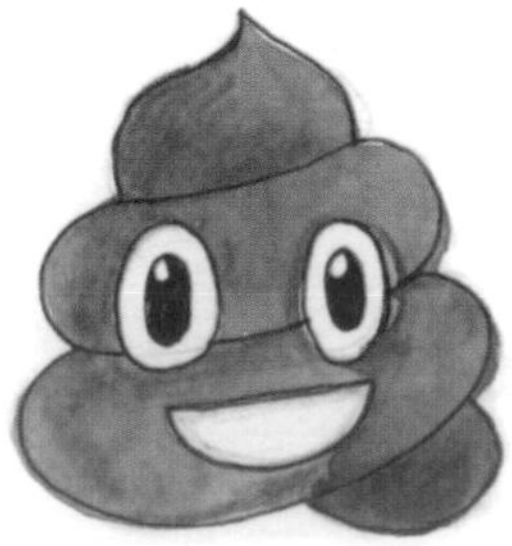

Poop is a sign of GOOD LUCK in Japan. Ergo, the famous smiling poop emoji.

• Professor Poop

There's a book called "Unko Kanji Doriru" that teaches kids a ton of phrases with the word UNKO ("poop") so they can learn the more than 1,000 kanji characters. (It's one of the 6 best-selling books on Amazon in Japan. O_O)

• Tokyo's National Museum of Emerging Sciences and Innovation had an exhibit on the digestive process. The kids could slide down a TOILET-shaped slide.

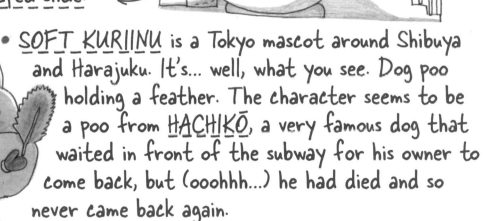

↳ Japanese kid with a poop cap.

Jump in, the water's fine!

• SOFT KURIINU is a Tokyo mascot around Shibuya and Harajuku. It's... well, what you see. Dog poo holding a feather. The character seems to be a poo from HACHIKŌ, a very famous dog that waited in front of the subway for his owner to come back, but (ooohhh...) he had died and so never came back again.

• POOP MAN

• The super famous ARALE with her friend UNCHI, Poop-Boy.

Akihiko Koseki made a video game, "Poo Pride," and to promote it he dressed up as Poop Man.

In a supermarket I found a comic whose protagonist is Butt Detective (Oshiri Tantei). He's a boy with a BUTT FACE, and when he finds something that's not quite right, he says: "I smell trouble..."

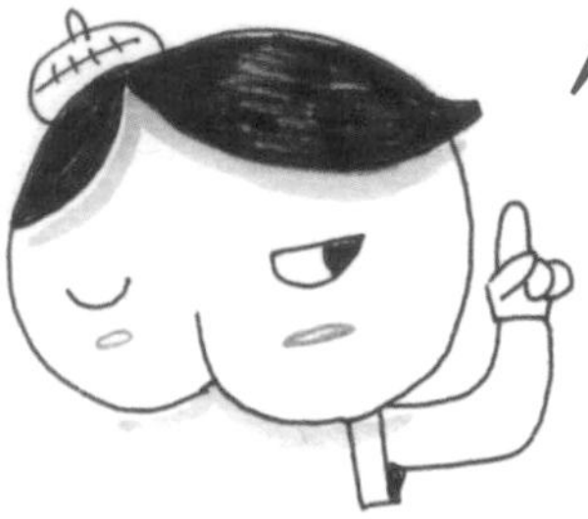

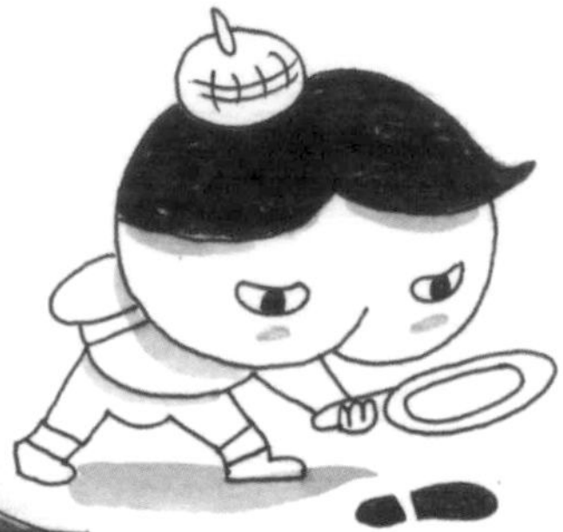

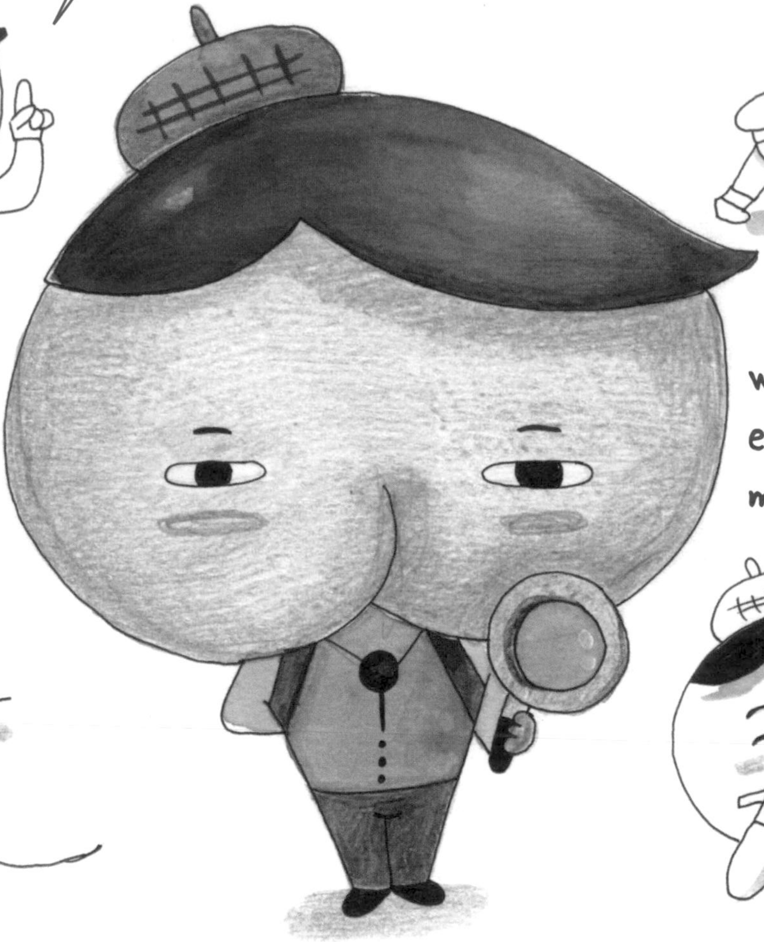

when he eats it's messed up.

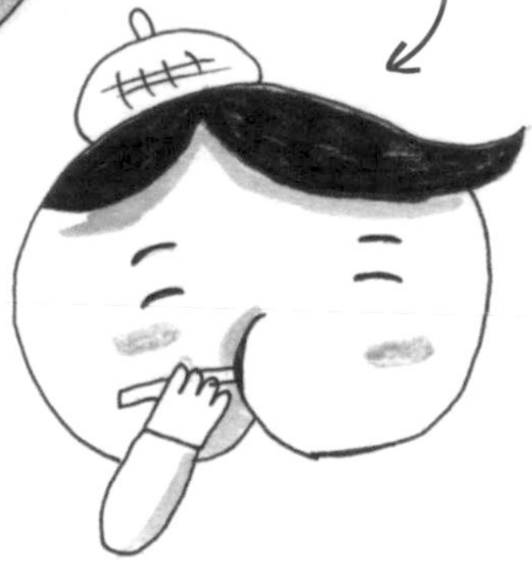

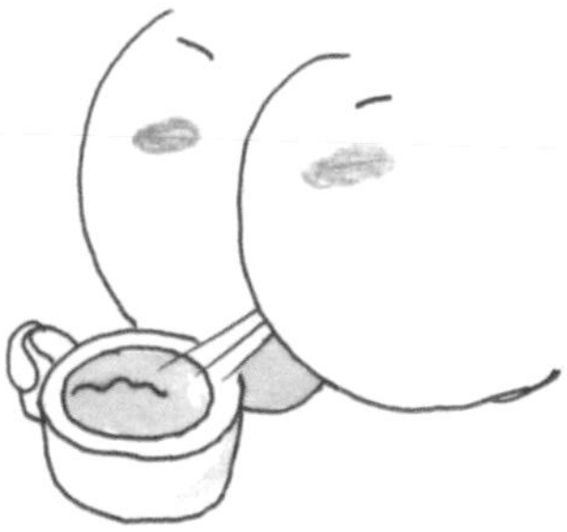

and when he blows on his coffee... a surreal work of art.

How did I end up talking about this?

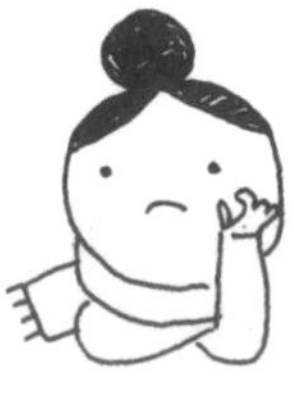

Going to the bathroom in Japan is an almost extraterrestrial experience.

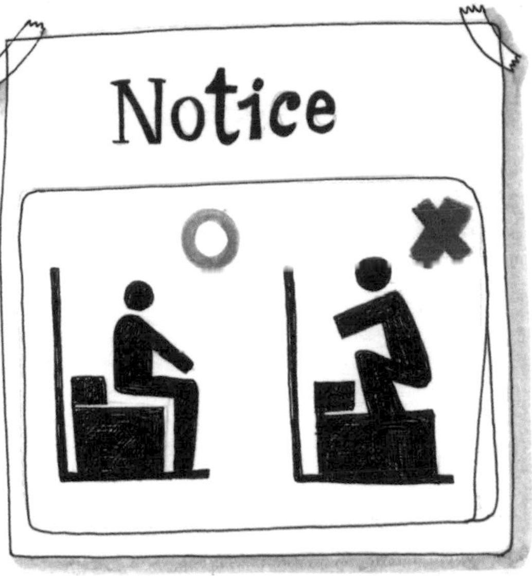
Notice

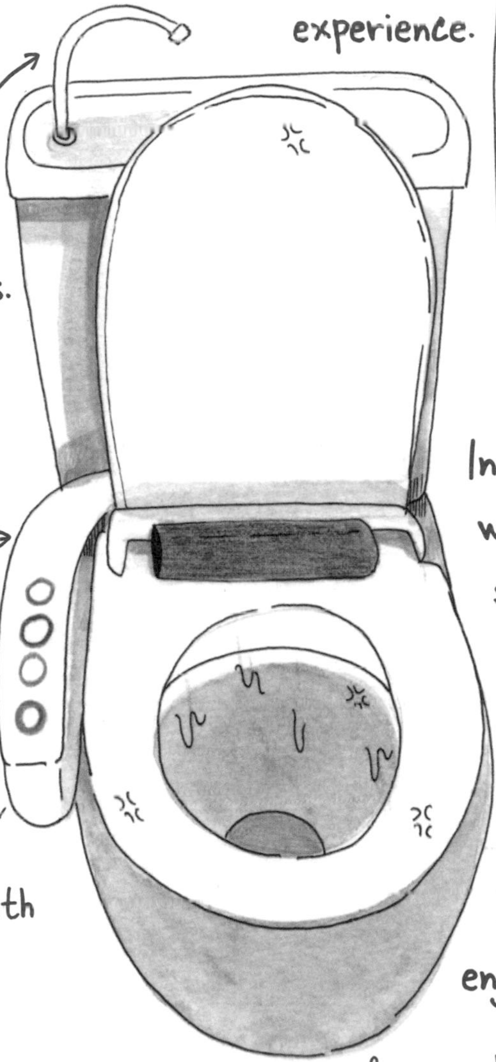

Little faucet for washing your hands.

I've gone into bathrooms where the lid opened by itself, thanks to a motion detector.

In Japanese cities chockablock with people packed in like sardines, going to the bathroom offers a moment of RARE PRIVACY. I think that's why they're so focused on these details, because they want to fully enjoy the moment.

Control with options.

Spray for cleaning your bum. // Spray for your vulva.

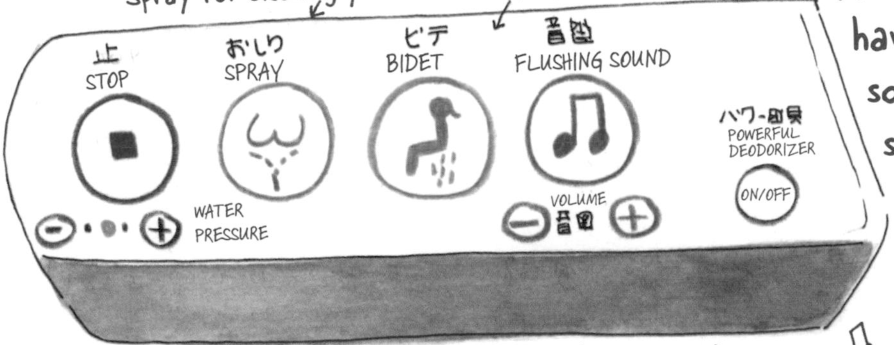
止
STOP
おしり
SPRAY
ビデ
BIDET
FLUSHING SOUND
POWERFUL DEODORIZER
ON/OFF
WATER PRESSURE
VOLUME

It must be horrible to have them hear you pee, so they have a sound system. It sounds like the tank is being flushed the entire time.

Some bathrooms (especially in homes) have slippers JUST for going to the bathroom (considered a "dirty area").

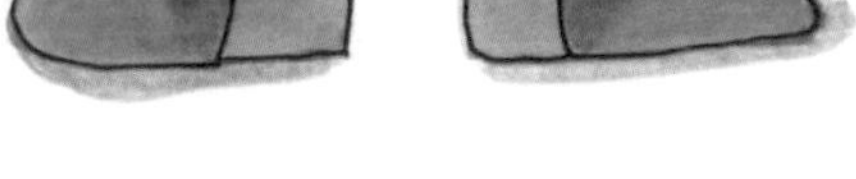

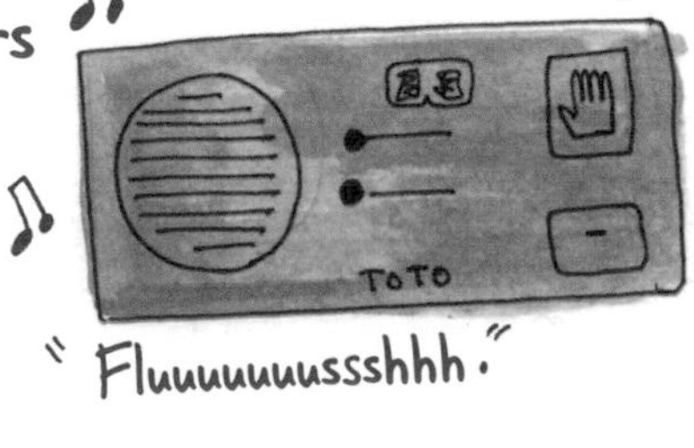
TOTO

"Fluuuuuuussshhh."

"Sudden Shower over Shin–Ōhashi Bridge and Atake"
  by Utagawa Hiroshige.   ┗ – – – – – – – – – – – →

"The Great Wave off Kanagawa"
  by Katsushika Hokusai (overleaf).

"The Fifty-Three Stations of the Tōkaidō "
  by Utagawa Hiroshige (second overleaf).

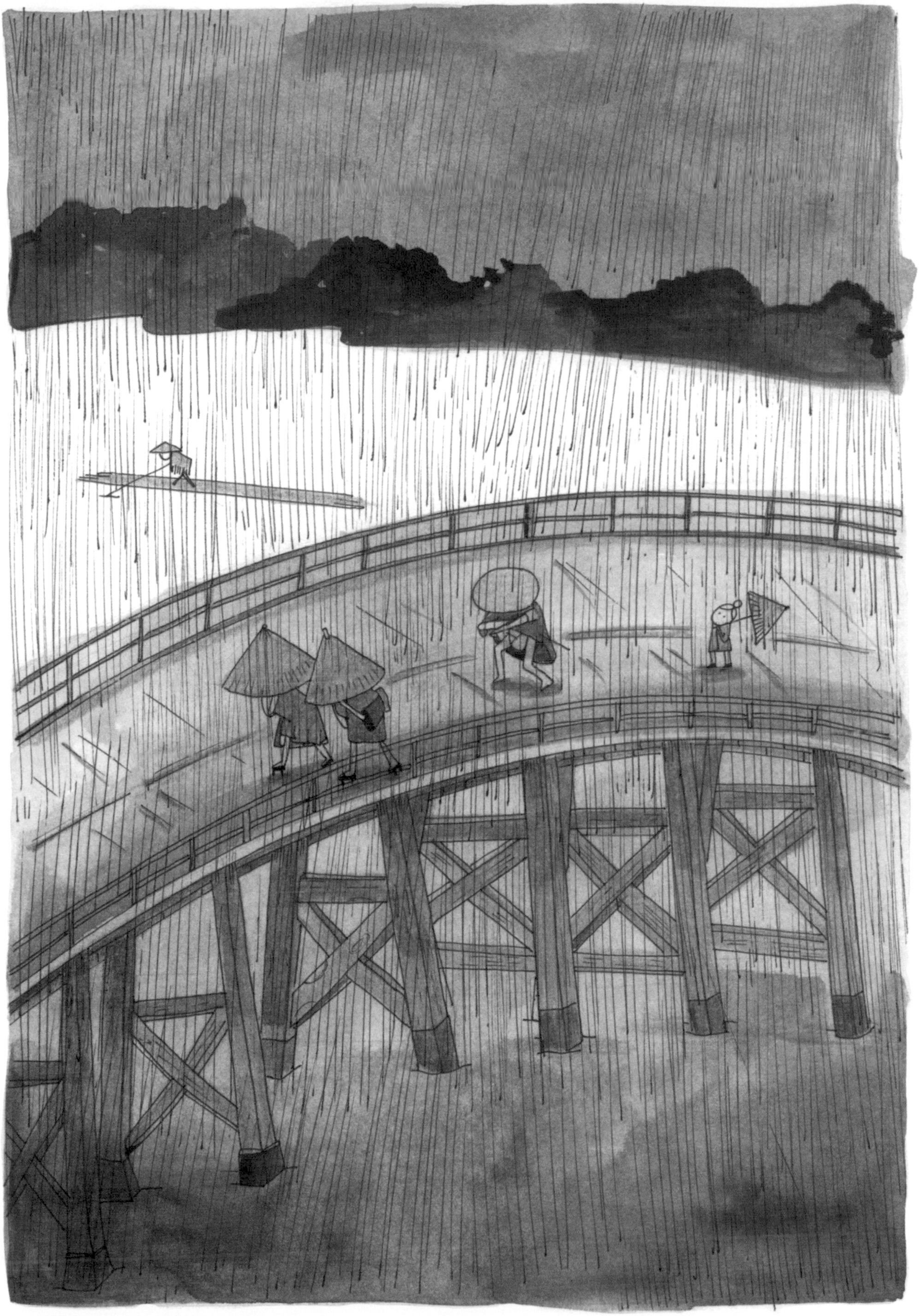

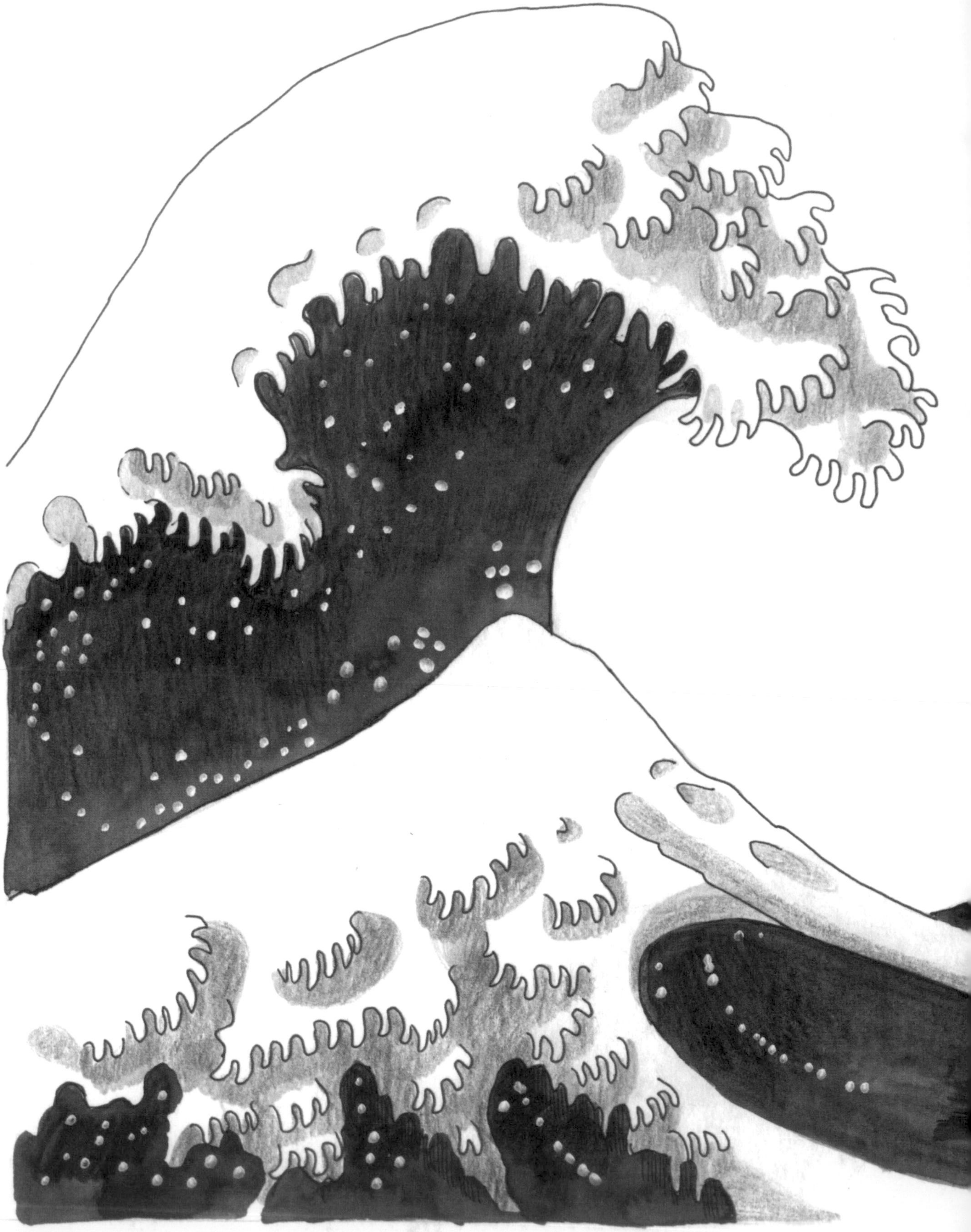

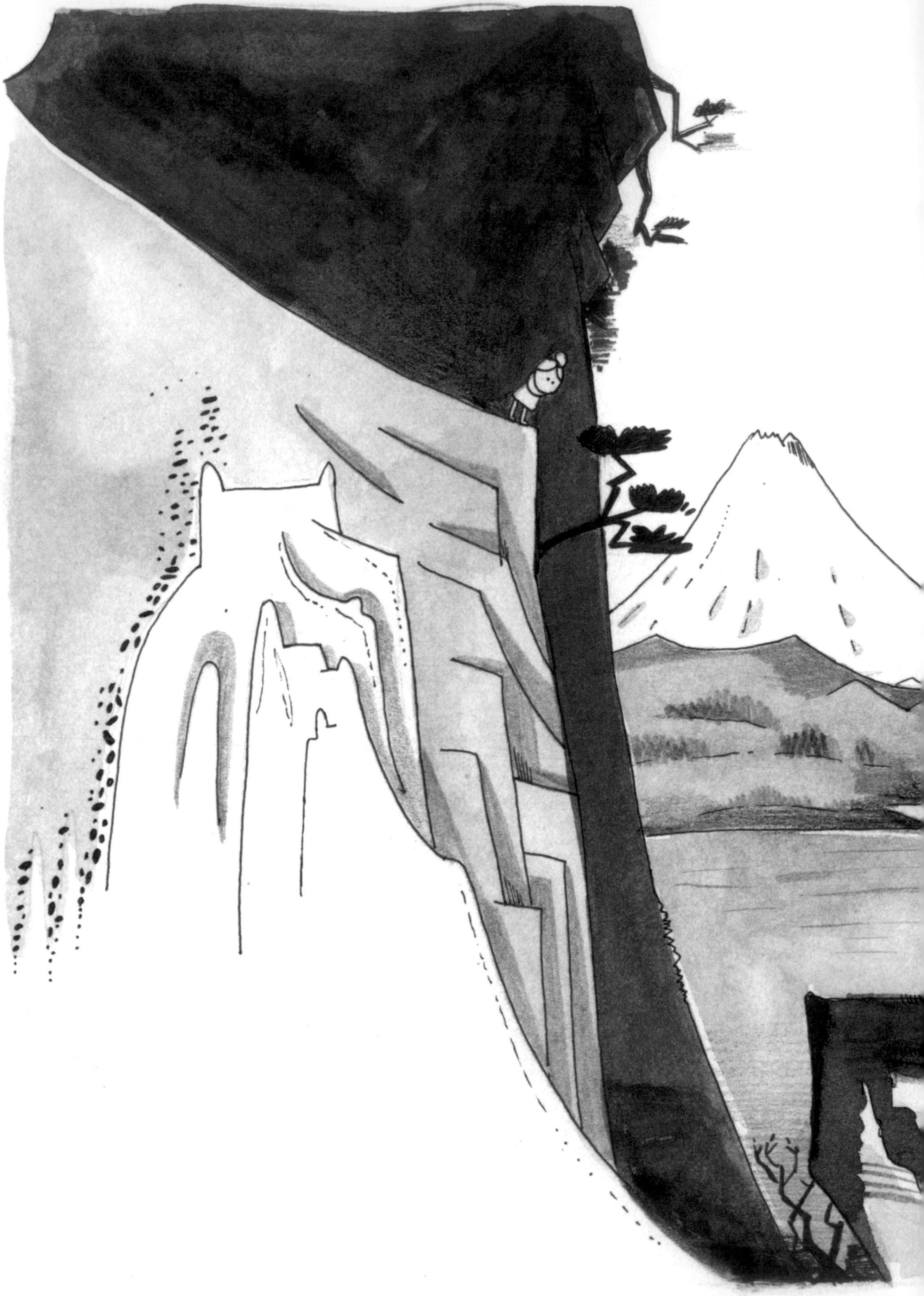

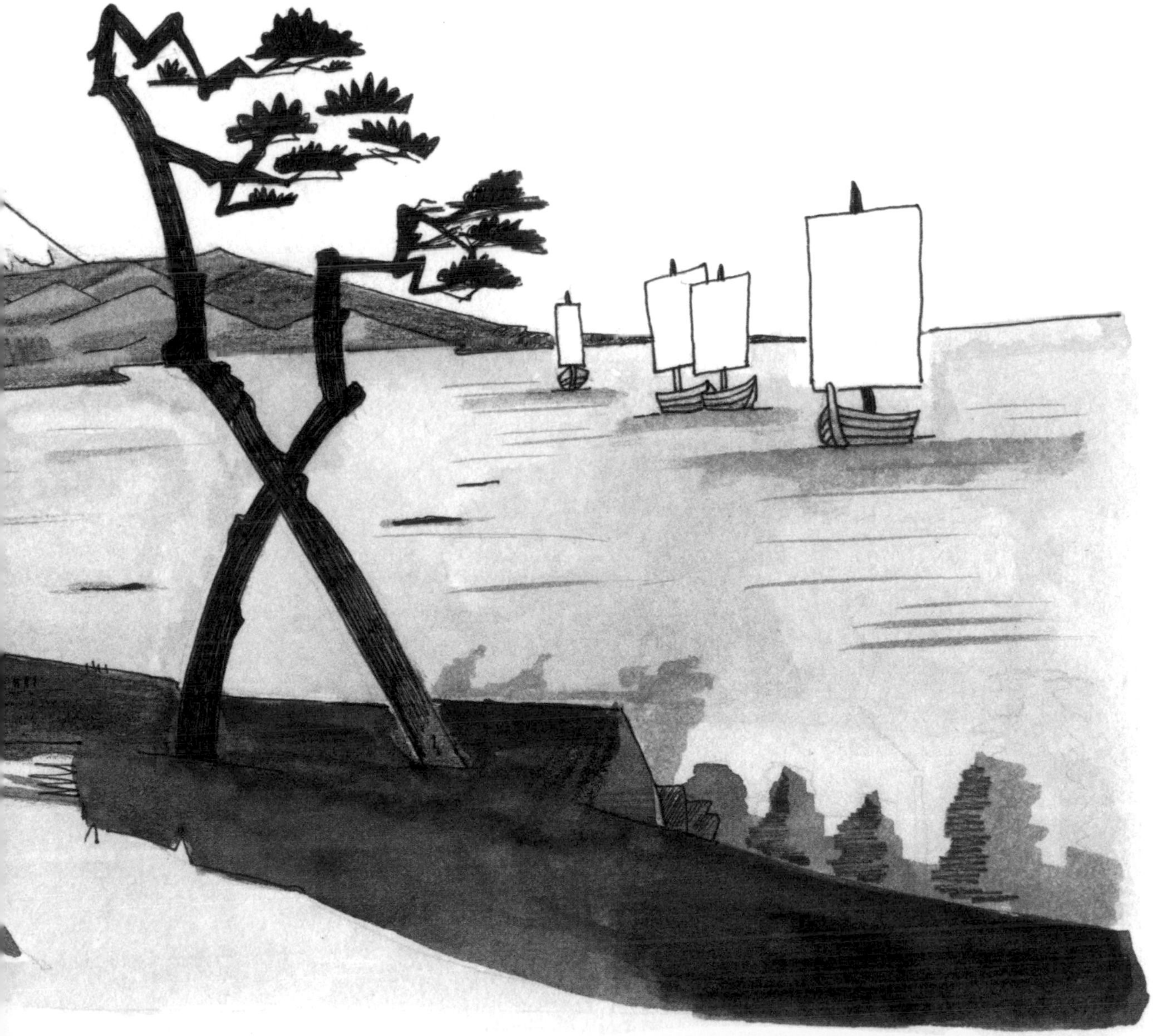

the UKiyo-e museum

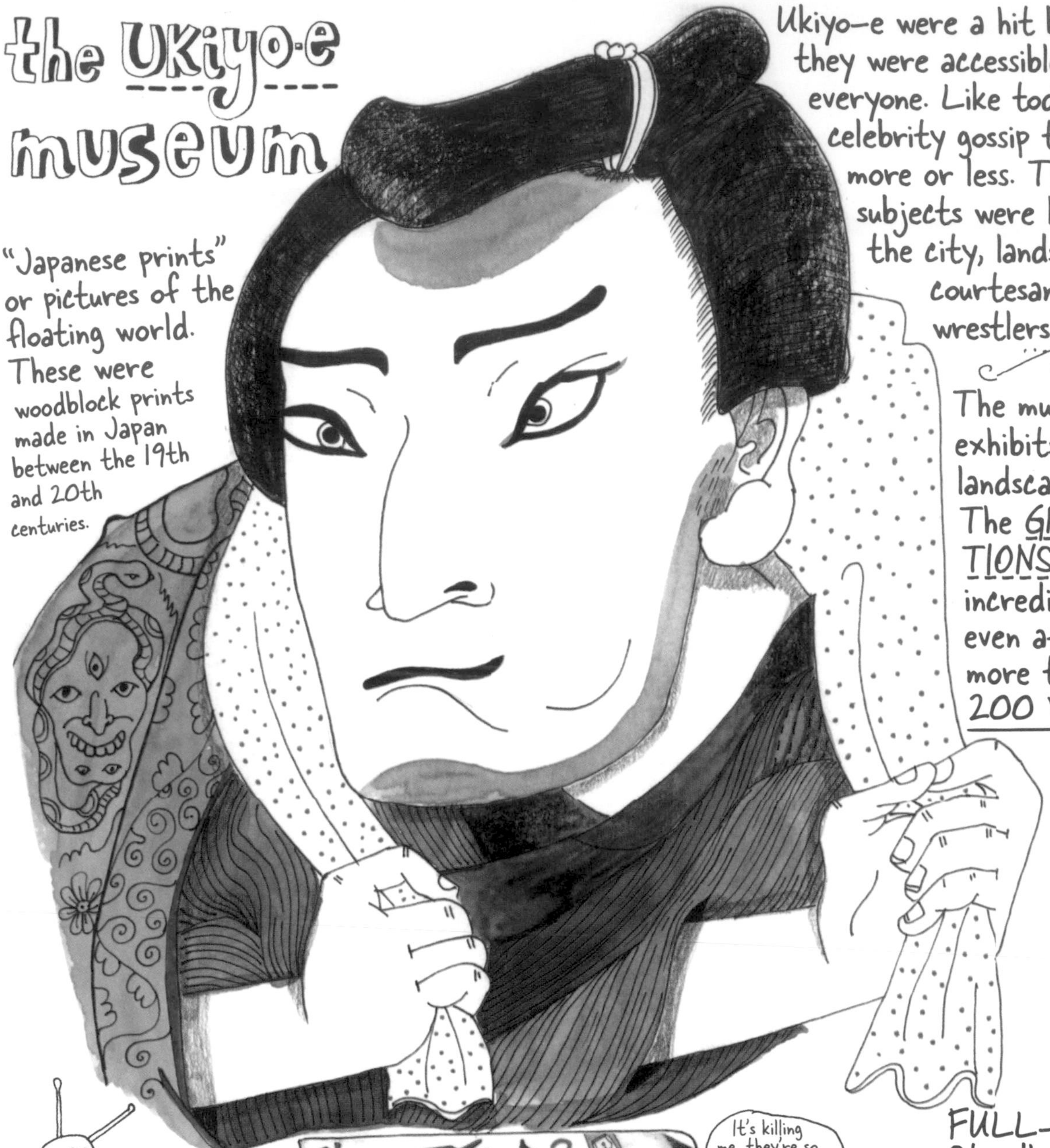

"Japanese prints" or pictures of the floating world. These were woodblock prints made in Japan between the 19th and 20th centuries.

Ukiyo-e were a hit because they were accessible for everyone. Like today's celebrity gossip tabloids, more or less. Their subjects were life in the city, landscapes, courtesans, sumo wrestlers...

The museum exhibits mainly landscapes. The GRADA-TIONS were incredible, even after more than 200 YEARS.

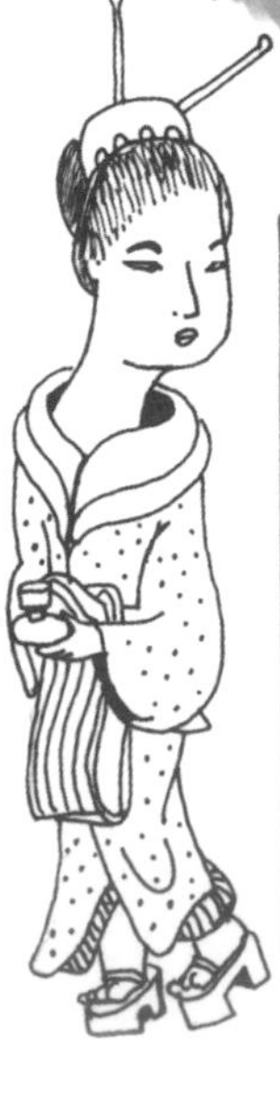

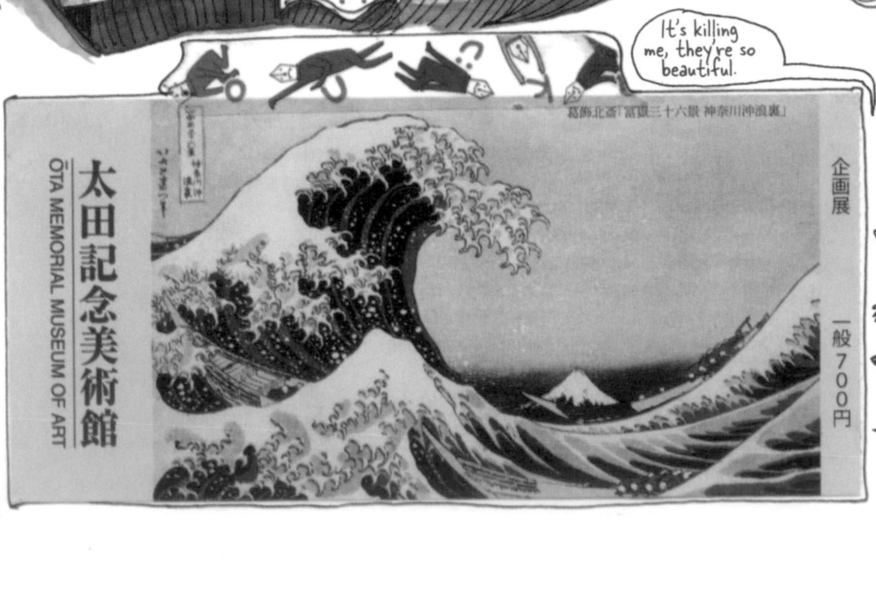

葛飾北斎「富嶽三十六景 神奈川沖浪裏」
太田記念美術館
ŌTA MEMORIAL MUSEUM OF ART
企画展
一般700円

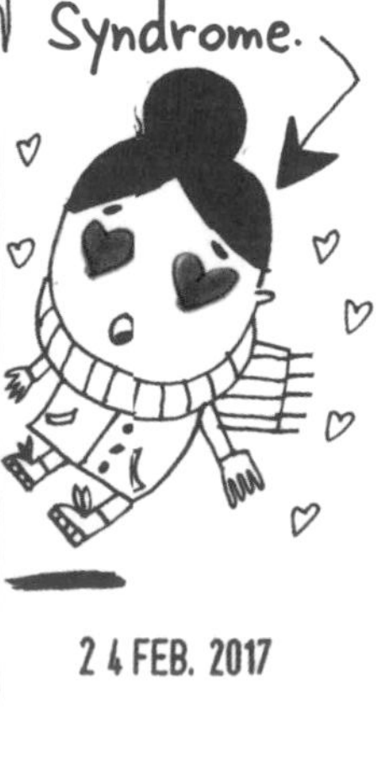

It's killing me, they're so beautiful.

FULL-ON Stendhal Syndrome.

2 4 FEB. 2017

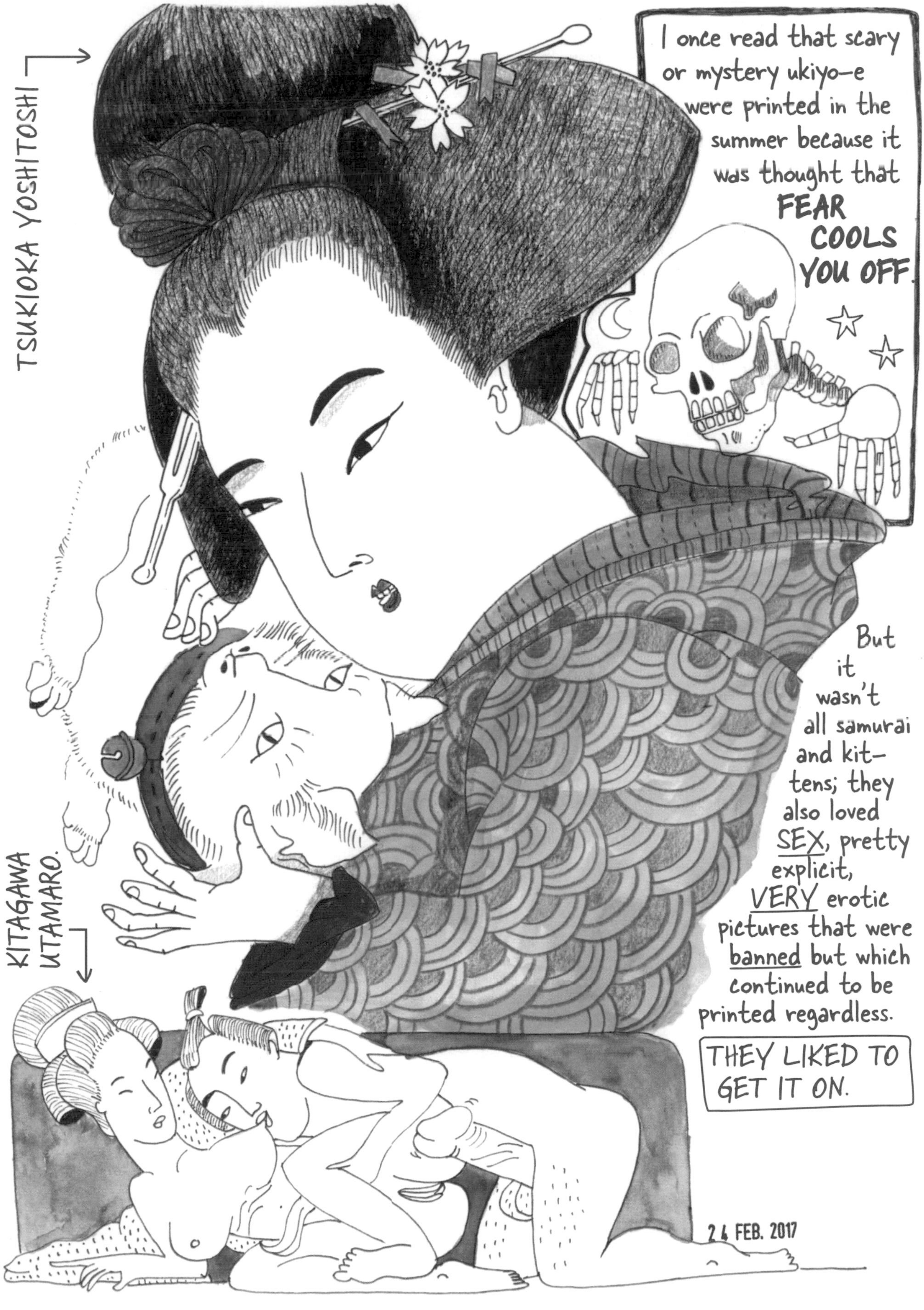

TSUKIOKA YOSHITOSHI
I once read that scary or mystery ukiyo-e were printed in the summer because it was thought that FEAR COOLS YOU OFF.
But it wasn't all samurai and kit-tens; they also loved SEX, pretty explicit, VERY erotic pictures that were banned but which continued to be printed regardless.
THEY LIKED TO GET IT ON.
KITAGAWA UTAMARO.
24 FEB. 2017

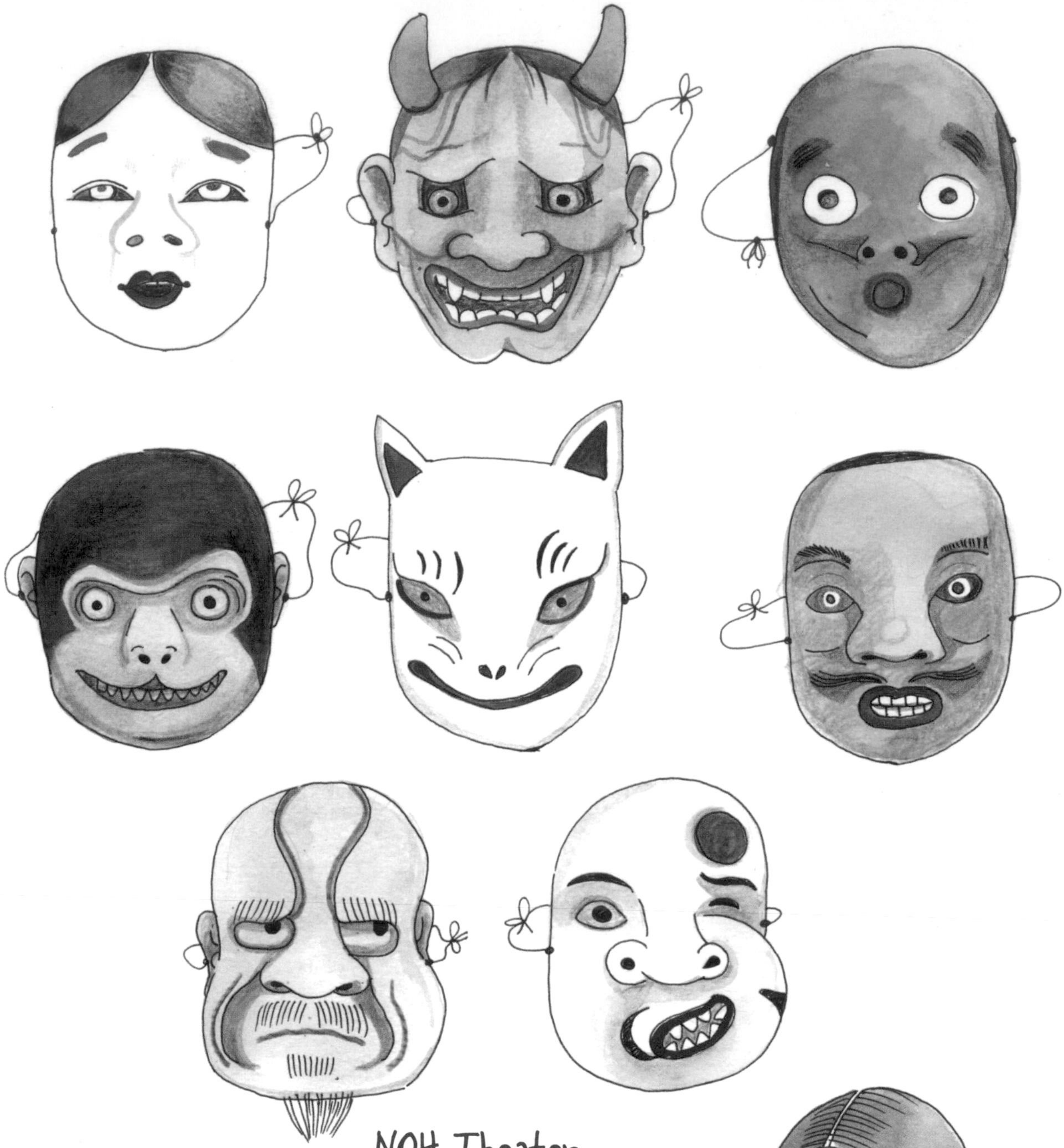

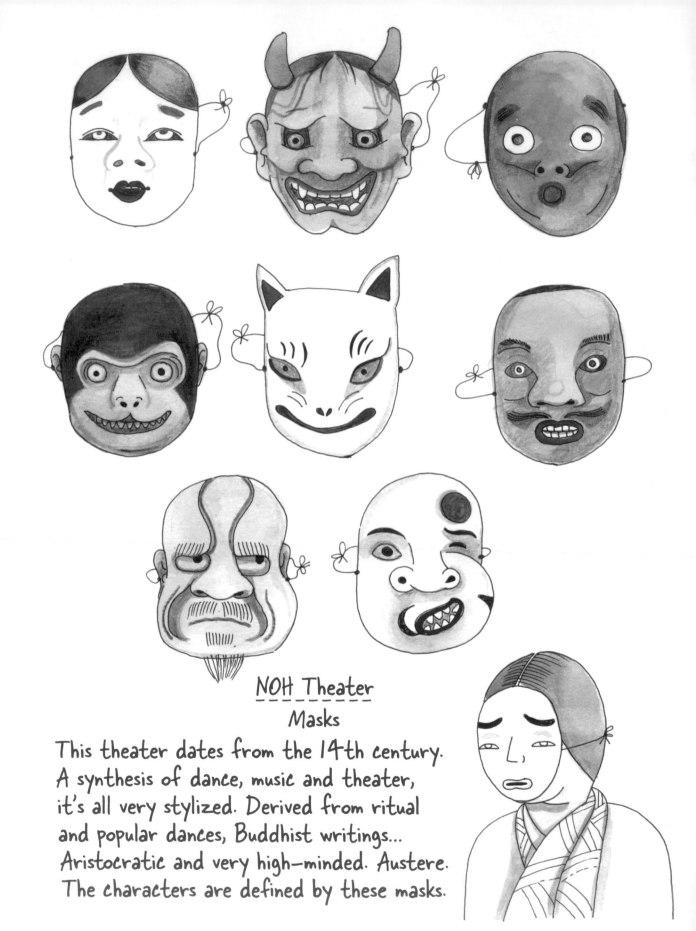

NOH Theater

Masks

This theater dates from the 14th century. A synthesis of dance, music and theater, it's all very stylized. Derived from ritual and popular dances, Buddhist writings... Aristocratic and very high-minded. Austere. The characters are defined by these masks.

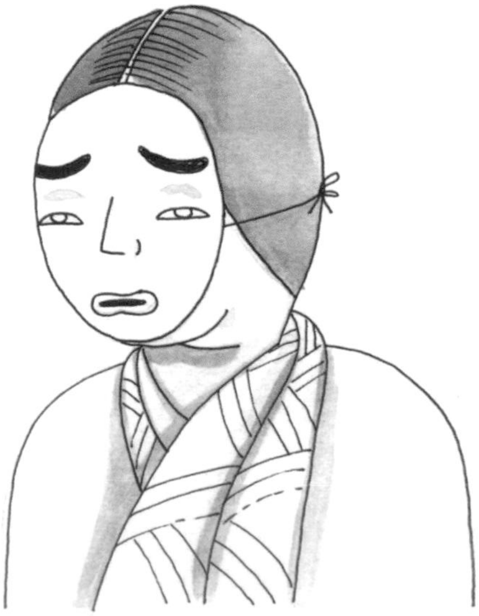

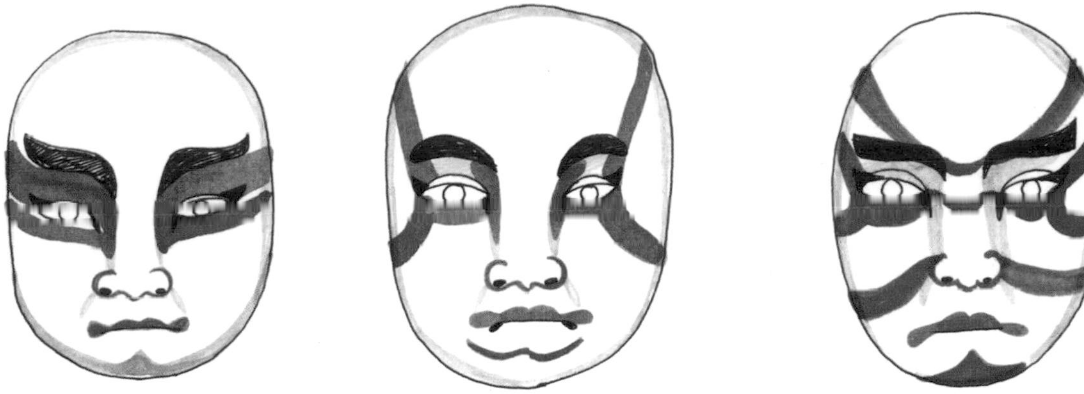

Some characters represent evil; others, consideration or calm; others, the passion of youth…

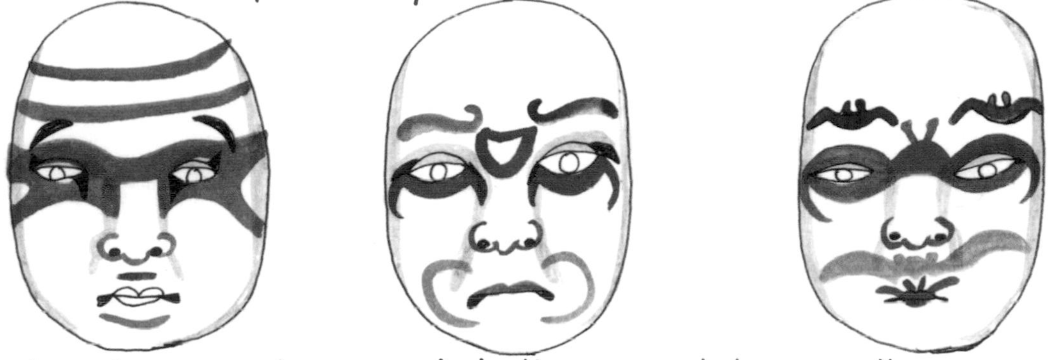

Some characters are gods.

And others are astute supervillains.

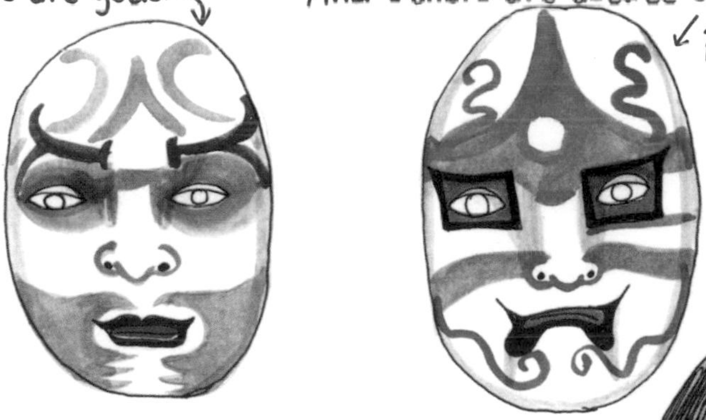

Each type of make-up represents certain values and has its own characteristics.

Kumadori Makeup in KABUKI THEATER

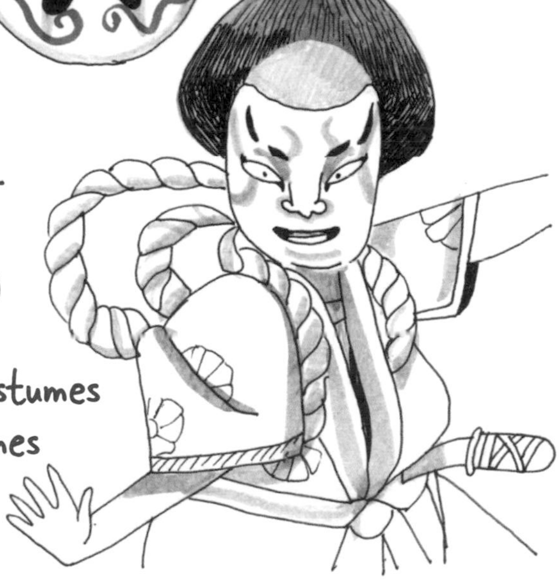

Much more popular than Noh. Despite having originated with Okuni, who was a woman, it ended up with women banned from performing in it. The colorful costumes reflect the tastes of merchants. Themes revolve around ordinary people and their obligations toward society.

Kabuki theaters tend to stage plays that deal with individuals and their obligations to the society around them, their responsibility toward the collective.

These are stories in which it's understood that to survive individually, one needs the community, TOGETHERNESS; one needs to accept whatever comes, to laugh, drive away fears, BE PATIENT.

Kabuki theaters may date back a couple of centuries; nevertheless, their message remains at the VERY HEART of Japanese behavior.

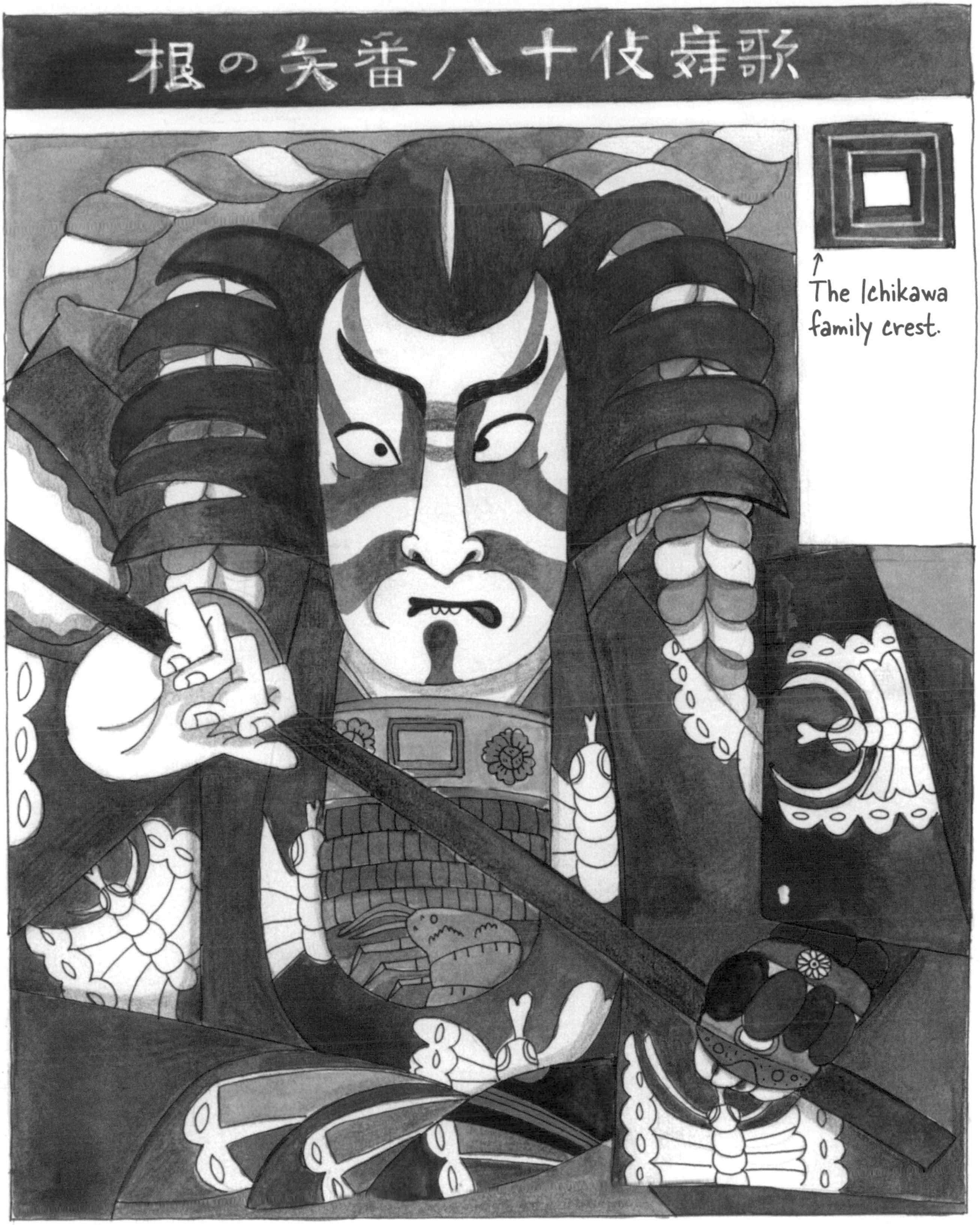
歌舞伎十八番矢の根
The Ichikawa family crest.

Poster from the early 20th century showing the Ichikawa Mimasu actor playing Soga Goro. The story of the Soga brothers includes vengeance, intrigue, adventure and a bit of romance. It became very popular.

Sumi—e, a monochromatic ink wash painting technique, came to Japan from China. ↙

A couple of years ago, I took a four-session course on shodō, Japanese calligraphy. I was able to attend by skipping out of the agency where I was working (I've never told this to anyone).
What you need to learn this technique is not just practice but also PEACE OF MIND.

The drawings are supposedly made with a single stroke.

What you draw is a reflection of your inner self. You need to be calm and have a clear head. On the first day the teacher told me I was very impulsive, that I had a great deal of character; on the second, she said I was a bit impulsive; and on the third, that I got carried away.
I didn't go back for the fourth class.

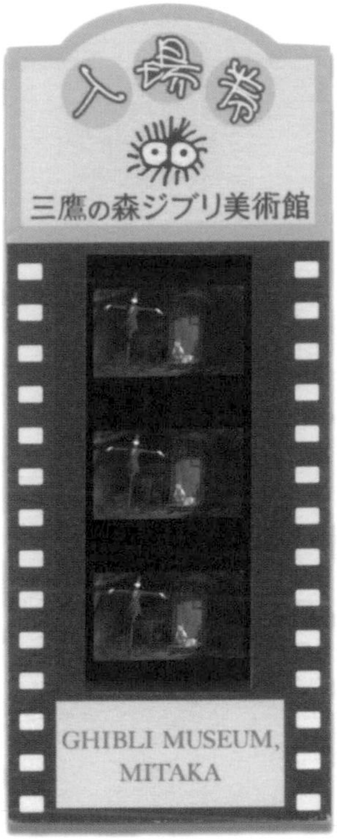
入場券
三鷹の森ジブリ美術館
GHIBLI MUSEUM,
MITAKA

One of the nicest things about the Ghibli Museum:
When you take your voucher, printed with the day and the time you're scheduled to go, they exchange it for this ticket.

A three-frame film strip from a Studio Ghibli film.

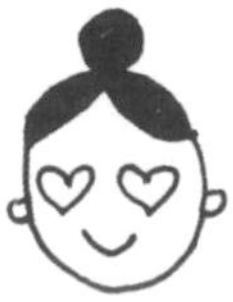

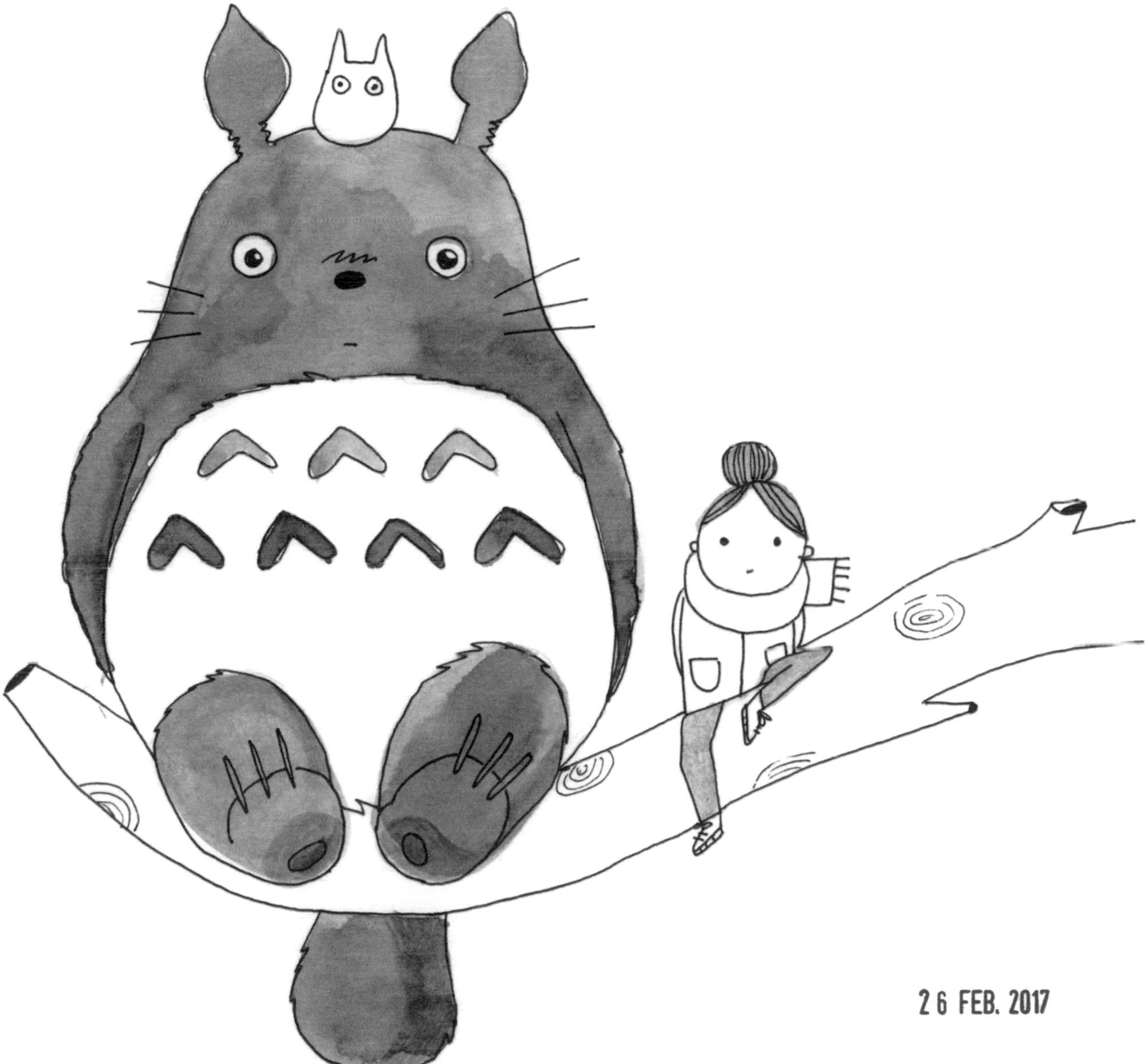

26 FEB. 2017

One of the Miyazaki characters I like the most is No Face or, as he's called in Japanese, **KAONASHI**.

It's a kind of shadow with a half-transparent mask that at first seems a bit friendly. Chihiro lets it into the gods' baths where she works, and the servants there discover that it can make GOLD. They fill it up until

it turns into some kind of foul, devouring, tyrannical MONSTER obsessed with CHIHIRO, who ignores it because she doesn't care about the gold. (Continues top right. ↗)

In the end it vomits everything and follows Chihiro on her adventure, having become completely docile, free from impulses, ambitions and appetites. I like it because I think almost everyone <u>has a NO FACE INSIDE</u>, and in life we often fight against certain

situations that bring out <u>the worst version of ourselves.</u>

At least in my case.

27 FEB. 2017

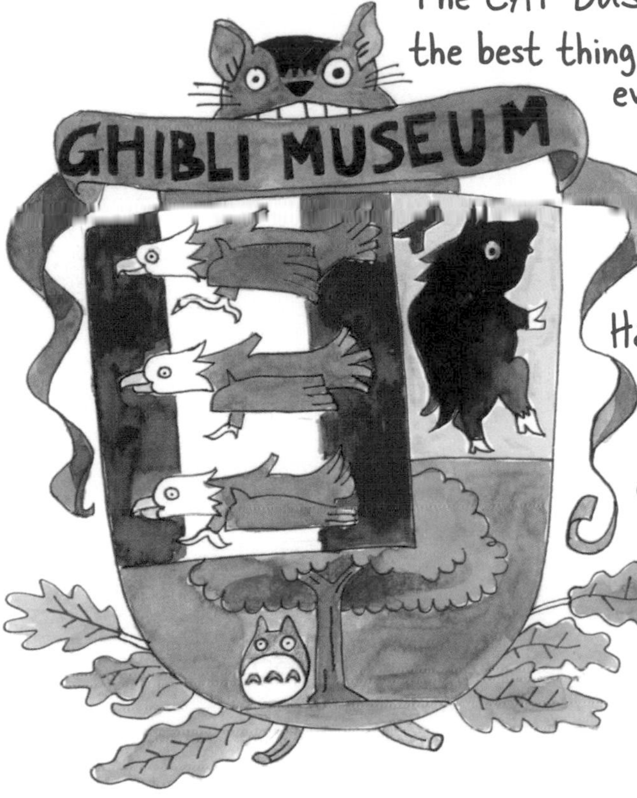
GHIBLI MUSEUM

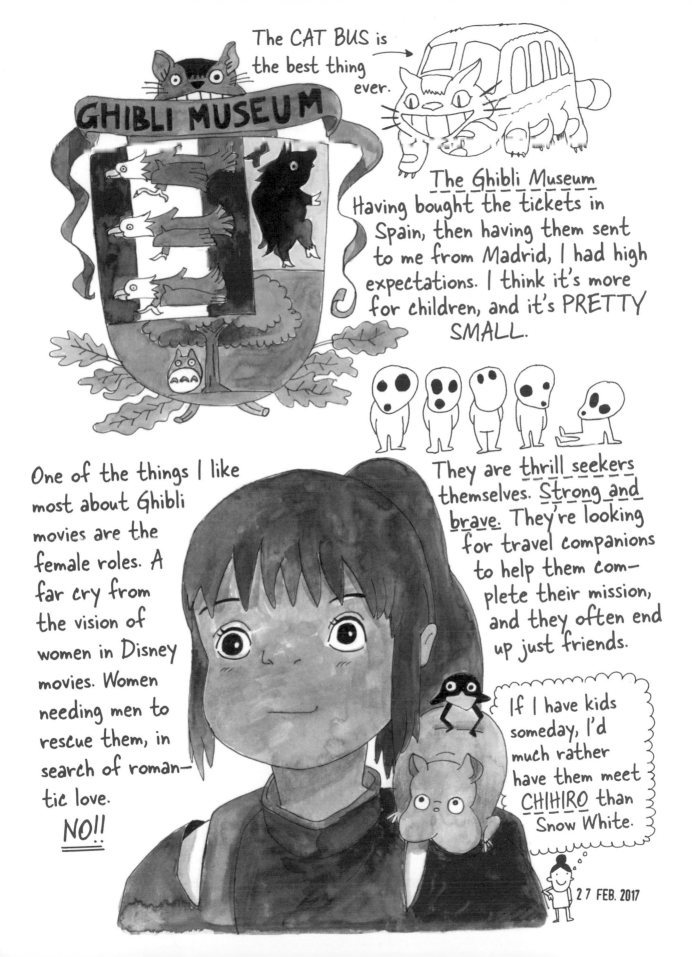

The CAT BUS is the best thing ever.

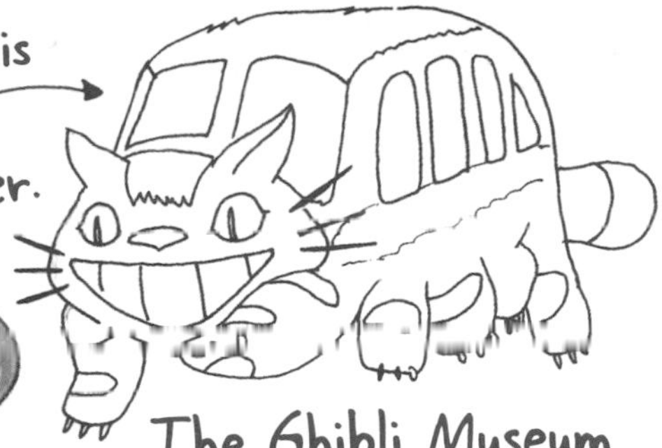

The Ghibli Museum

Having bought the tickets in Spain, then having them sent to me from Madrid, I had high expectations. I think it's more for children, and it's PRETTY SMALL.

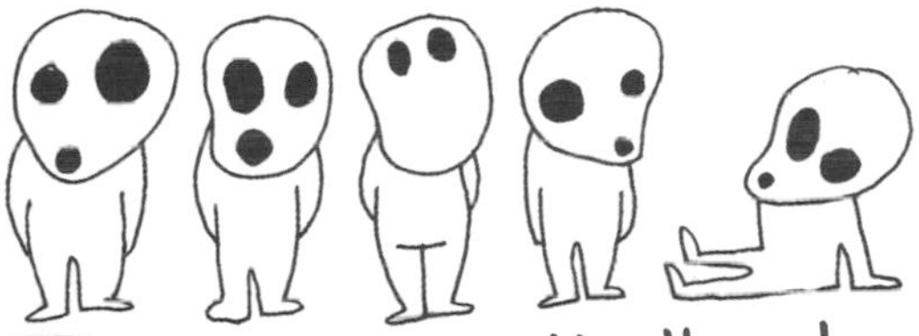

They are thrill seekers themselves. Strong and brave. They're looking for travel companions to help them complete their mission, and they often end up just friends.

One of the things I like most about Ghibli movies are the female roles. A far cry from the vision of women in Disney movies. Women needing men to rescue them, in search of romantic love.

NO!!

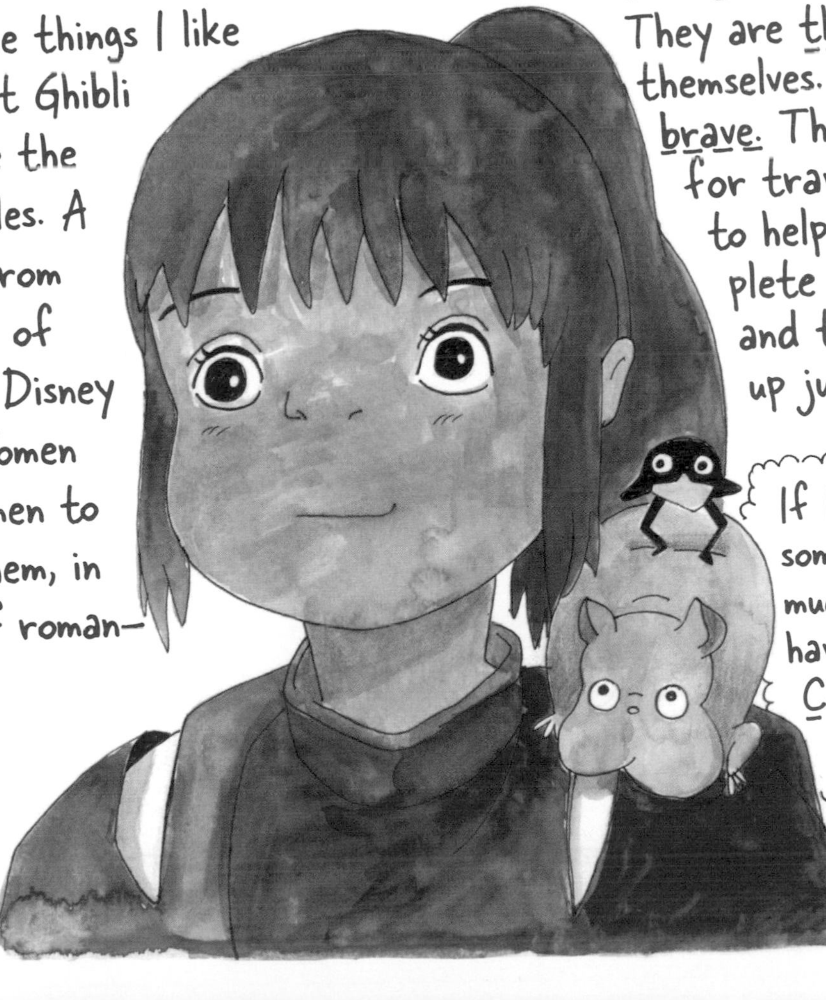

If I have kids someday, I'd much rather have them meet CHIHIRO than Snow White.

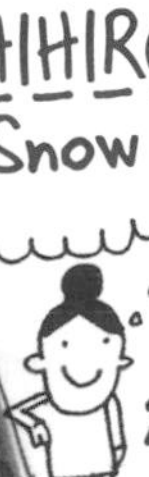

27 FEB. 2017

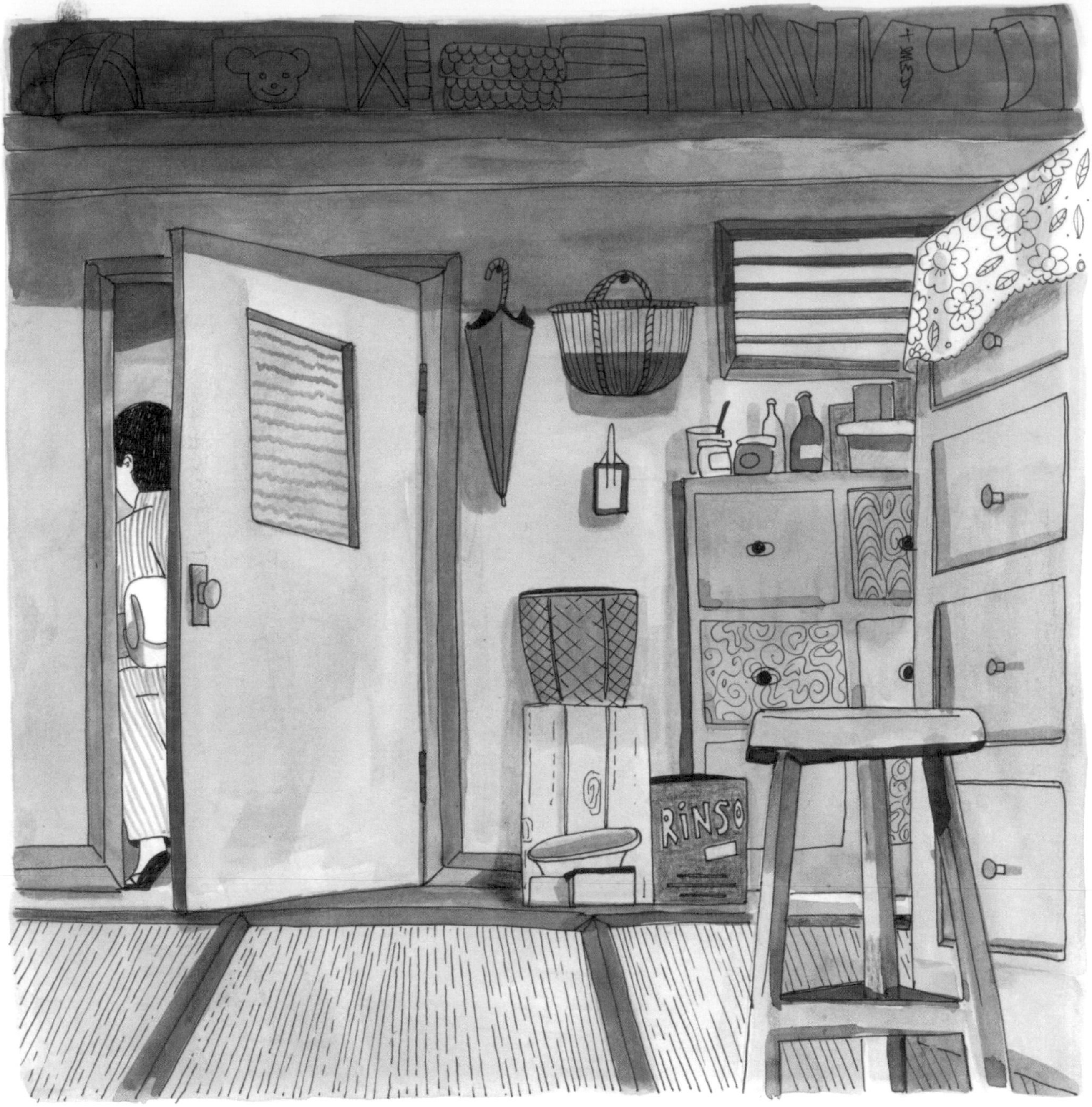
RINSO

Still from "Tokyo Story," by Yasujirō Ozu.

This is a beautiful movie that deals with the relationships between generations in one family. The parents leave their village to visit their children in Tokyo, where the latter are too busy to pay any attention to them.

Some might think it's too long, but it's perfect to help understand the conflict between the traditional values of the 50s and the

The only one paying attention to the parents is NORIKO, their son's widow.

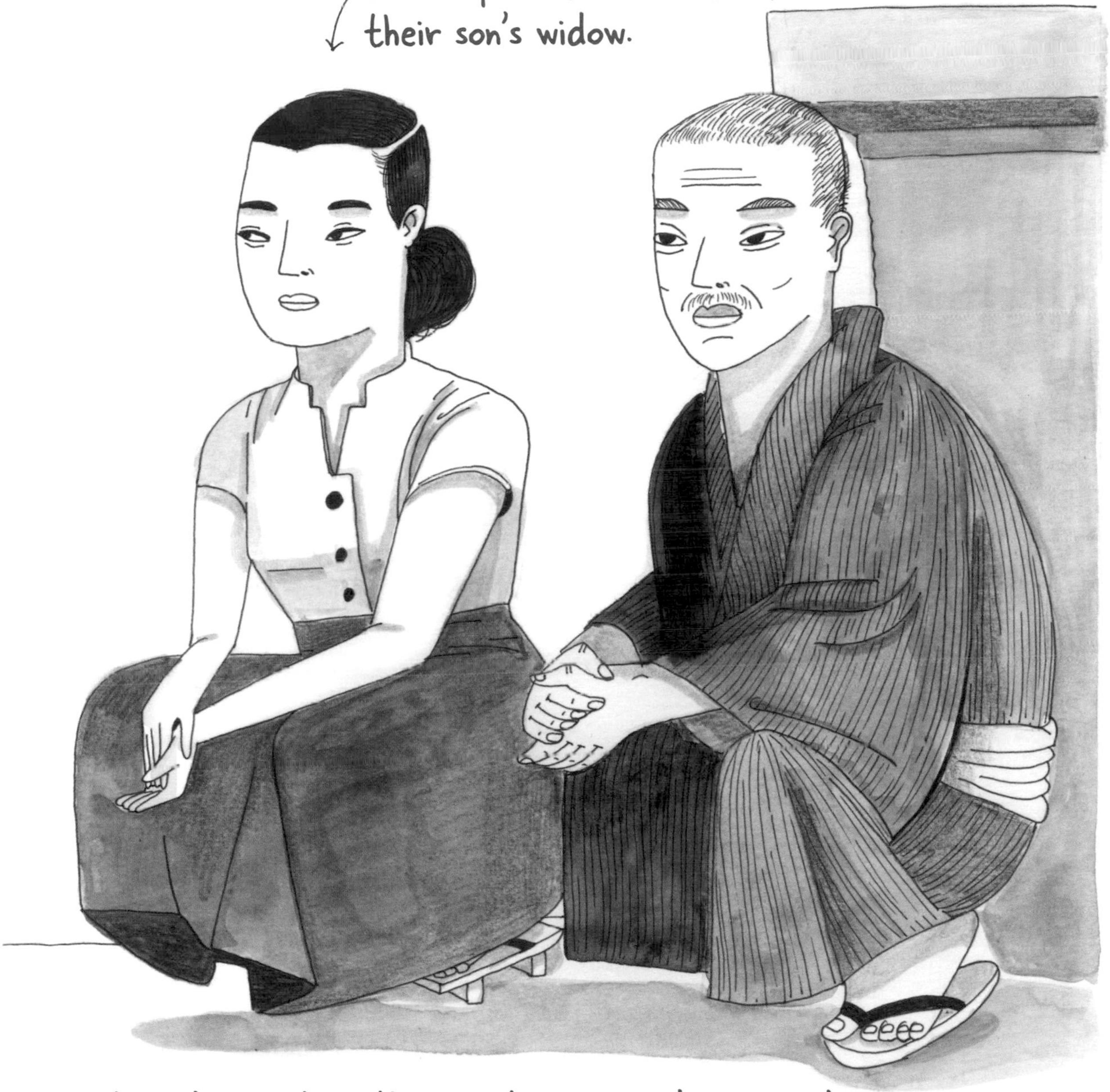

rampant modernization the country was undergoing: Japan seemed to be tearing itself apart.

Ozu always filmed his movies 35 inches (90 cm) from the ground, which is the height of a man sitting (obviously) on a tatami.

(Well, kneeling.)

I love this.

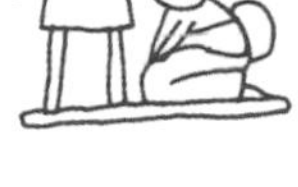

Takahashi-san is one of the patrons of my residency, a fairly important member of the residents' association. He's about 70 years old. He's the one who showed the most interest in and kindness towards me.

When I painted the mural in the train passageway, he stayed with me the whole time, standing on the first day, sitting in a camping chair the second day.

He came with his little dog, adorned with hairclips and clasps, tucked in his jacket.

He ate next to nothing, but one day he took me to an izakaya in Matsudo. I don't know how many kinds of ramen and sake I tried. He doesn't speak English, but we understood each other because he always carried around an electronic dictionary.

As I was painting the mural, I told him that I really liked the little bags you shook and stuck to your clothes for warmth. I said I hadn't seen them in Spain, and that my mother, who was always cold, would love them.

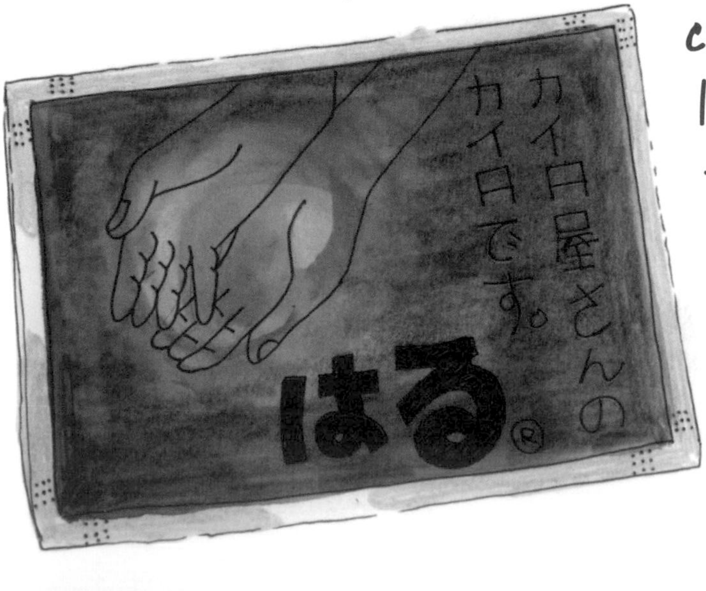
カイロ屋さんの
カイロです。
はる®

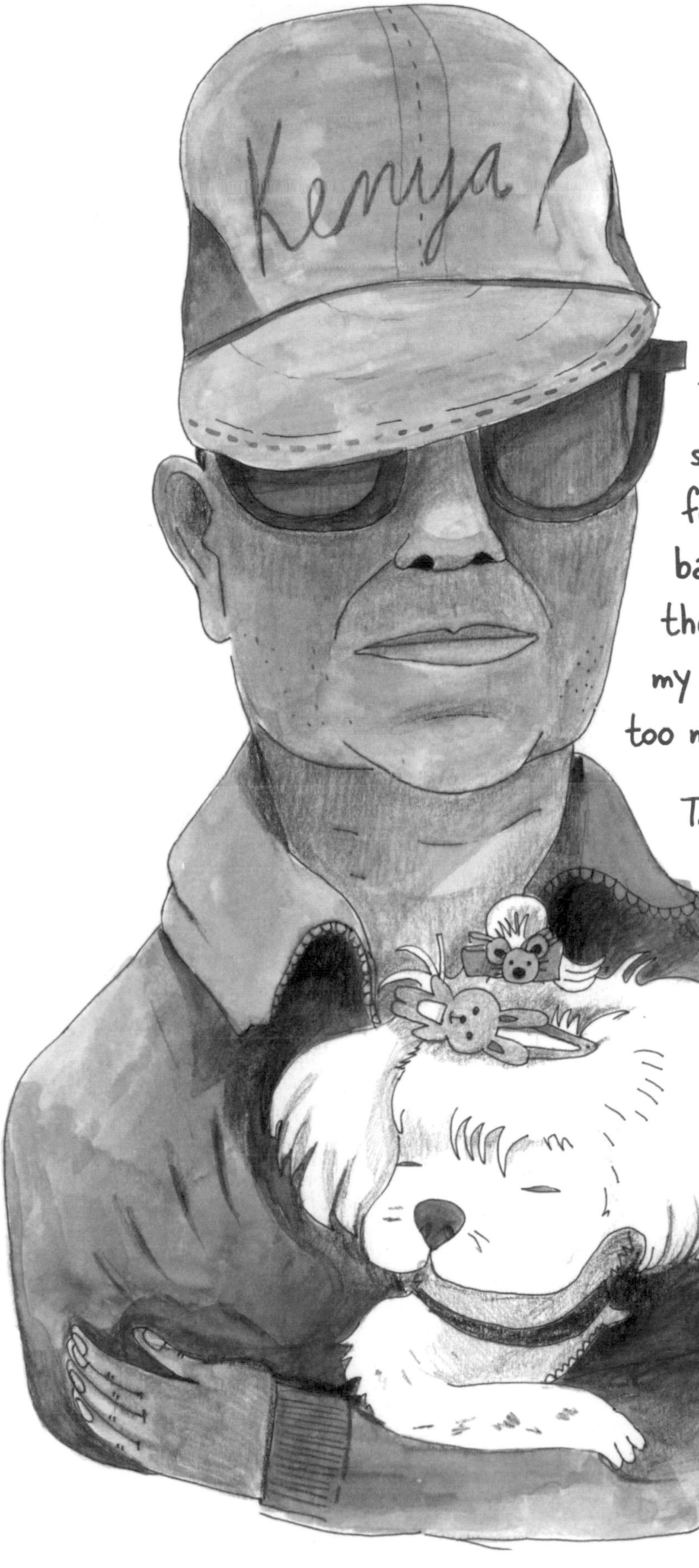
Kenya

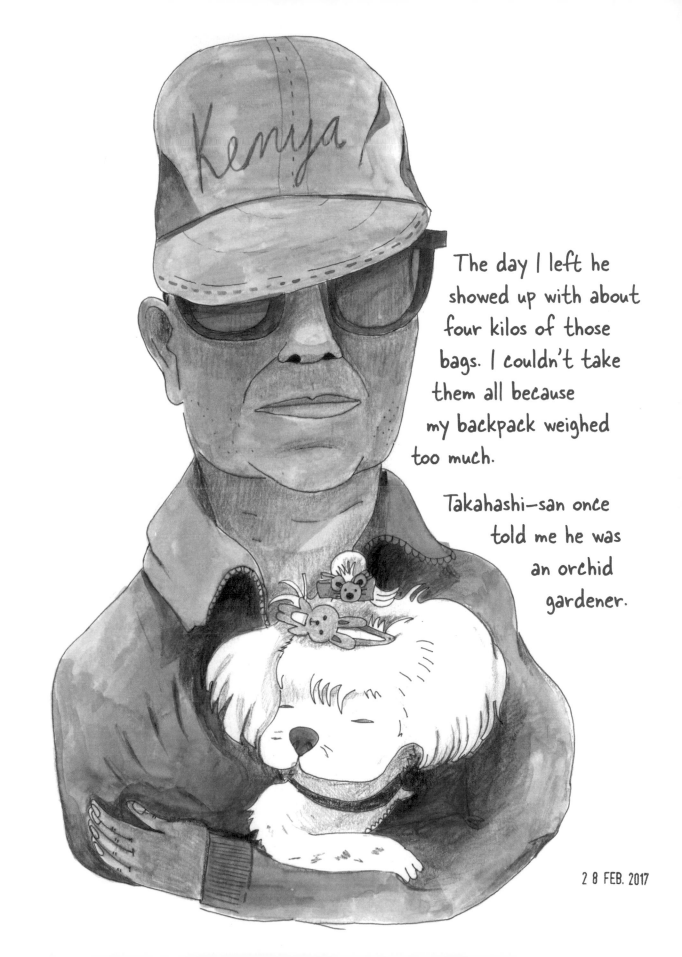

The day I left he showed up with about four kilos of those bags. I couldn't take them all because my backpack weighed too much.

Takahashi-san once told me he was an orchid gardener.

2 8 FEB. 2017

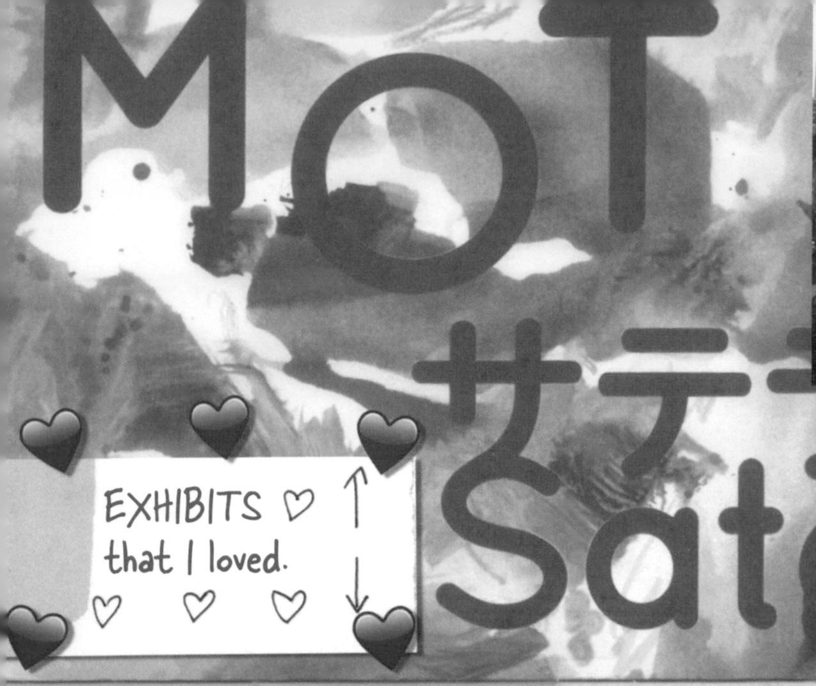
MOT
Satellite

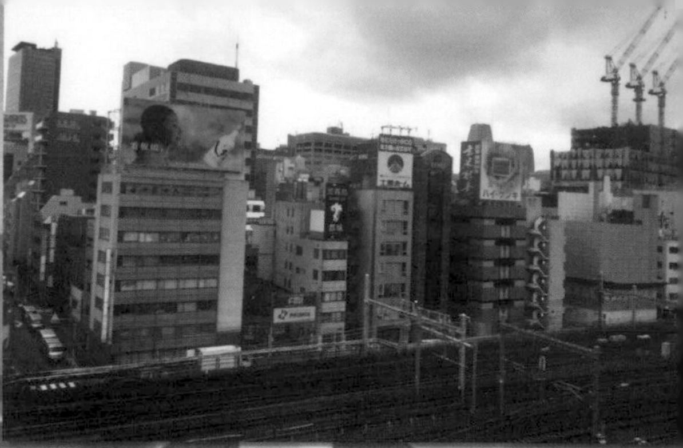

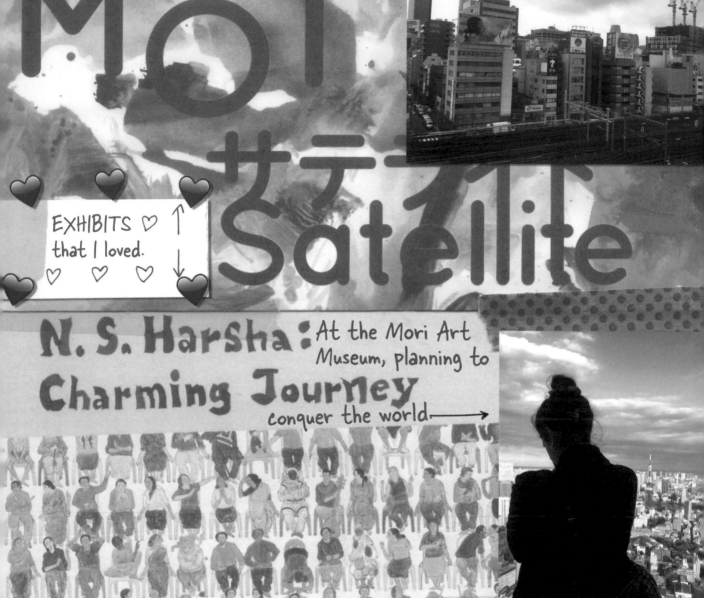

EXHIBITS ♡
that I loved.
♡ ♡ ♡

N. S. Harsha: Charming Journey

At the Mori Art Museum, planning to conquer the world →

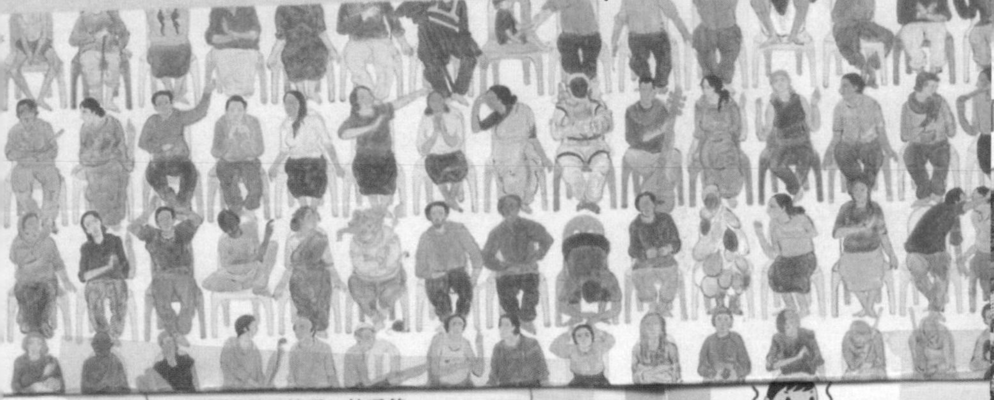

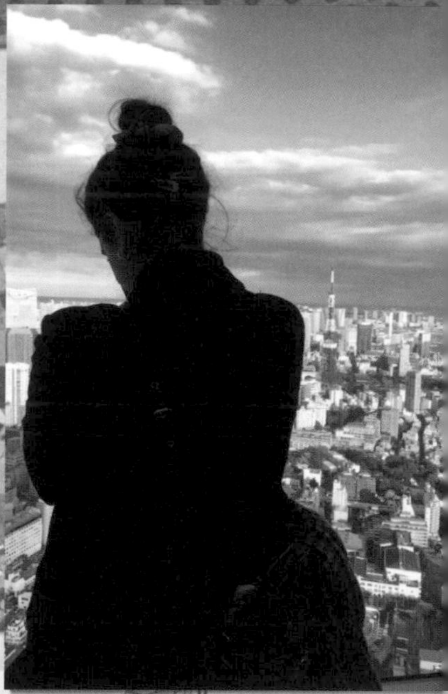

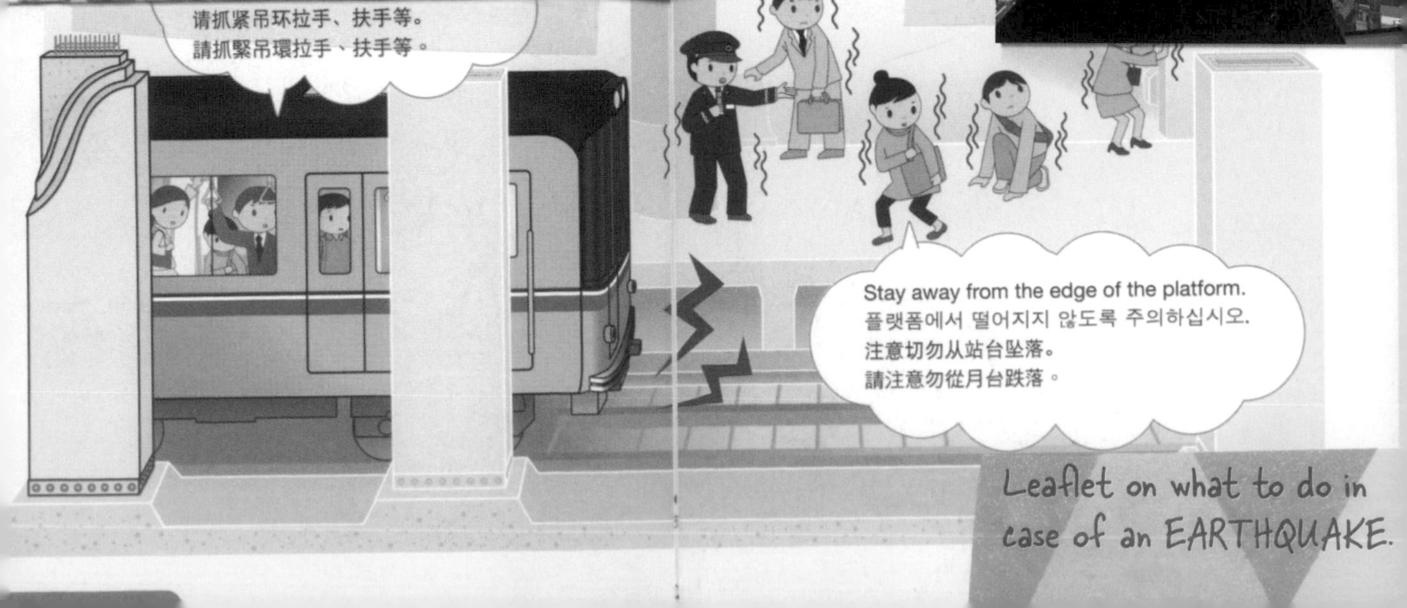
请抓紧吊环拉手、扶手等。
請抓緊吊環拉手、扶手等。
Stay away from the edge of the platform.
플랫폼에서 떨어지지 않도록 주의하십시오.
注意切勿从站台坠落。
請注意勿從月台跌落。

Leaflet on what to do in case of an EARTHQUAKE.

Week 3

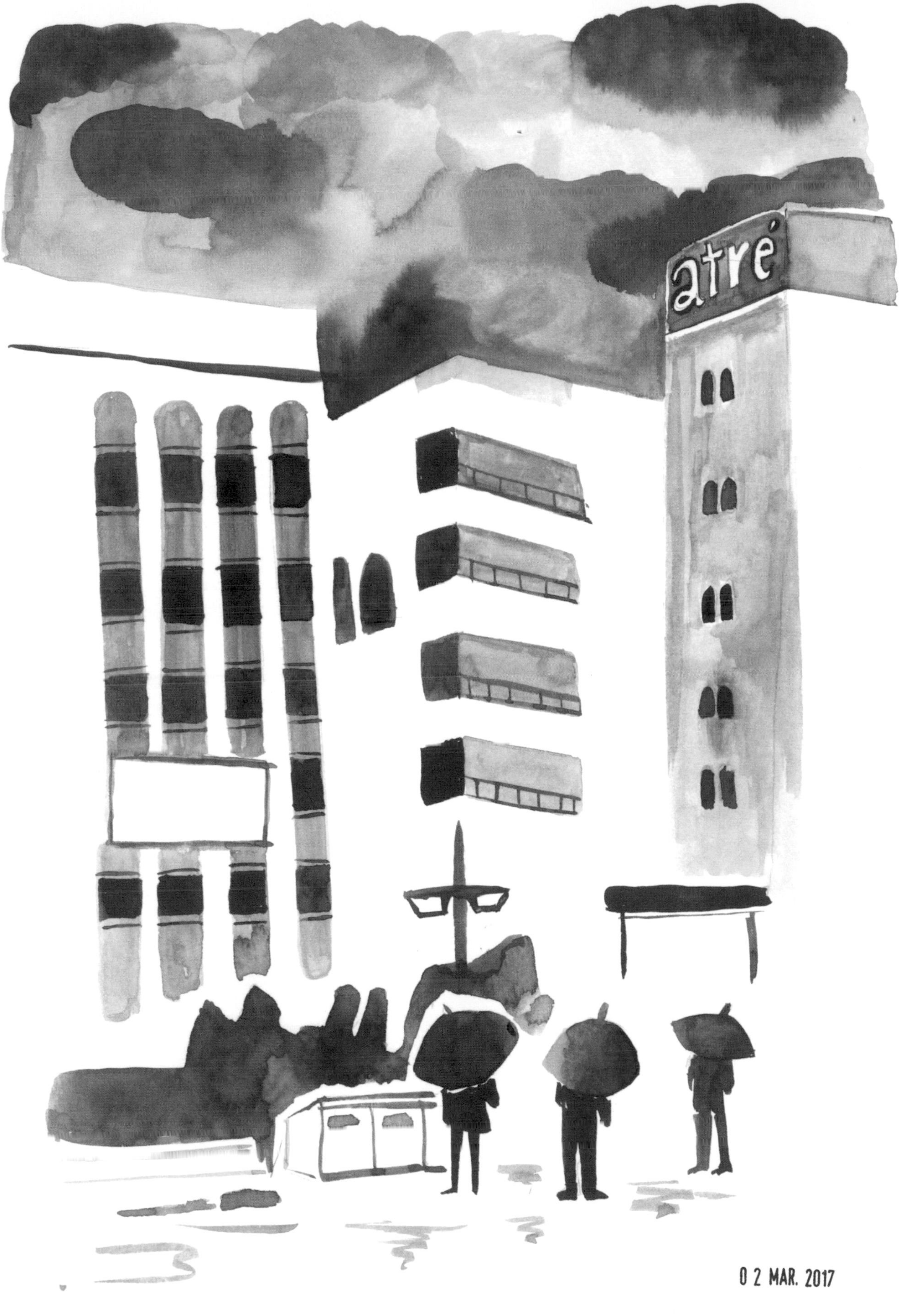
atré

0 2 MAR. 2017

This morning there was a pretty big <u>earthquake</u>.
I didn't notice because I was asleep.

Japan
has about 1,500 earthquakes
a year.

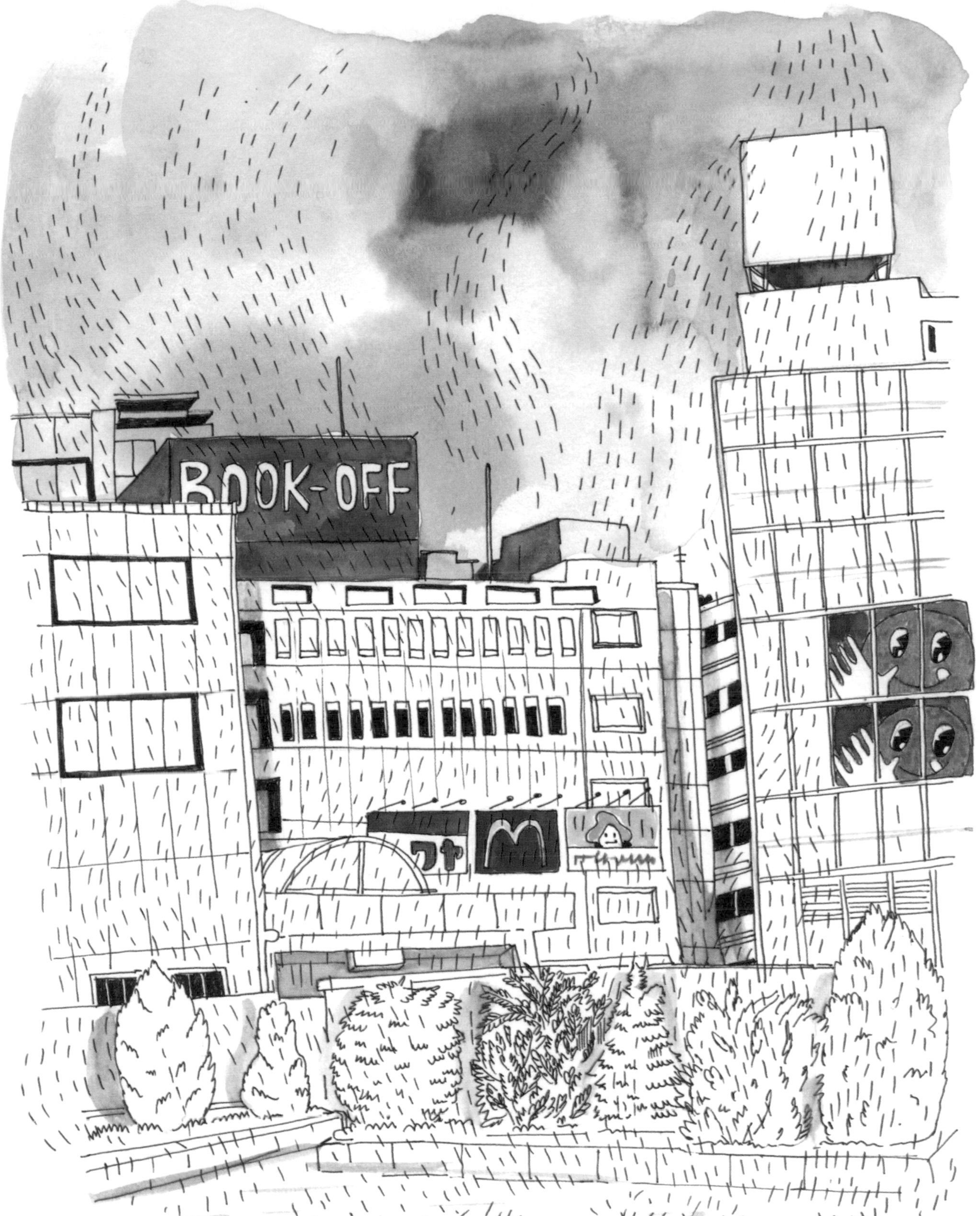
BOOK-OFF

Rainy Matsudo.
Itzi is gone.

0 2 MAR. 2017

Today is

HINA MATSURI

or Doll's Day
or Girl's Day.

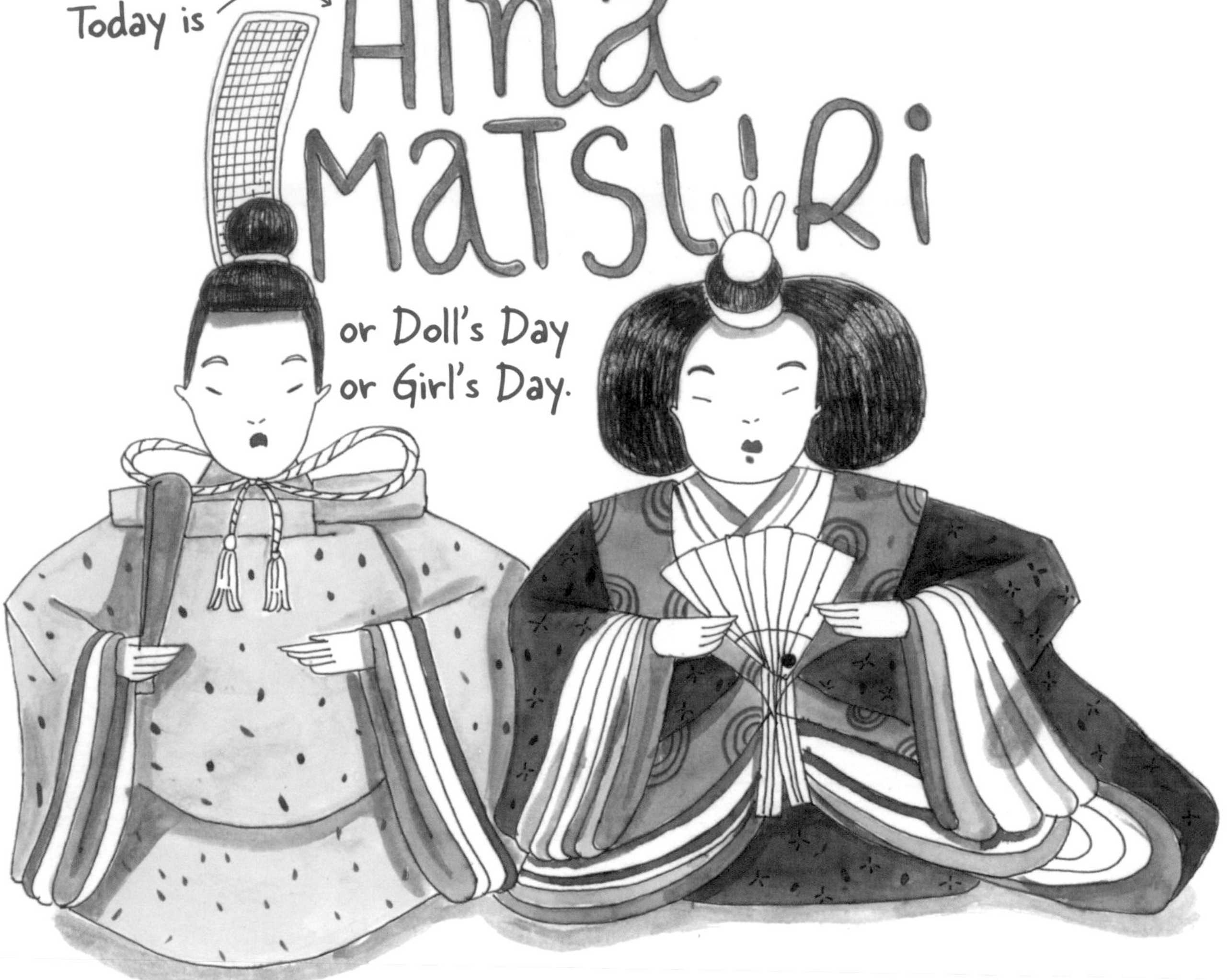

They used to think these dolls could hide evil spirits in their bodies, so tradition dictated that you had to get rid of them by sending them on a boat down a river.

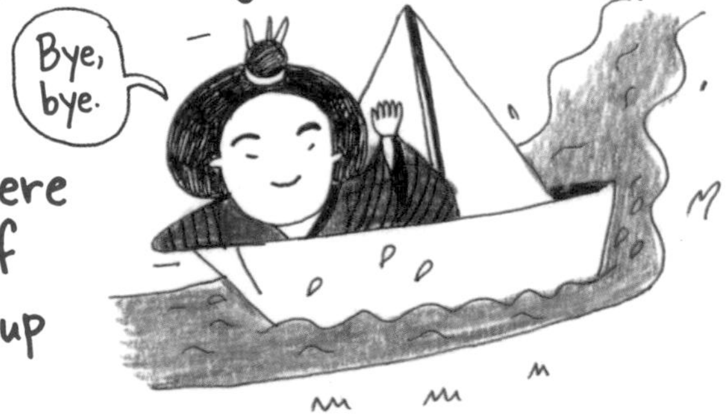
Bye, bye.

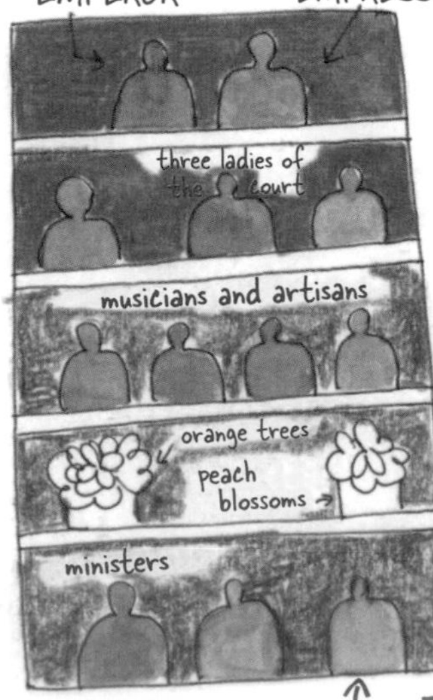
EMPEROR
EMPRESS
three ladies of the court
musicians and artisans
orange trees
peach blossoms
ministers

Those are dolls.

In homes where there are girls, a kind of stage is set with up to seven tiers to petition for their health and happiness. But, **OOPS**, if you're too slow in taking it down, things get turned around and they could end up old maids.

03 MAR. 2017

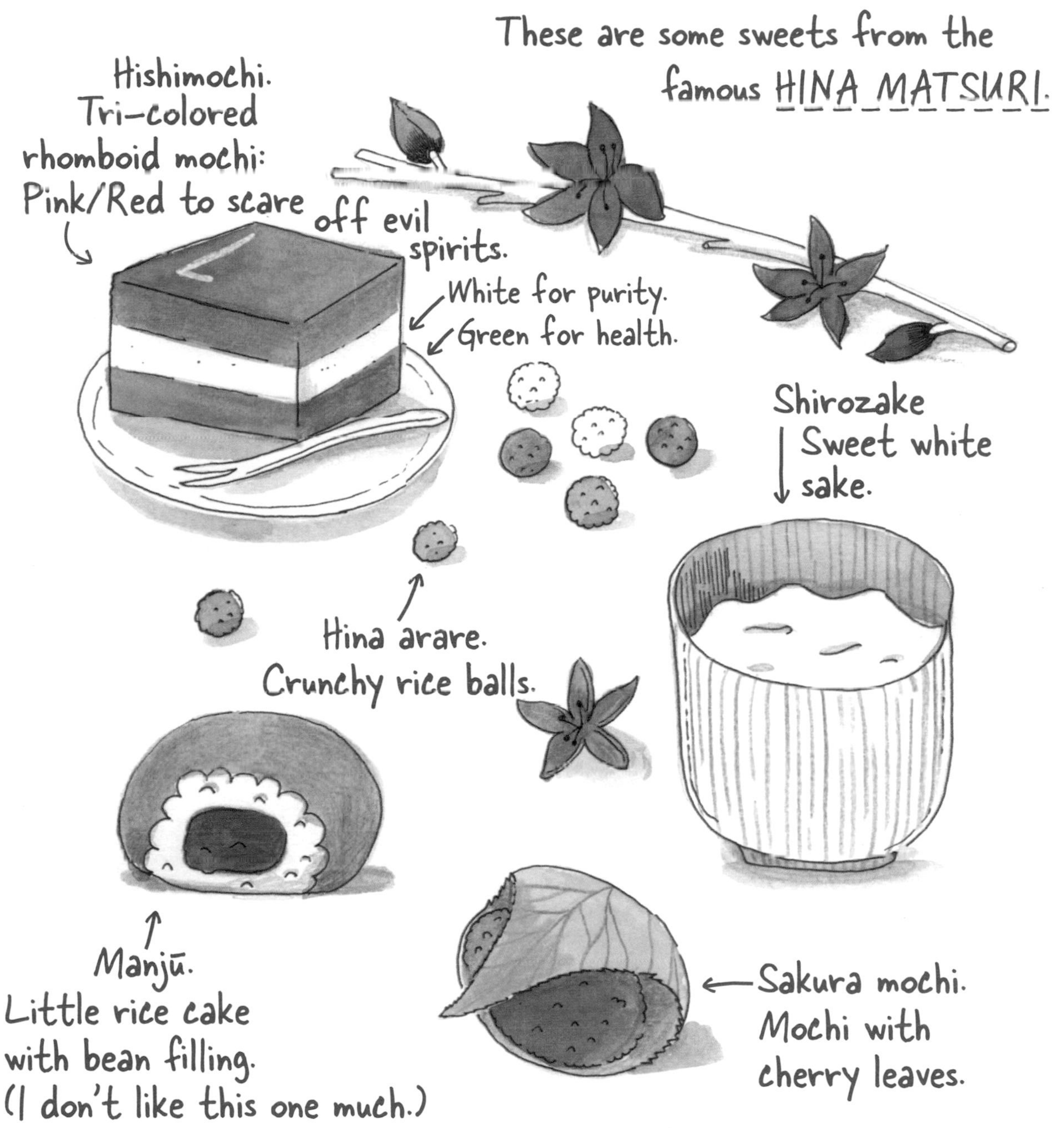
These are some sweets from the famous HINA MATSURI.
Hishimochi.
Tri-colored rhomboid mochi:
Pink/Red to scare off evil spirits.
White for purity.
Green for health.
Shirozake
Sweet white sake.
Hina arare.
Crunchy rice balls.
Manjū.
Little rice cake with bean filling.
(I don't like this one much.)
Sakura mochi.
Mochi with cherry leaves.

March is an important month in Japan, the month in which everything begins to blossom; it's spring, the cold weather is over...

March 3rd is when HINA MATSURI is celebrated, the 14th is WHITE DAY, and the end of the month is the start of HANAMI, the tradition of viewing cherry blossoms.

Woodblock print by <u>KITAGAWA UTAMARO</u> (1753-1806).
He was famous for his portraits of women from the
Yoshiwara neighborhood, the red-light district in <u>Edo</u>,

what today we
call Tokyo.

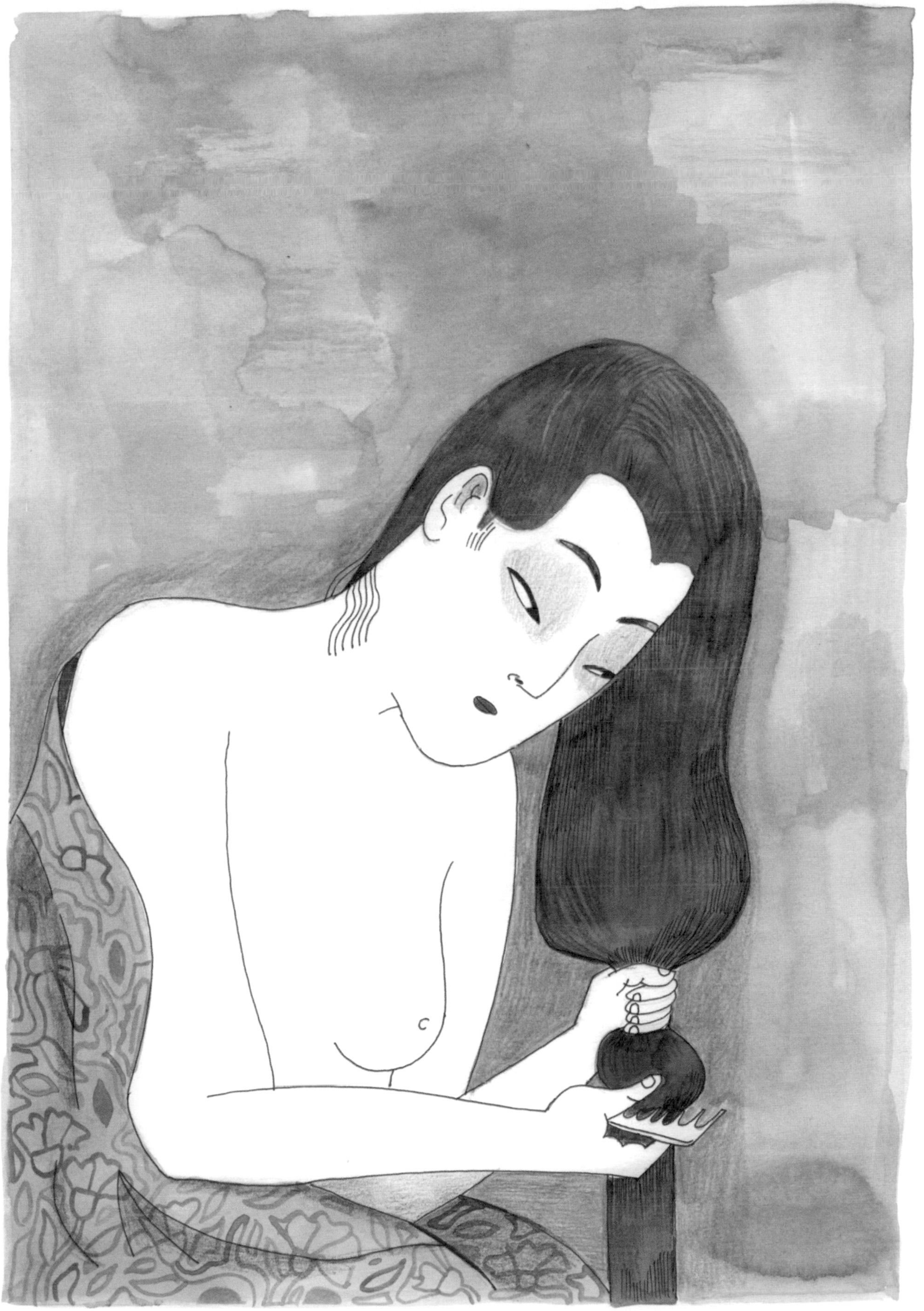

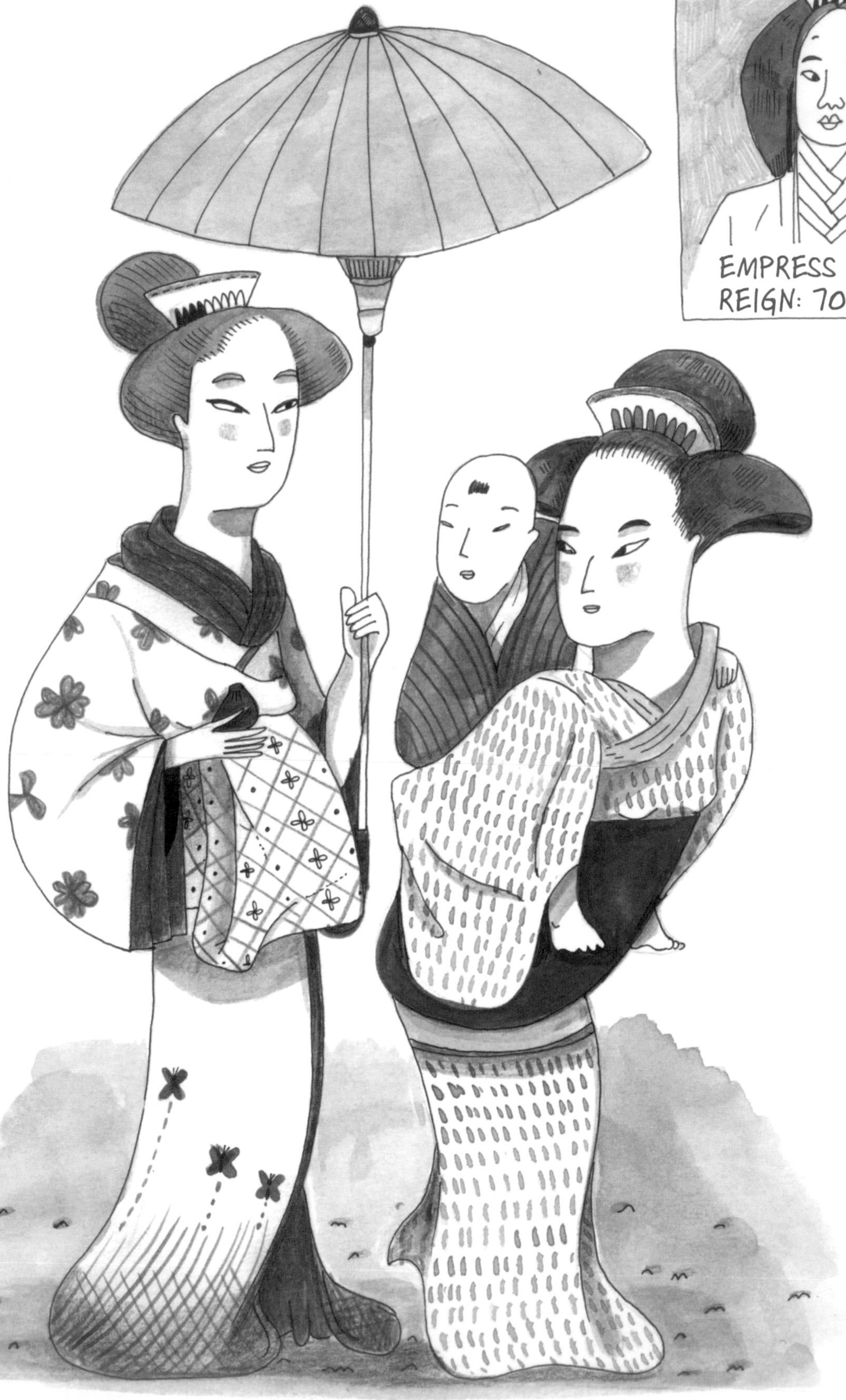

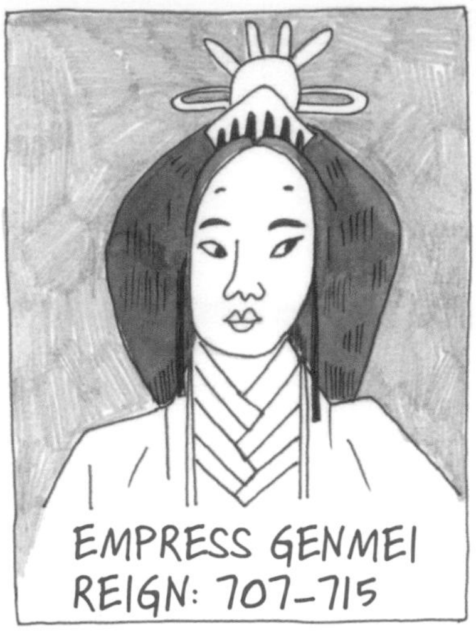
EMPRESS GENMEI
REIGN: 707–715

WOMEN in Japan have gone through different stages. For over 12 centuries they had a fundamental role: there were 5 empresses between 754 and 1770. They were not required to marry royalty, they could even remain unmarried.

The arrival of CONFUCIANISM and the introduction of roles for individuals to find their place within the common good changed everything. A model of the "perfect woman" was designed. The (hateful) ONNA DAIGAKU was published, a text directed towards young marriageable women or full-fledged wives.

(In my opinion.)

This established three paths of blind obedience for women: to their fathers (if they were single), to their husbands (if they were married) and to their sons (if they were widowed).

There were also seven reasons why a woman could be driven out of the family:

- Disobeying her mother-in-law.
- Being infertile.
- Talking too much.
- Stealing.
- Engaging in lewd activities.
- Being jealous.
- Having an incurable disease.

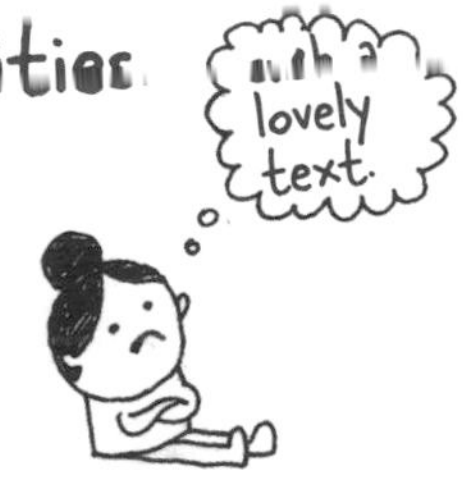
lovely
text.

Dainty and delicate, like a porcelain doll, that's what women were like.

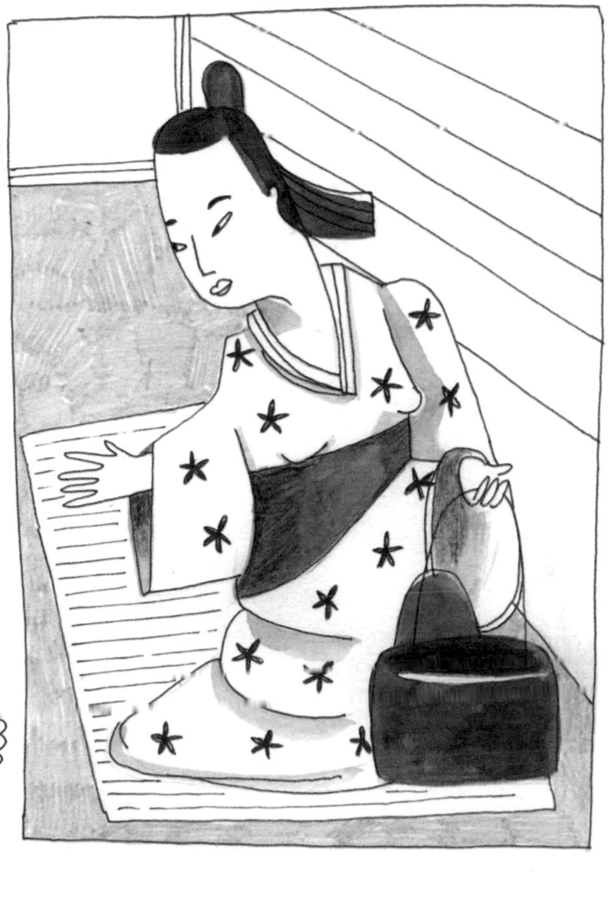

This young lady is called Tomeo Gozen and she was a samurai warrior between 1180 and 1185. As well as being a beauty, she was said to be an excellent archer, and as a swordswoman she was one in a million. A star.

I wonder what the <u>ONNA-BUGEISHA</u> would think of that book. They were female samurai warriors trained to use weapons and protect family and honor.

They would slash the book apart with their NAGINATA,

which is a small katana.

Obvious.

GEISHAS

GEISHAS are women who are prepared to entertain at meetings. They speak well, know music, traditional Japanese arts... They begin training at 15 years of age as apprentices, or <u>MAIKOS</u>.

Don't confuse geishas with <u>OIRAN</u>, who were also young women trained to entertain, but they were experts in sexual matters as well. Like high-class courtesans.

They were differentiated by their dress, hairstyles and makeup.

For example, the <u>OBI</u> (belt), which geishas wore in back and oiran wore in front.

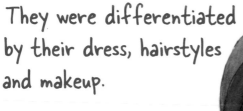

Oiran styled their hair with a widow's peak so their faces would be heart shaped.

Another difference (in case you see them from the back): both apply makeup to the nape of their neck to enhance eroticism, but ① geishas use this design and ② oiran use this other one.

Geishas generally wear more discreet kimonos and hairstyles than their apprentices, the MAIKOS. Why?

Because a geisha is an experienced woman who knows she's valued more for her qualities than for her physical appearance.

She hooks clients with what she has inside.

The essence of a geisha is IKI. Iki is an unabashed but elegant style. You have iki, you don't learn it. What the apprentice tries to do is improve it.

Geisha EROTICISM has a lot to do with iki. Being very subtle: it could be a look, a lock of hair falling on her cheek, a peek at the nape of her neck pointing the way toward the flesh...

Iki is understood to be a kind of elegance based on subtlety and insinuation.

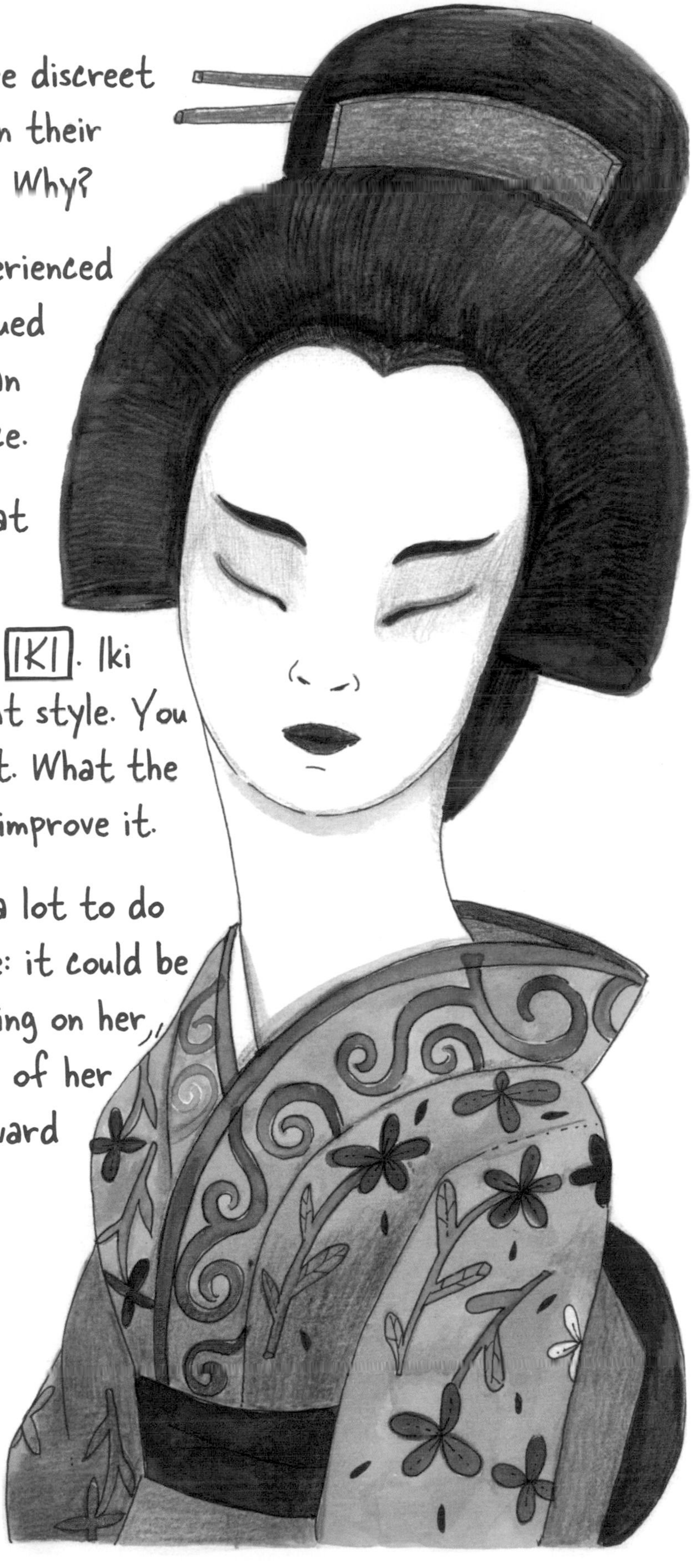

One of the best-known geishas is the main character of the Italian opera <u>MADAME BUTTERFLY</u>, by Puccini.

It tells the (heartbreaking) love story of a geisha, Cio-Cio-San, who marries American Marine officer Pinkerton, for whom this wedding is just an amusing "divertimento" in a country that wasn't his. For her, it's <u>ABSOLUTE LOVE.</u>

He leaves Japan, but she waits for him.

When he finally returns three years later, he's come with his new wife to take back the child he had with Cio-Cio-San.

Cio-Cio-San gives her son to him, then kills herself by committing <u>HARAKIRI</u>.

Bye, bye.

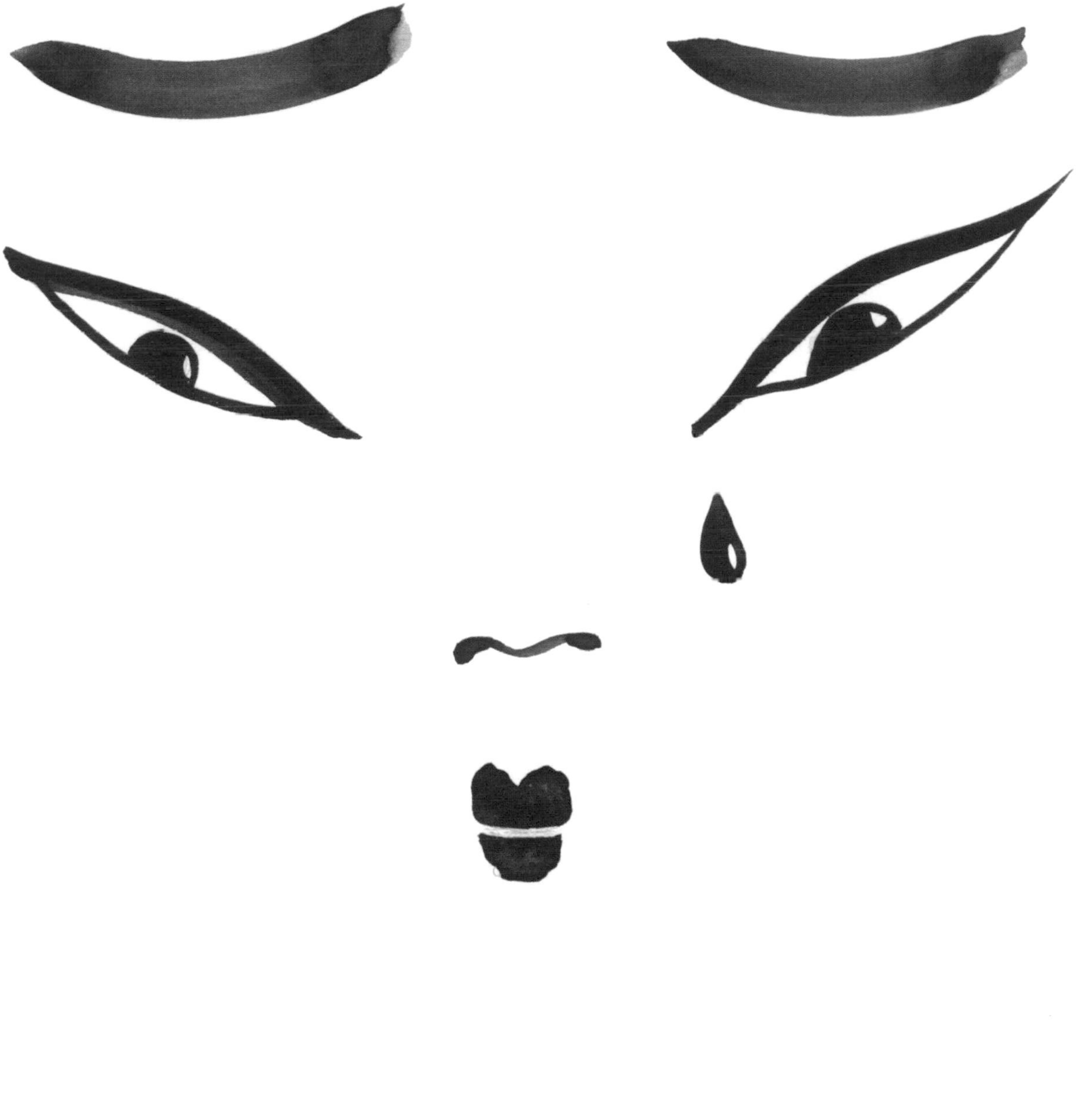

Entrance to Kabukicho, considered the red-light district of Tokyo. Full of restaurants, bars and nightclubs. There's adult entertainment for women as well as men. − − − − − − − − − − − − − − − − − →

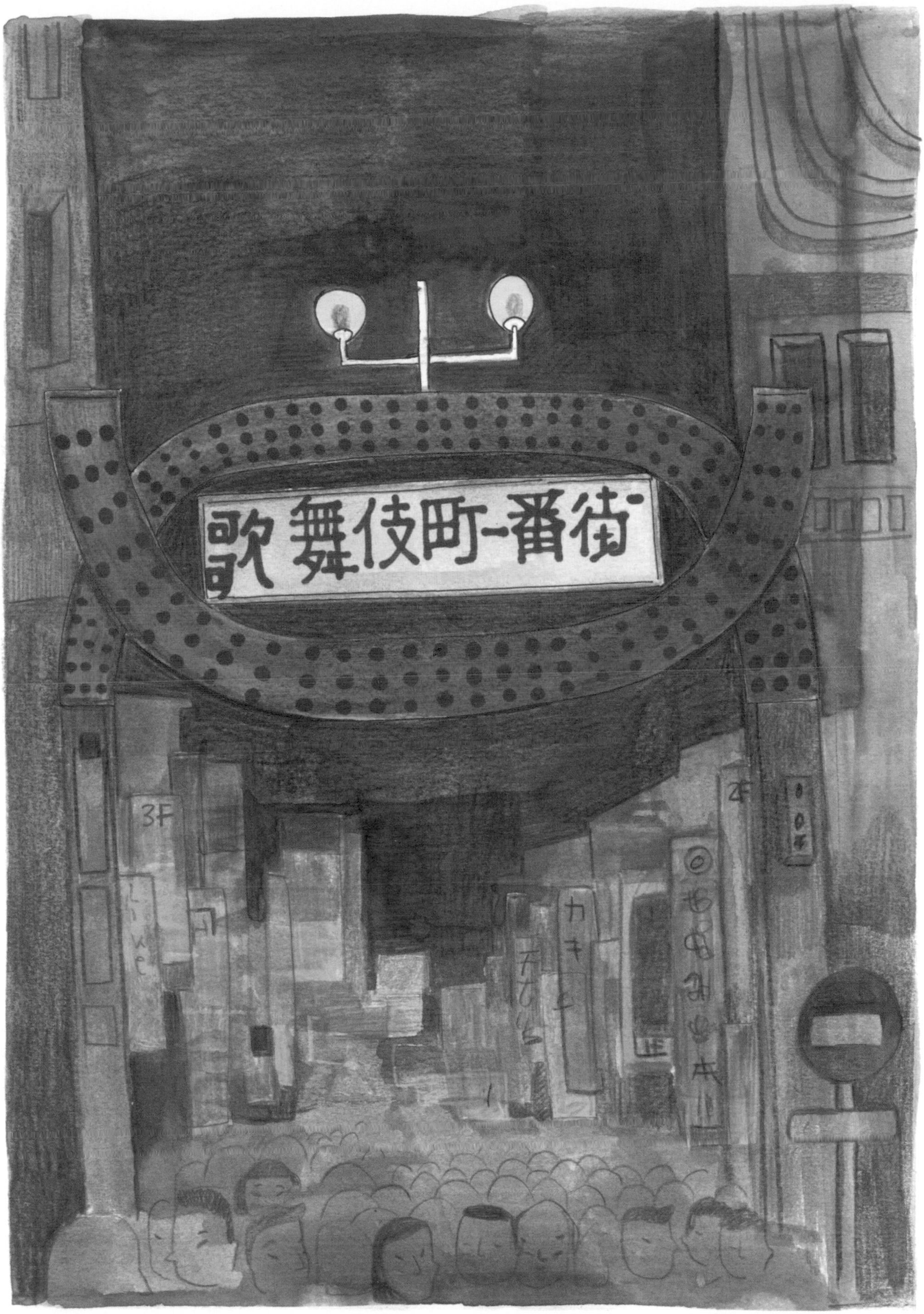
歌舞伎町一番街
3F

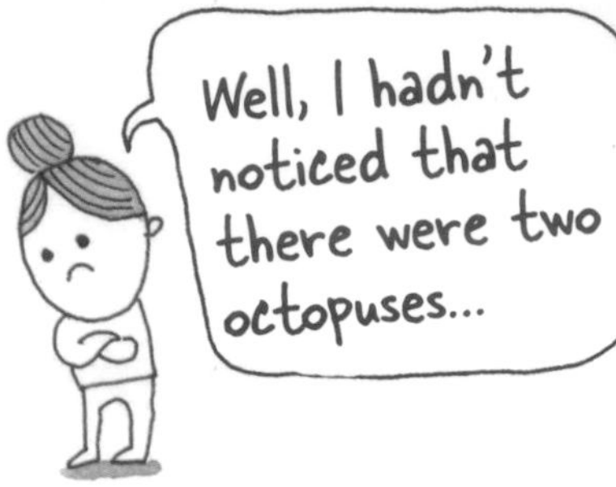
Well, I hadn't noticed that there were two octopuses...

"The Dream of the Fisherman's Wife" by Hokusai, 1814.
This is an example of SHUNGA, a type of ukiyo-e with an erotic theme.

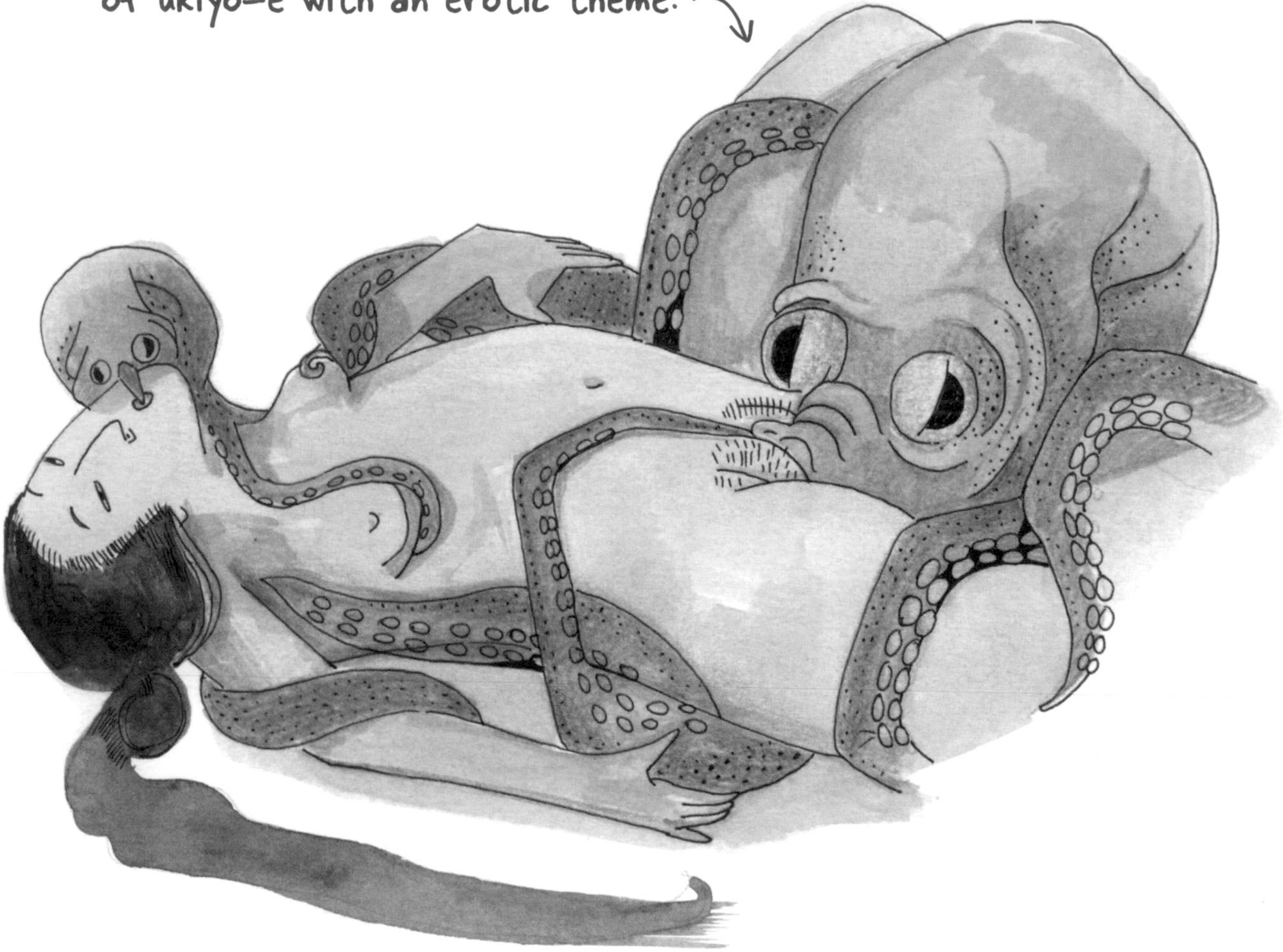

SEX in Japan is not QUIIITE as taboo as you might think. In SHINTO, one of the two main religions practiced, it's not frowned upon, but is treated very naturally.

No Smoking sign in the street.

Sign advertising erotic massages found in the Kanda area.

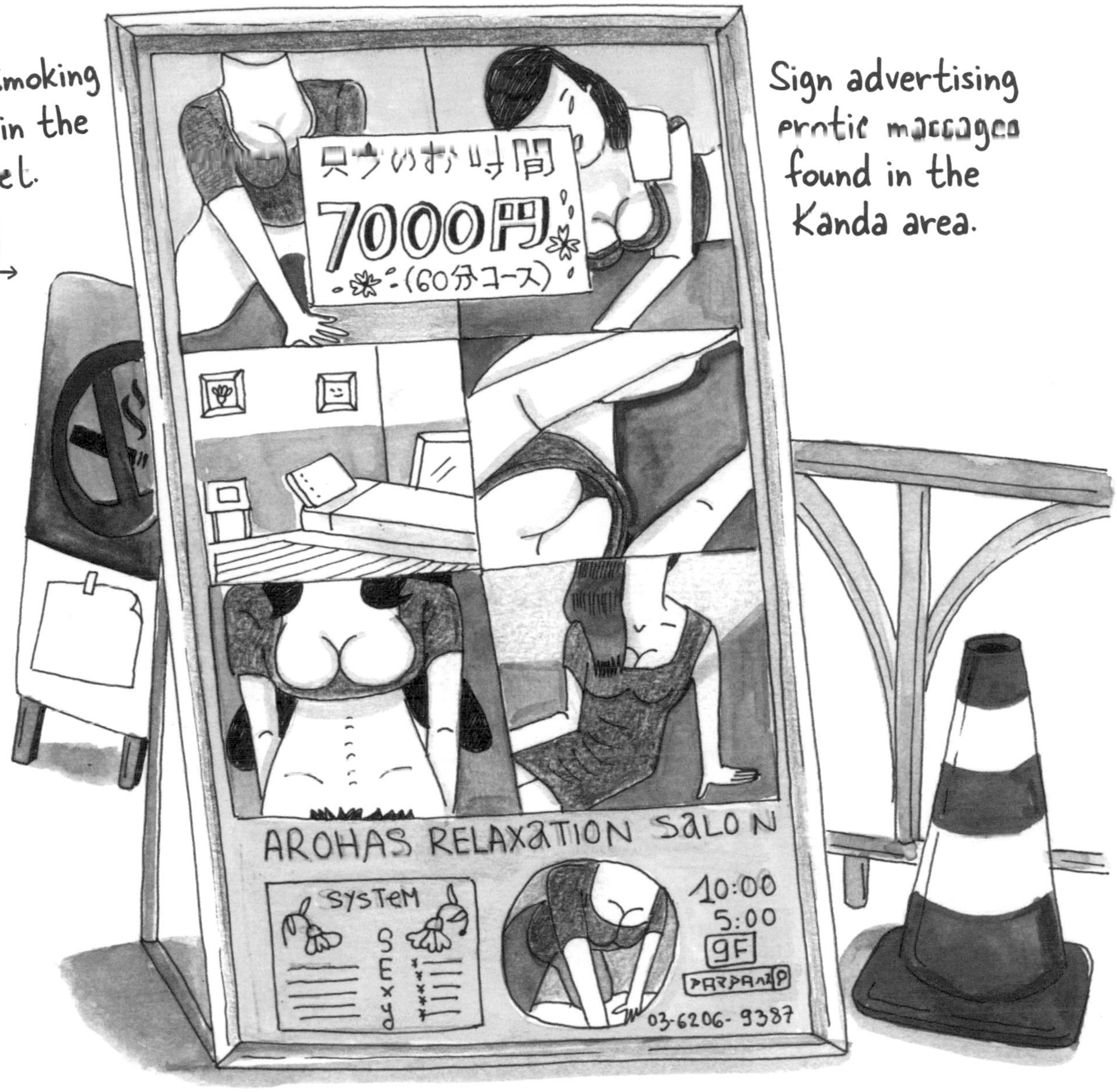
7000円
(60分コース)
AROHAS RELAXATION SALON
SYSTEM
SEXY
10:00
5:00
9F
03-6206-9387

Up until 1956, brothels were legal. That year, the ANTI-PROSTITUTION law was enacted, which prohibited ONLY coitus. Then businesses offering "OTHER THINGS" started up, such as SOAPLAND, massage parlors, PINK SALONS...

Places where they soap you up to the happy ending.

Fellatio bars.

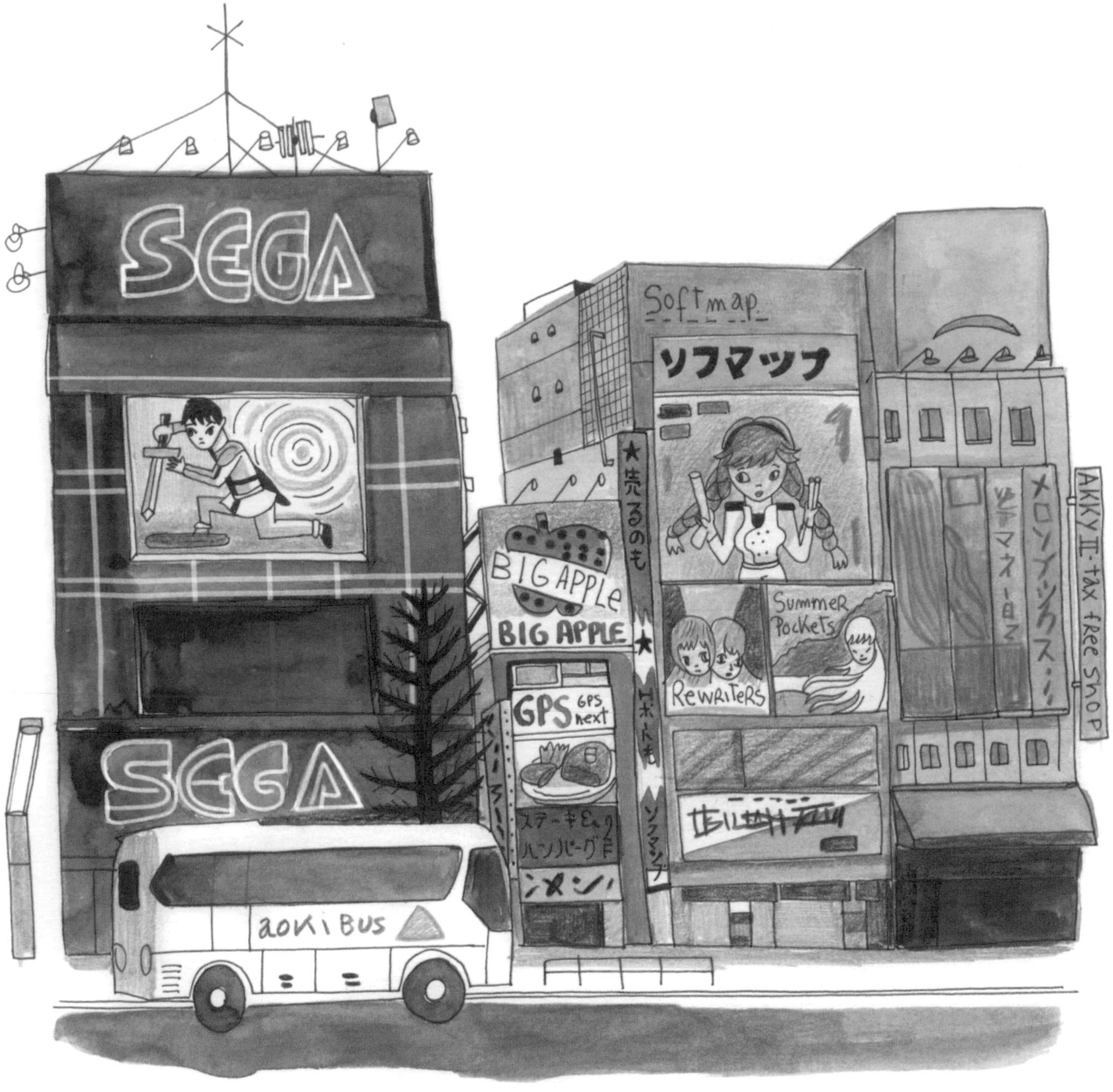
SEGA
Softmap
ソフマップ
BIG APPLE
BIG APPLE
GPS
GPS next
Summer Pockets
Rewriters
メロンブックス
AKKY II tax free shop
SEGA
aoki BUS

It's really hard to draw Akihabara.

I came across this action figure in a game center in Akihabara. FUJIKO MINE is a character from the series Lupin III.

Her name means "peaks of Mount Fuji."

Very subtle...

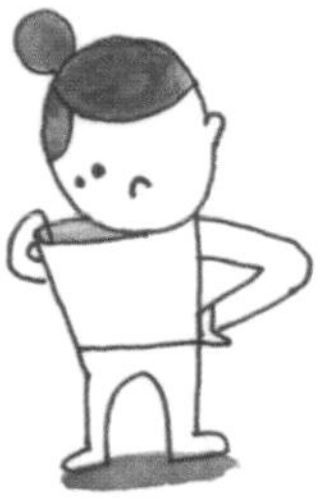

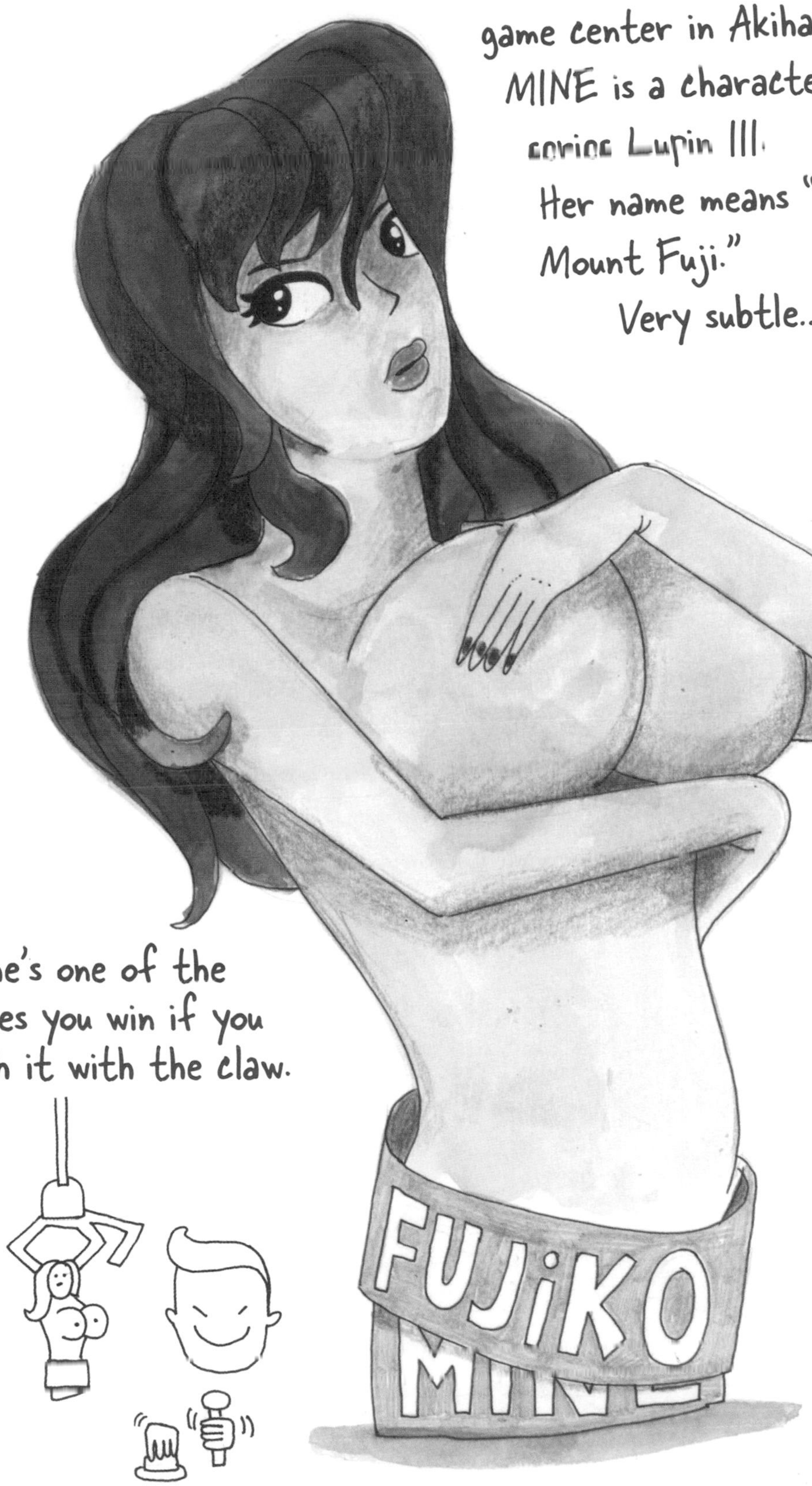
FUJiKO
MINE

She's one of the figures you win if you catch it with the claw.

They love these games.

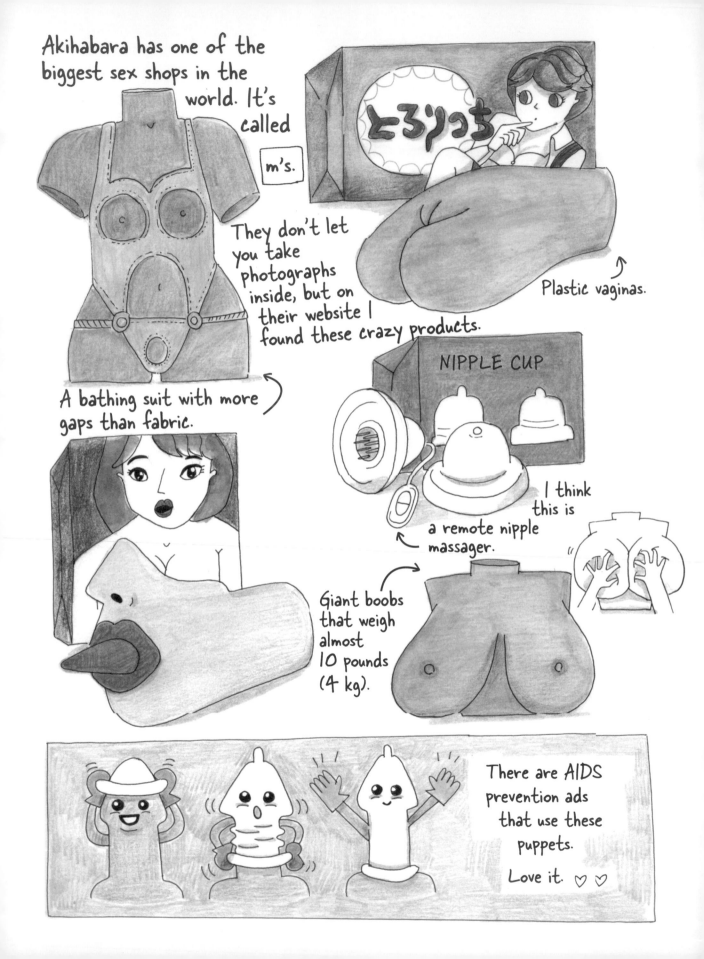

Akihabara has one of the biggest sex shops in the world. It's called

m's.

They don't let you take photographs inside, but on their website I found these crazy products.

Plastic vaginas.

A bathing suit with more gaps than fabric.

NIPPLE CUP

I think this is a remote nipple massager.

Giant boobs that weigh almost 10 pounds (4 kg).

There are AIDS prevention ads that use these puppets.

Love it. ♡ ♡

Sign in one of the women-only passenger cars.

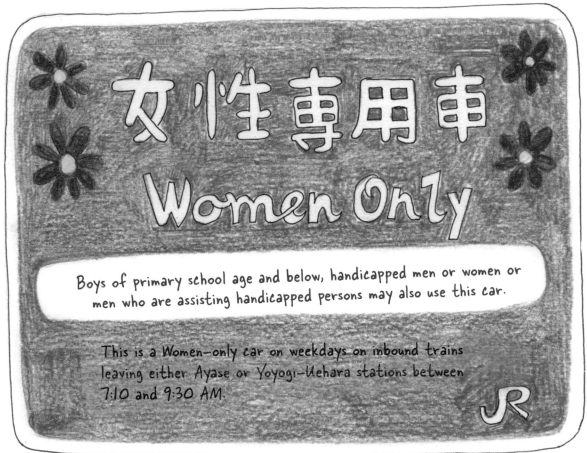

女性専用車

Women Only

Boys of primary school age and below, handicapped men or women or men who are assisting handicapped persons may also use this car.

This is a Women-only car on weekdays on inbound trains leaving either Ayase or Yoyogi-Uehara stations between 7:10 and 9:30 AM.

JR

└ Obviously it's also in Japanese, but I can't be bothered to copy it.

Japan is full of "pervs." Harassing women became so extreme that cars had to be designated just for them during rush hour.   These men are called CHIKAN and there's increasing awareness about calling them out ON SITE.

YOU PIG!

Room in a LOVE HOTEL (obviously I found it on a website). The PENIS LAMP deserves special mention.

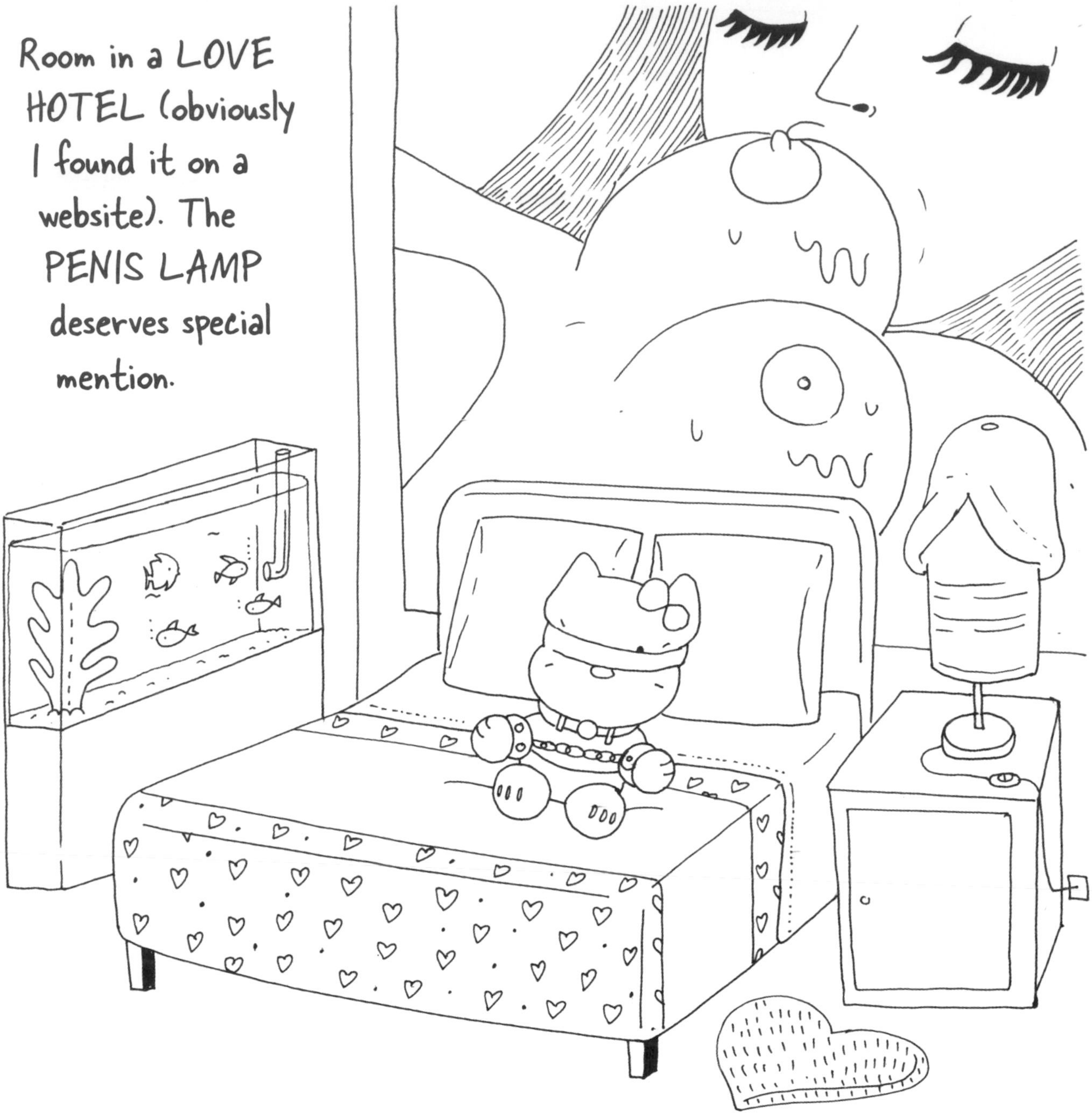

There are studies proving Japan's HUGE problem: the tough economic situation is such that many men resign themselves to NOT having a partner, and to sex... by themselves. Having a partner is an expense many can't take on in a patriarchal society where it's assumed the man must support the family.

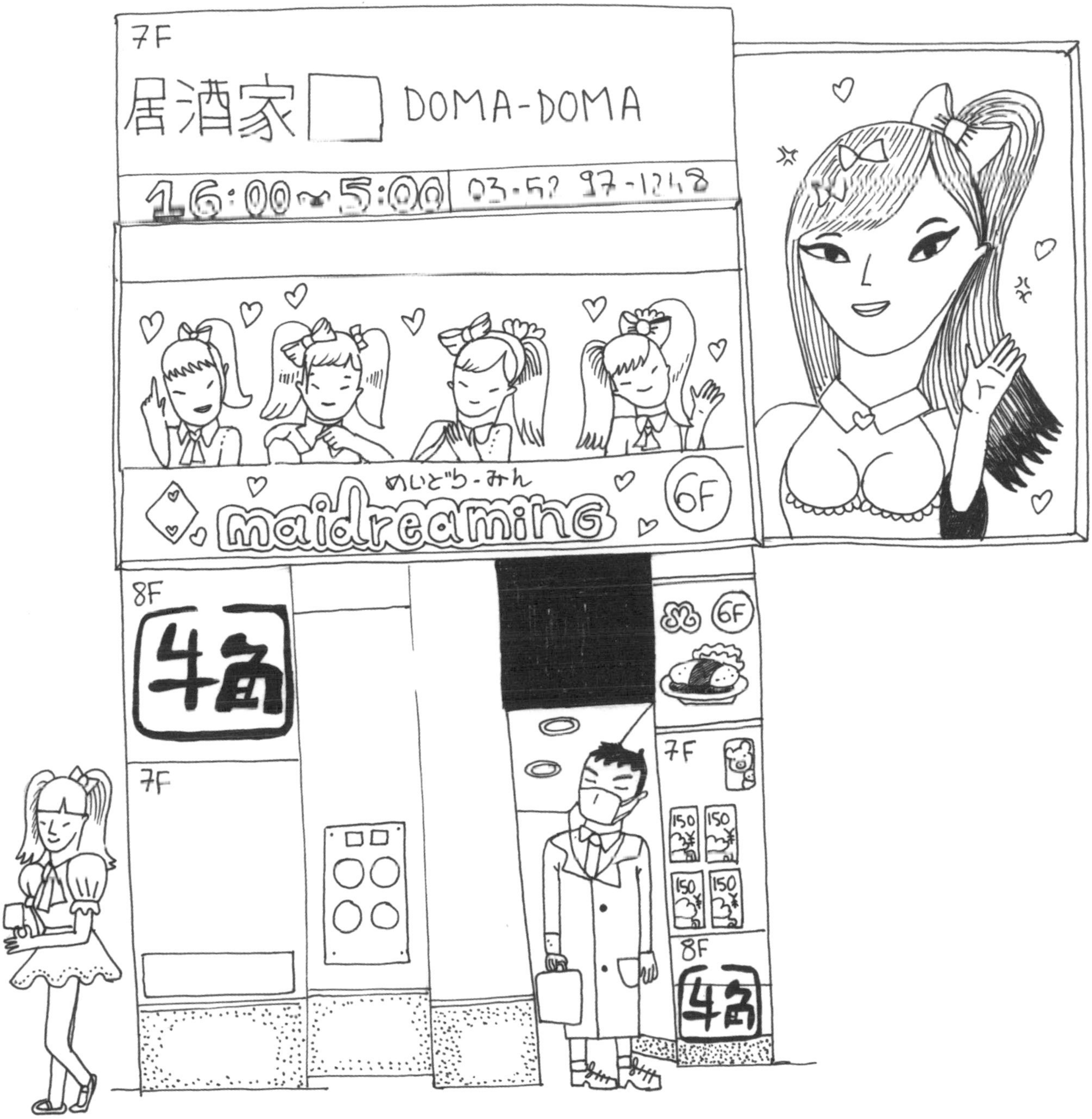
7F
居酒家
DOMA-DOMA
16:00~5:00
めいどり-みん
maidreaming
6F
8F
牛角
7F
6F
7F
150
150
150
150
8F
牛角

The government warns: 69% of men and 59% of women do not have a partner. 40% of men younger than 34 ARE VIRGINS. This causes a very low birth rate in a country where living over the age of 90 is fairly common.

I found out about ikigai from a photograph my sister sent to my phone from Spain.

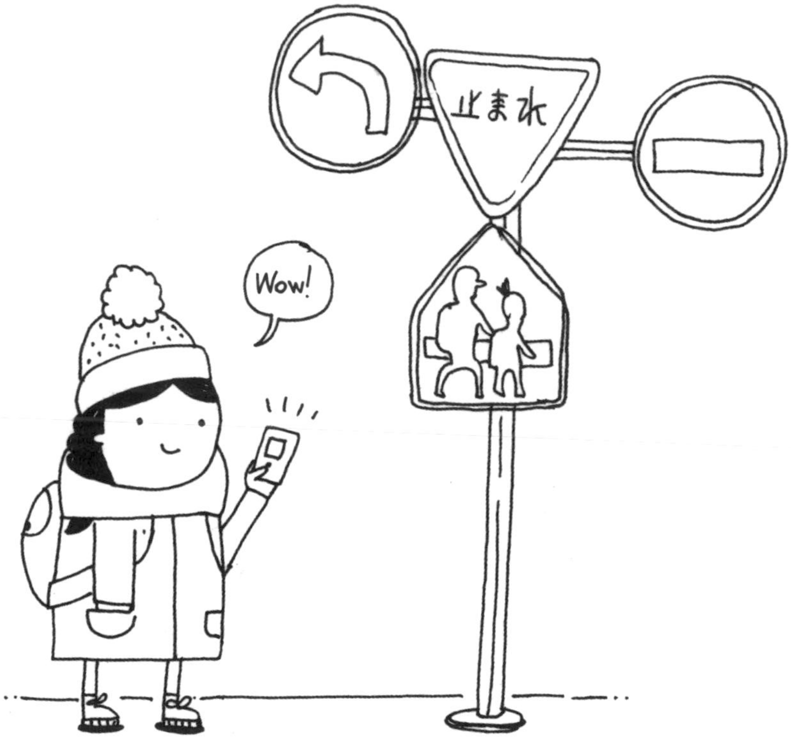
止まれ
Wow!

IKIGAI literally means "Reason for Living." A search within oneself, a search that can last an entire lifetime. Etymologically, it comes from

IKIRU + KAI
↓
To live.

Materialization of what one expects.

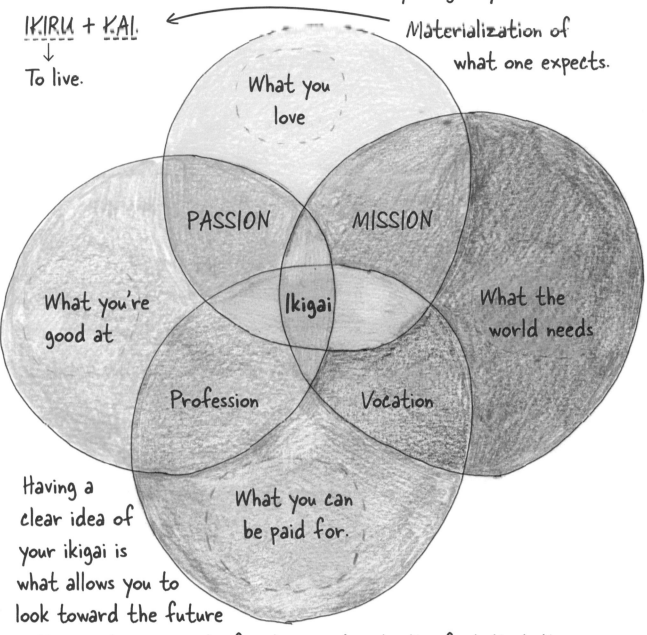

What you love

PASSION

MISSION

What you're good at

Ikigai

What the world needs

Profession

Vocation

What you can be paid for.

Having a clear idea of your ikigai is what allows you to look toward the future with a certain amount of optimism, despite the fact that the present might look VERY dark. Reassessing your ikigai now and again is necessary. I understand it to be a way of asking yourself the basic questions: Who am I? Where am I going? Why do I do what I do?

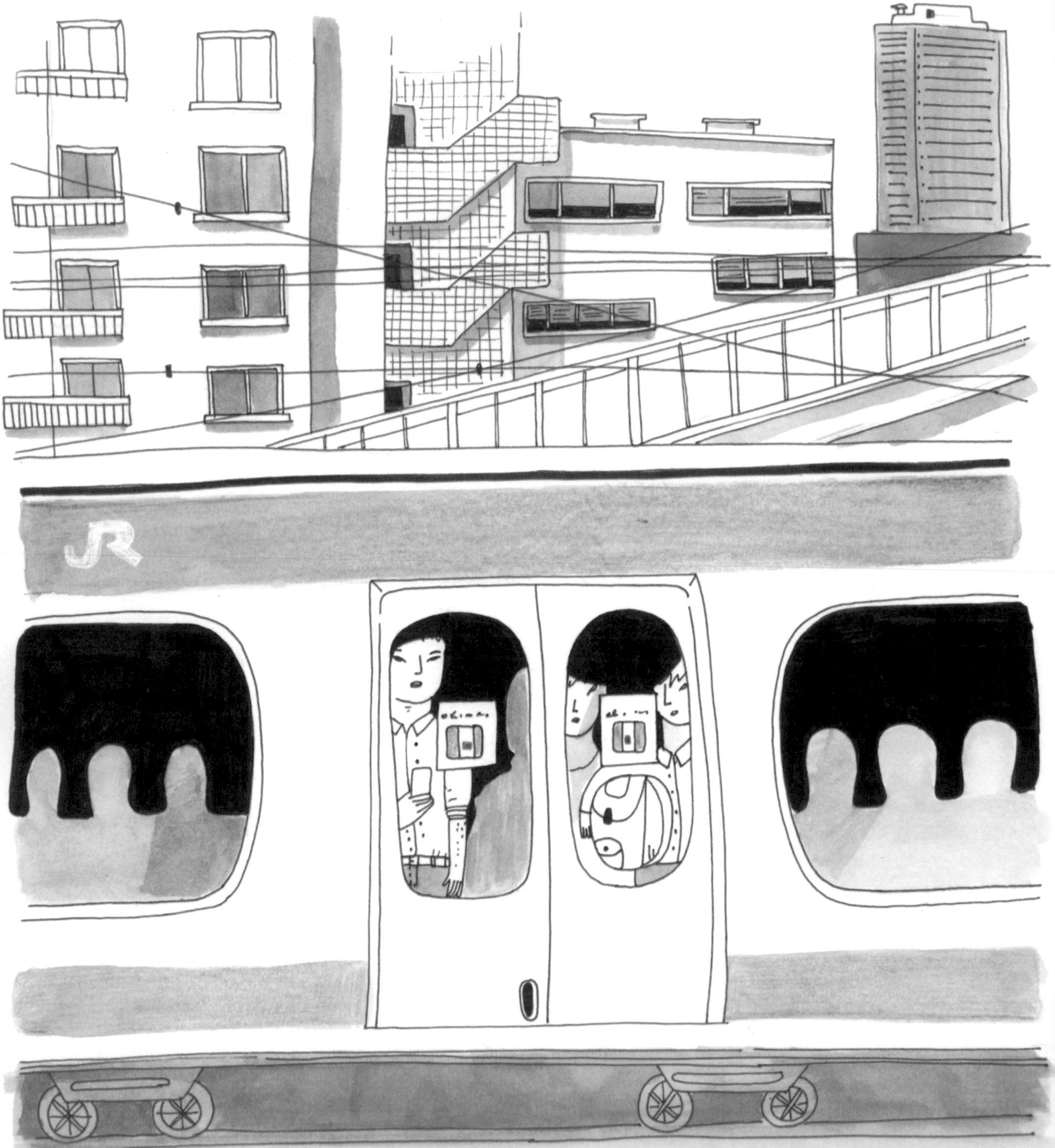
JR

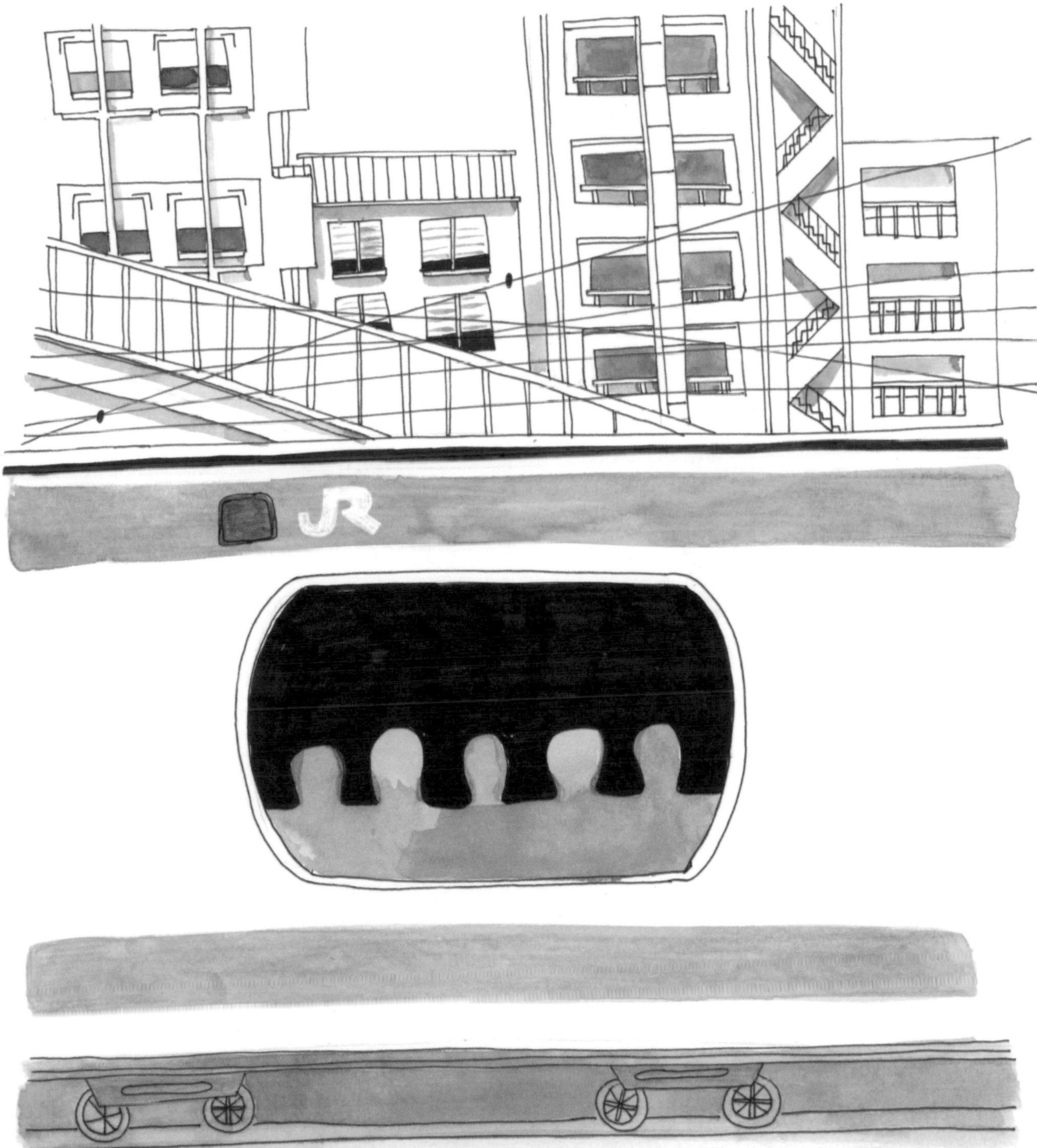
JR

It was thought that the I̲K̲I̲G̲A̲I̲ of women was to be at home dedicating themselves to their families, and that of men was business and work. But this is more true of another era; of post-war Japan, when the whole country had to be reconstructed through effort, hard work and a very conventional idea of family.

This was the era of the s̲a̲l̲a̲r̲y̲m̲e̲n̲, men who worked for the same company all their lives. Dedicated and long-suffering, low-level executives. The boss was god, and the corporation they worked for was where they spent their entire professional career (and social life). I̲n̲t̲e̲r̲m̲i̲n̲a̲b̲l̲e̲ ̲h̲o̲u̲r̲s̲ and e̲n̲d̲l̲e̲s̲s̲ ̲w̲o̲r̲k̲d̲a̲y̲s̲. They didn't know much about their families; the wife was in charge of everything having to do with the home.

On an individual level, this suffering was worth it because, on a collective level, the country had to be rebuilt.

ZZZZZ...   ZZZZZ...

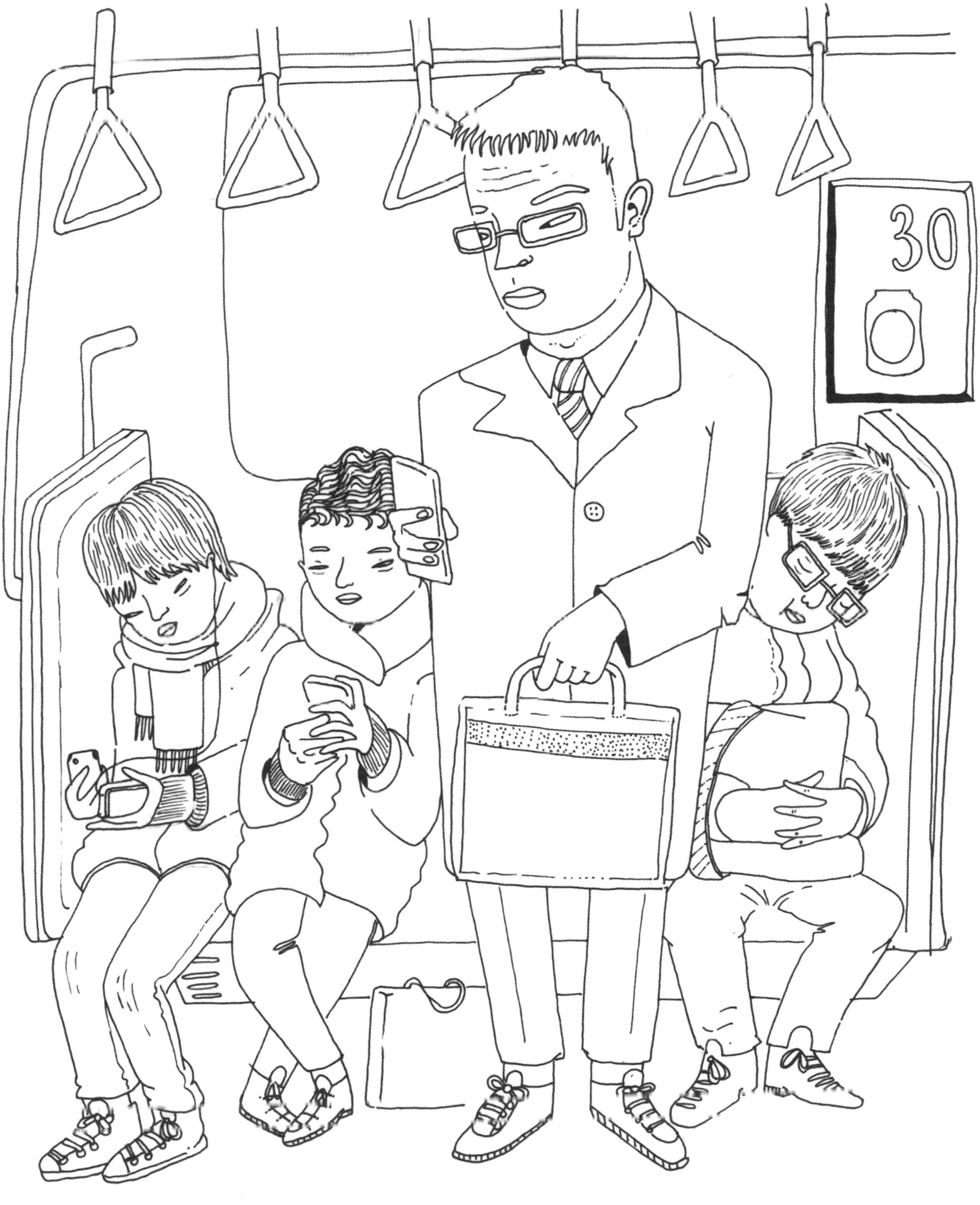
30

<u>But</u> in 1991, when the real estate bubble burst, the Japanese MAN (the middle-class heterosexual male with an administrative position) lost his hegemony, his reign. Gone were those contracts lasting an entire lifetime, and the individual therefore lost <u>his identity</u>.

The fact that women entered the labor market, and the increase in more precarious jobs with finite durations, made many men feel their <u>reason for living</u> (which up until then had been work) had failed them.

And the suicide rate went up.

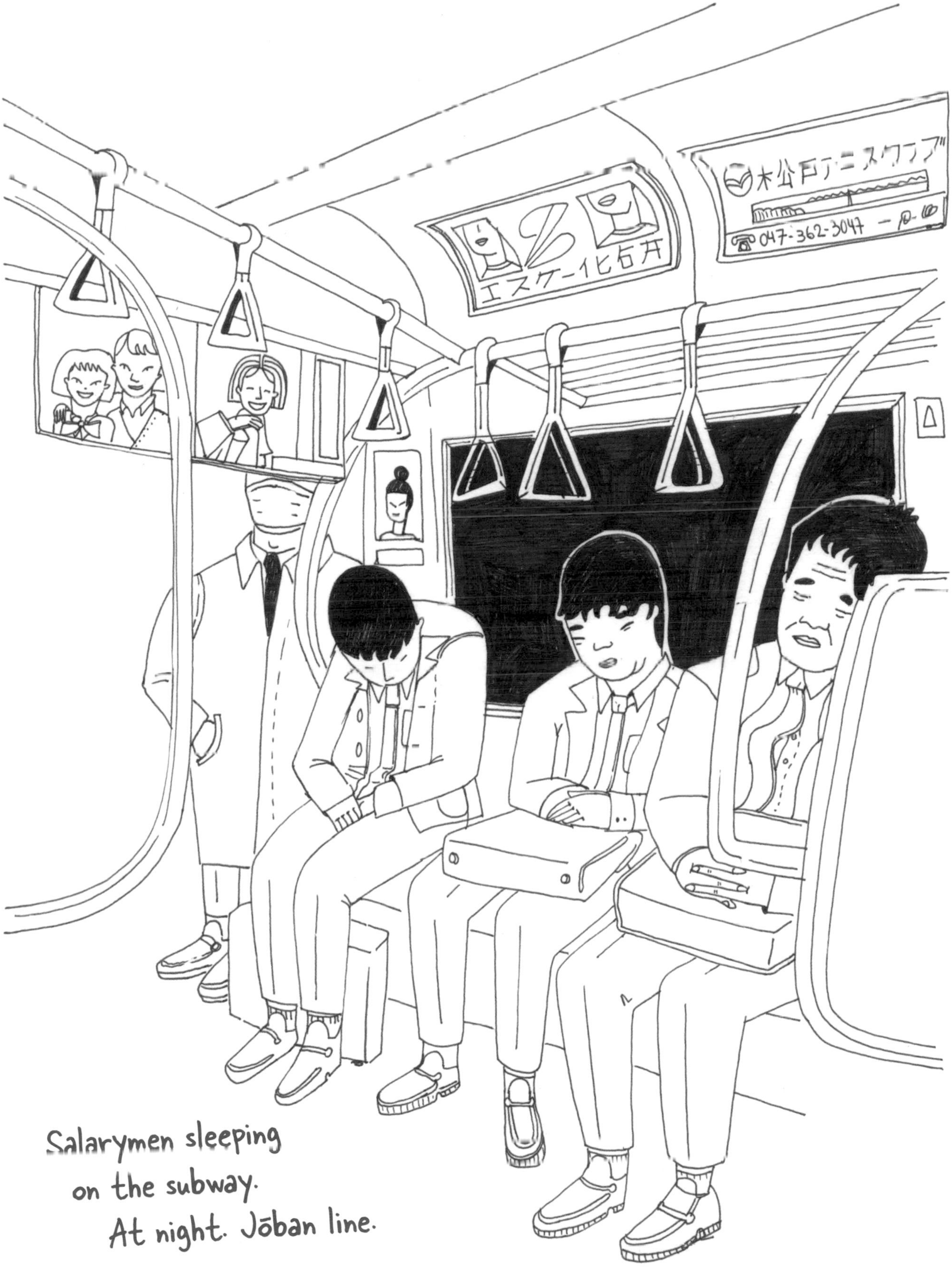
エスケー化石井
松戸テニスクラブ
047-362-3047

Salarymen sleeping
on the subway.
At night. Jōban line.

Sign found in the subway at Matsudo station.

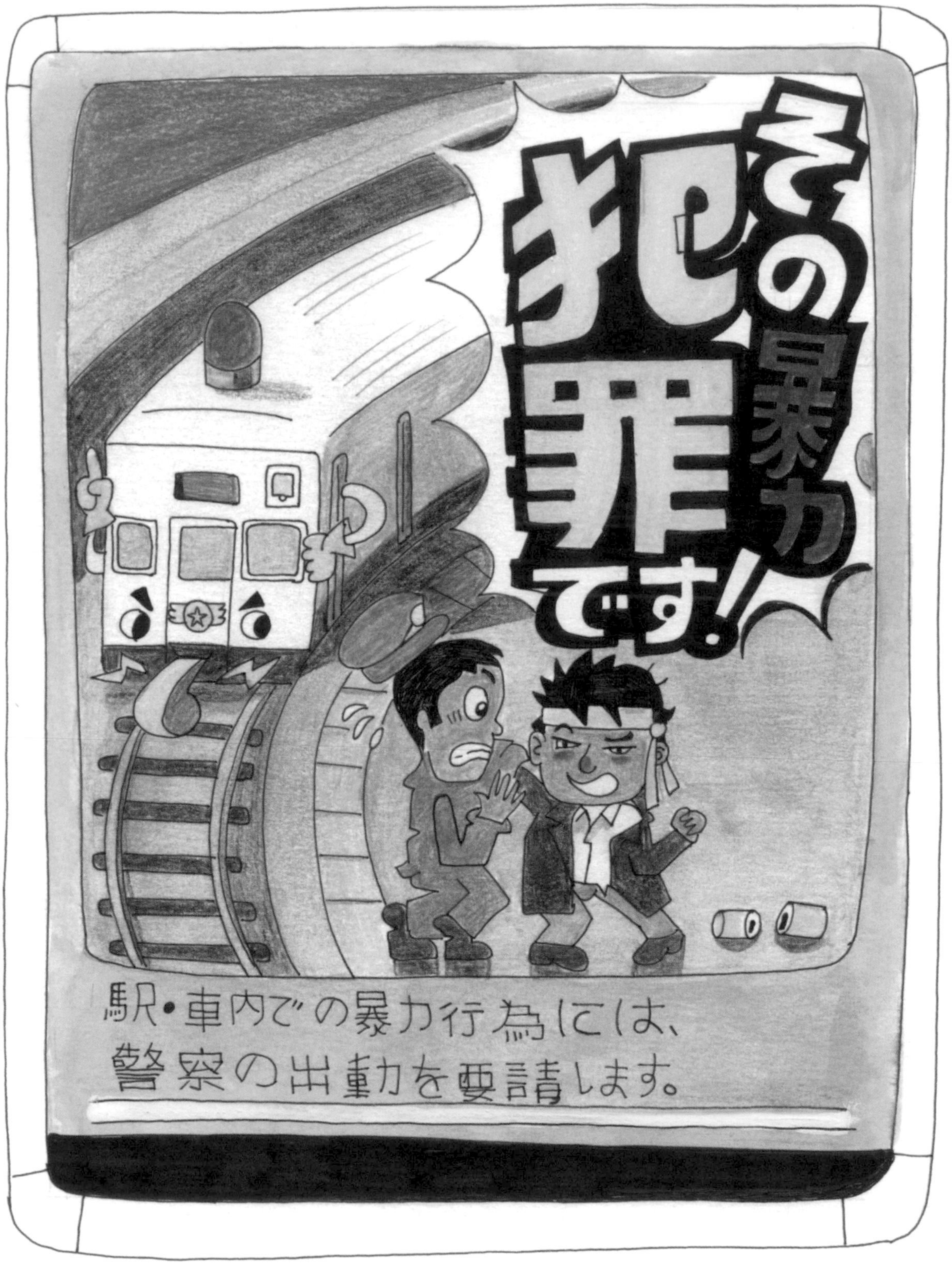
その暴力
犯罪です!
駅・車内での暴力行為には、
警察の出動を要請します。

I'm not sure exactly what it says, but you get the picture of what's going on...

This one I saw in the Sumiyoshi subway station.

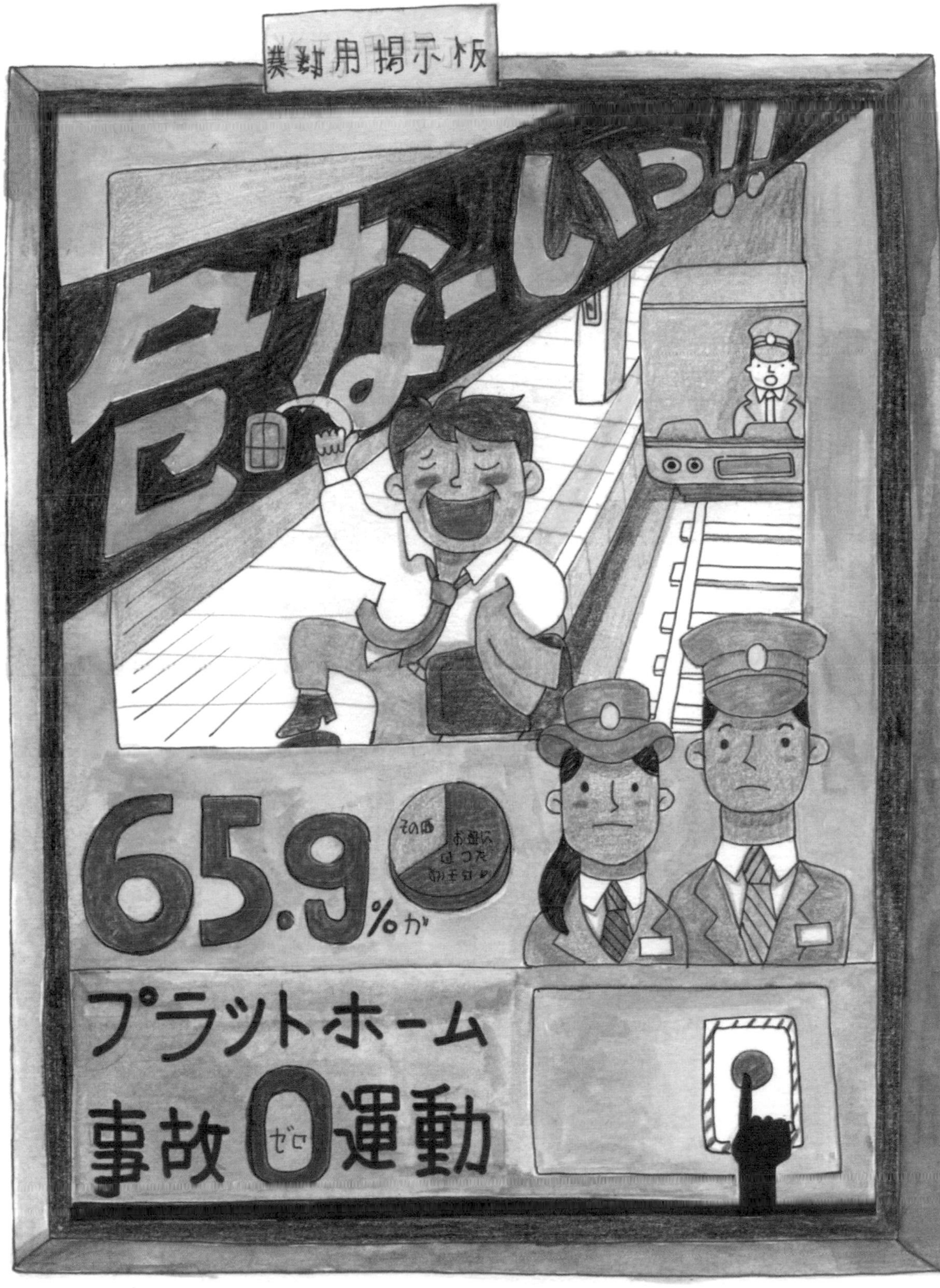
危なーいっ!!
65.9%が
プラットホーム
事故0運動
ゼロ

with statistics and an emergency button in case things get really ugly.

KAROSHI or TO DIE WORKING

Death from work-related stress was officially recognized by the Japanese Ministry of Health in 1987.

We're talking about KAROSHI when an employee suffers a heart attack or a stroke after working an average of over 65 hours a week for at least a month.

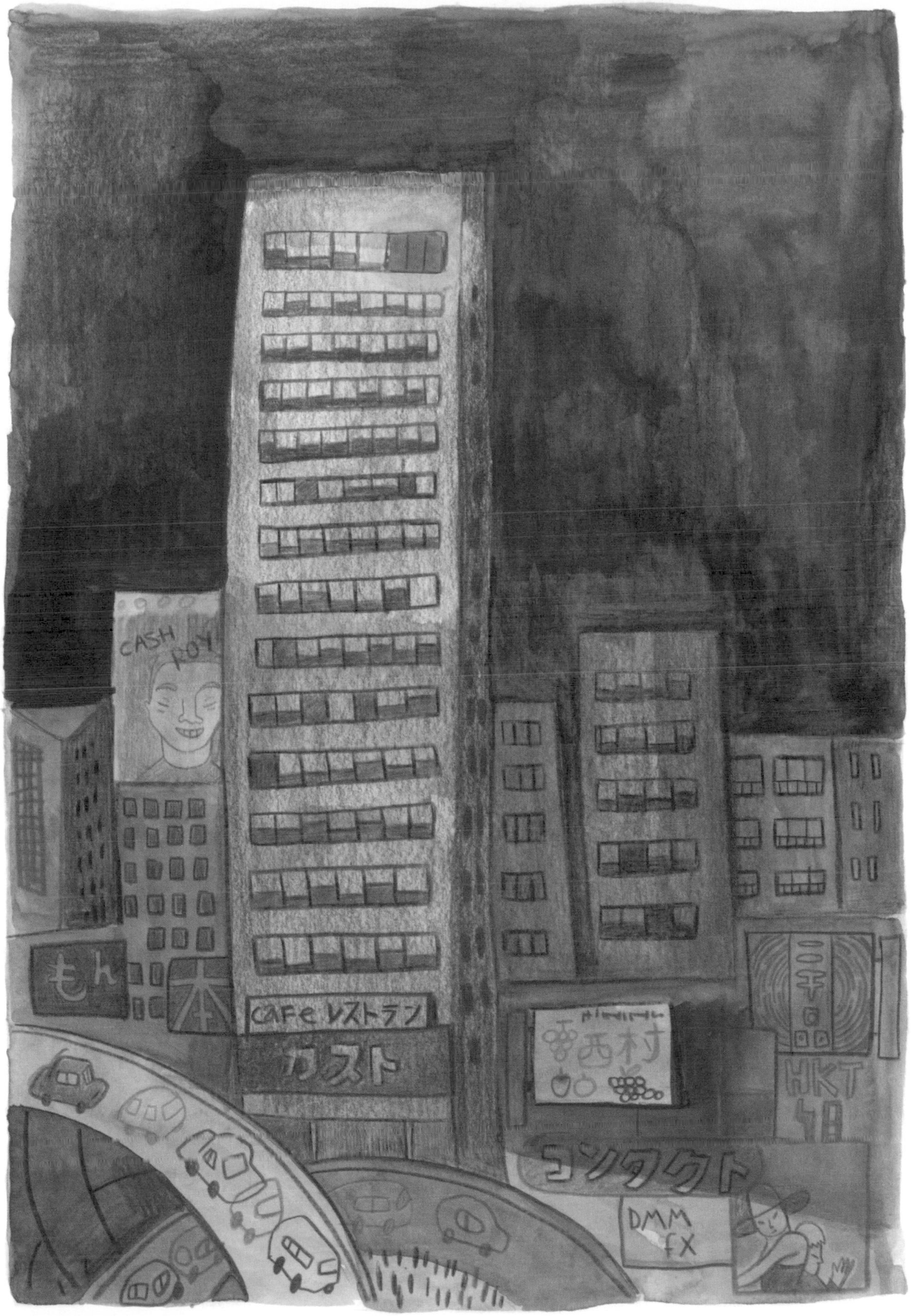
CASH BOY
もん
本
CAFE レストラン
ガスト
コンタクト
DMM FX
HKT 48

From the time I get up until I go to bed, opposite my window I see the office/desk of this woman who's tied to her paperwork and telephone.

I come home and there she is; I leave and she's still there... It reminds me of Amélie Nothomb's book "Fear and Trembling." The character of the young woman who ends up reporting

Amélie because she realized she could outdo her...

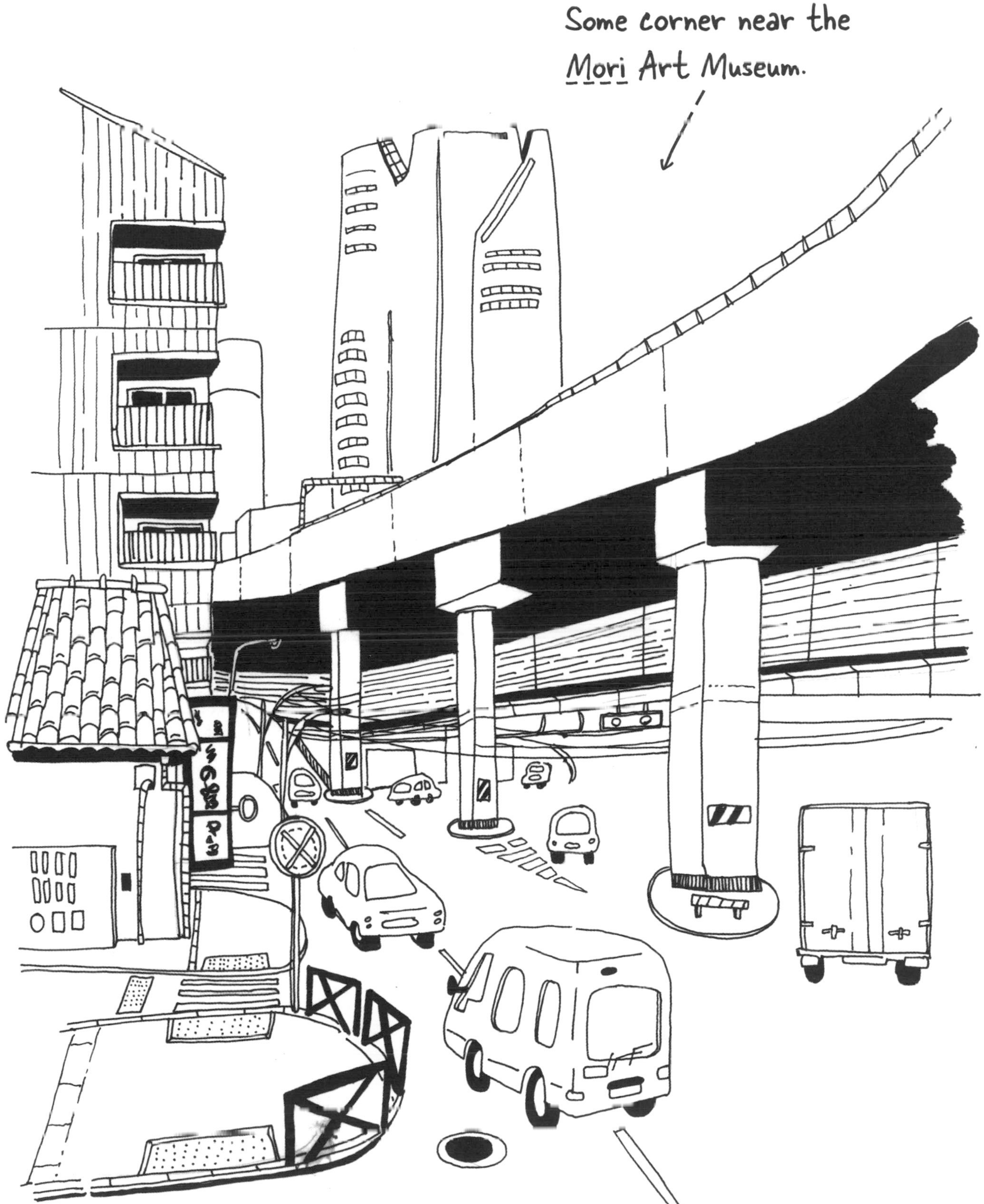
Some corner near the
Mori Art Museum.

This is **PIPO-KUN** the Japanese police mascot for the Tokyo Police Department. His name comes from PEOPLE + POLICE. He was born in 1987 and is EVERYWHERE. He's the definitive mascot. Big ears to hear people's problems, a sort of antenna for detecting motion.

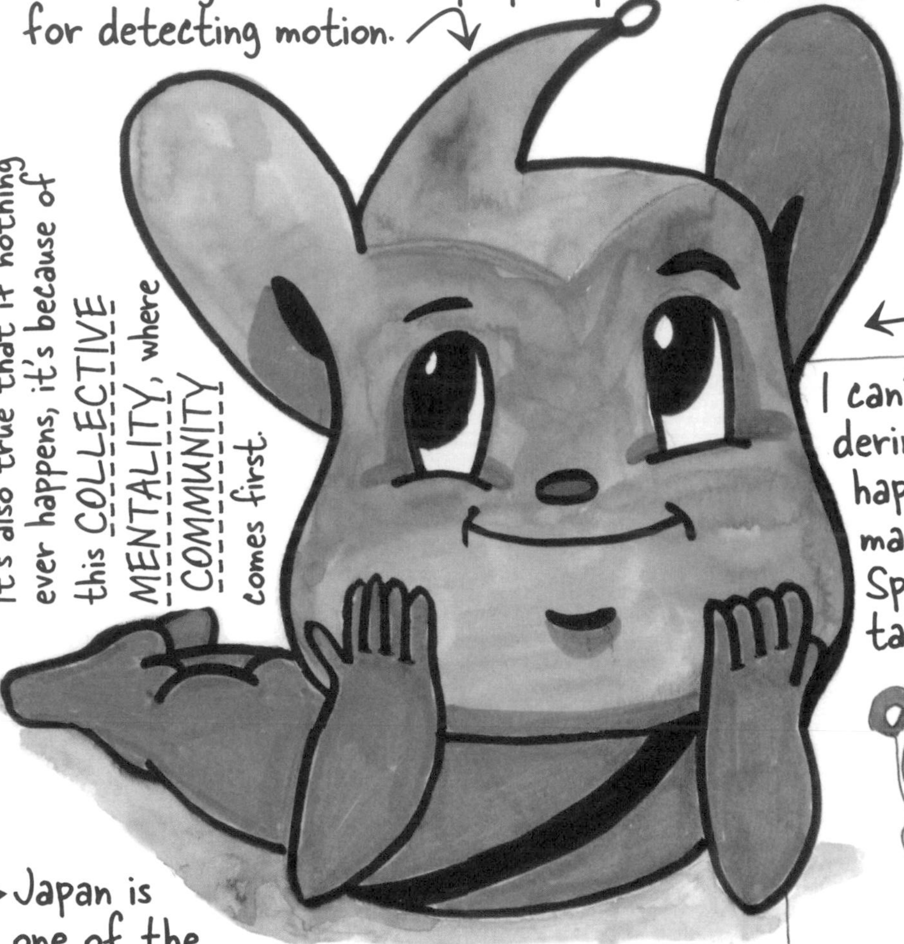

And huge eyes to see "every corner of society."

It's also true that if nothing ever happens, it's because of this COLLECTIVE MENTALITY, where COMMUNITY comes first.

I can't stop wondering what would happen if we had a mascot like this in Spain. Would people take it seriously?

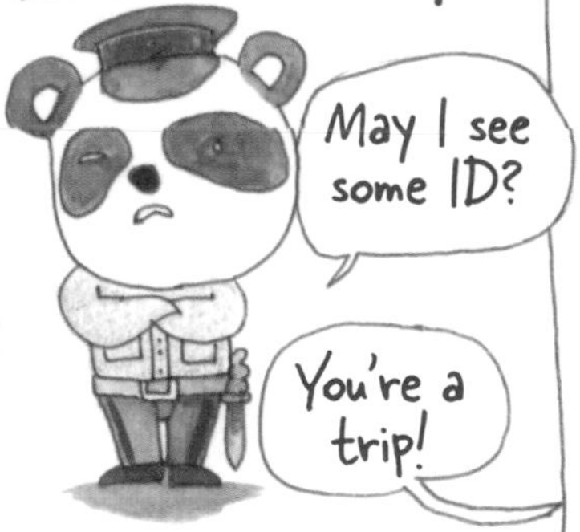
May I see some ID?
You're a trip!

Japan is one of the safest places, with the lowest crime rate in the world. I can't get over how "CUTESY" the police mascots are in a system where laws are extremely strict and penalties are very harsh.

The newspapers reported on a man who was arrested for sticking his finger in one of the pots where they cook things.

A-R-R-E-S-T-E-D.

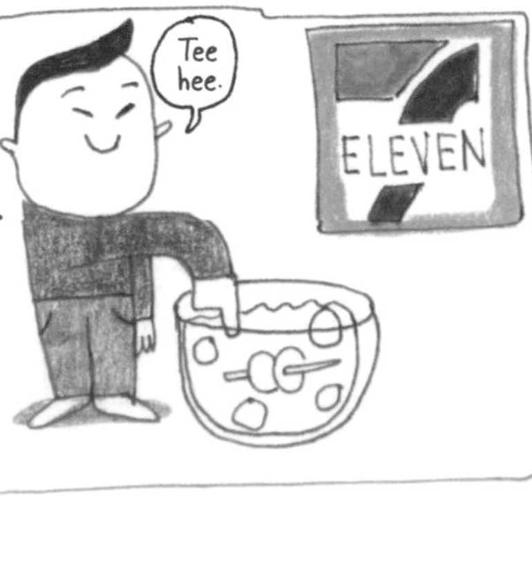
Tee hee.
ELEVEN

0 4 MAR. 2017

And speaking of delinquency and community, I read that when delinquents are arrested, they feel more ashamed of having failed their people than of themselves. What they do then is apologize through the famous BOWING. There are 4 levels of apologies and bows:

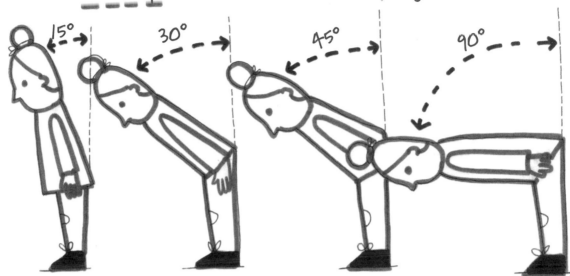

15°   30°   45°   90°

ESHAKU (15°)
To greet a
co-worker or
a subordinate.

FUTSUUREI
(30°)
To greet a
corporate
superior or to
greet clients.

TEINEIREI
(45°)
To thank
someone for
doing something
for us or to
apologize.

SAIKEIREI
(90°)
To apologize
for serious
misconduct.

And then there's DOGEZA, a bow where you kneel with your head touching the floor. This is reserved for very serious mistakes.

One of the few times this was used in public was in response to the Fukushima incident, when the nuclear power plant managers apologized to the Japanese people on camera.

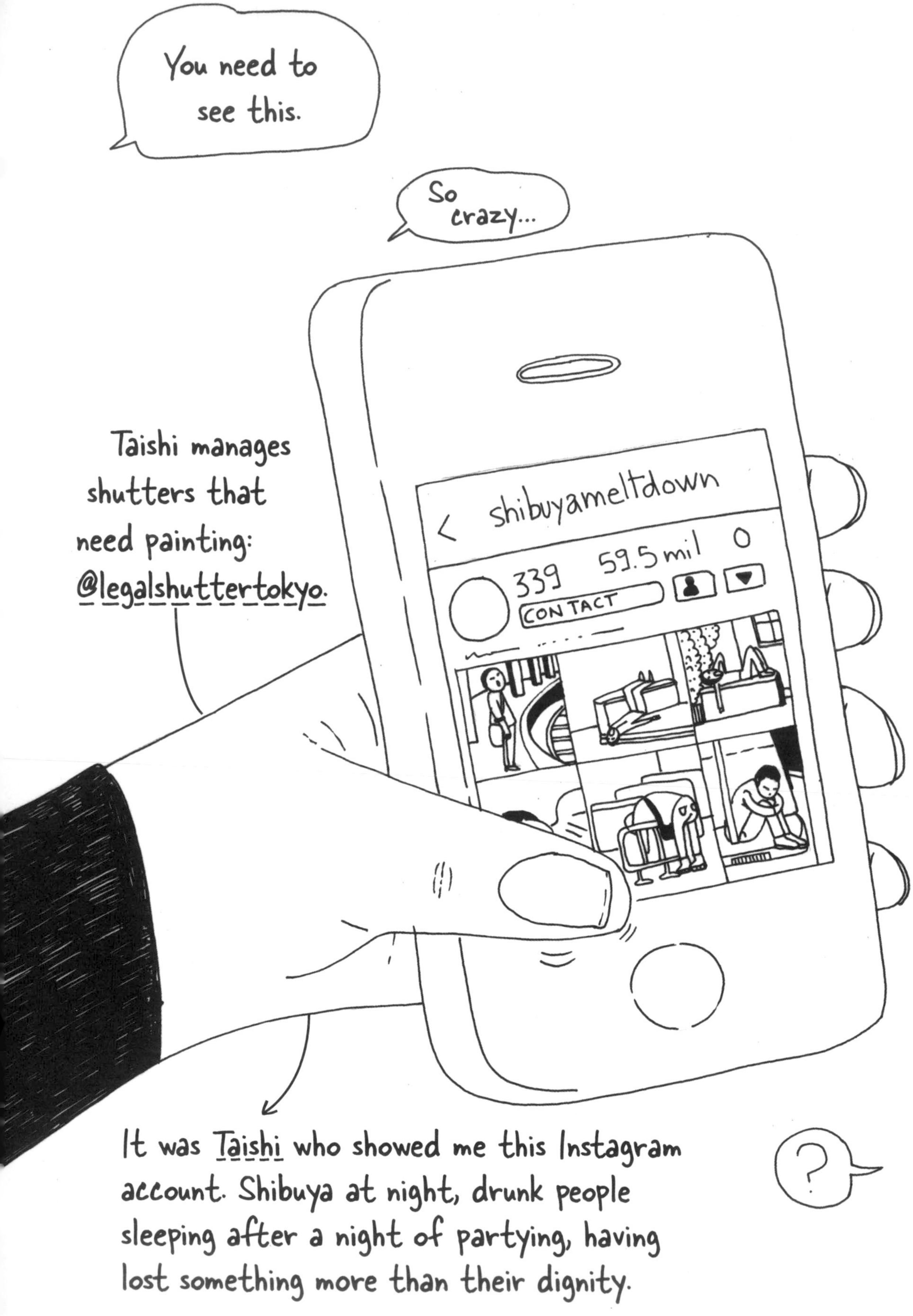
You need to see this.
So crazy...
Taishi manages shutters that need painting: @legalshuttertokyo.
shibuyameltdown
339
59.5 mil
0
CONTACT
?
It was Taishi who showed me this Instagram account. Shibuya at night, drunk people sleeping after a night of partying, having lost something more than their dignity.

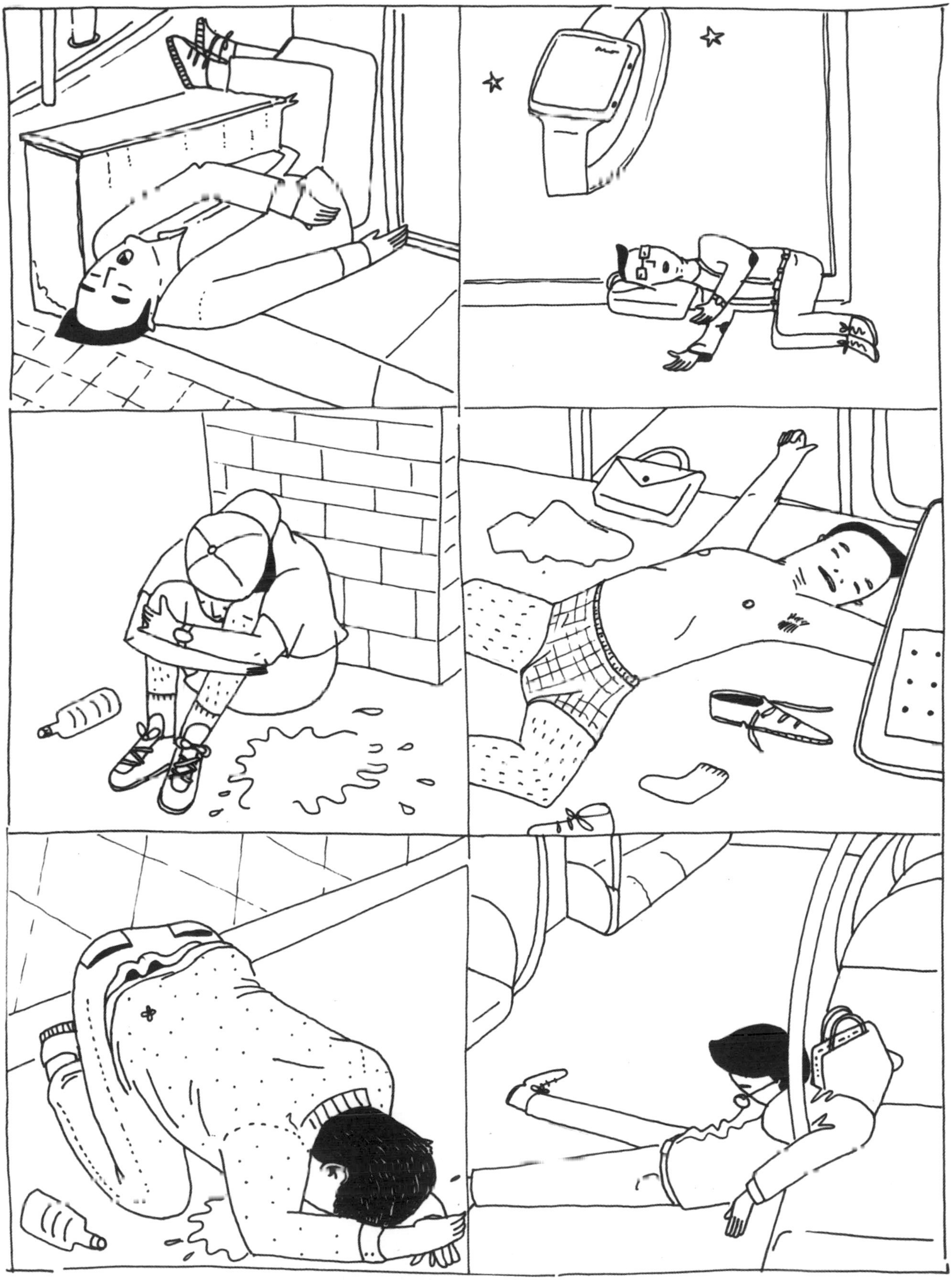

A bona fide social phenomenon.

Junpei and Shoji, from Paradise Air.

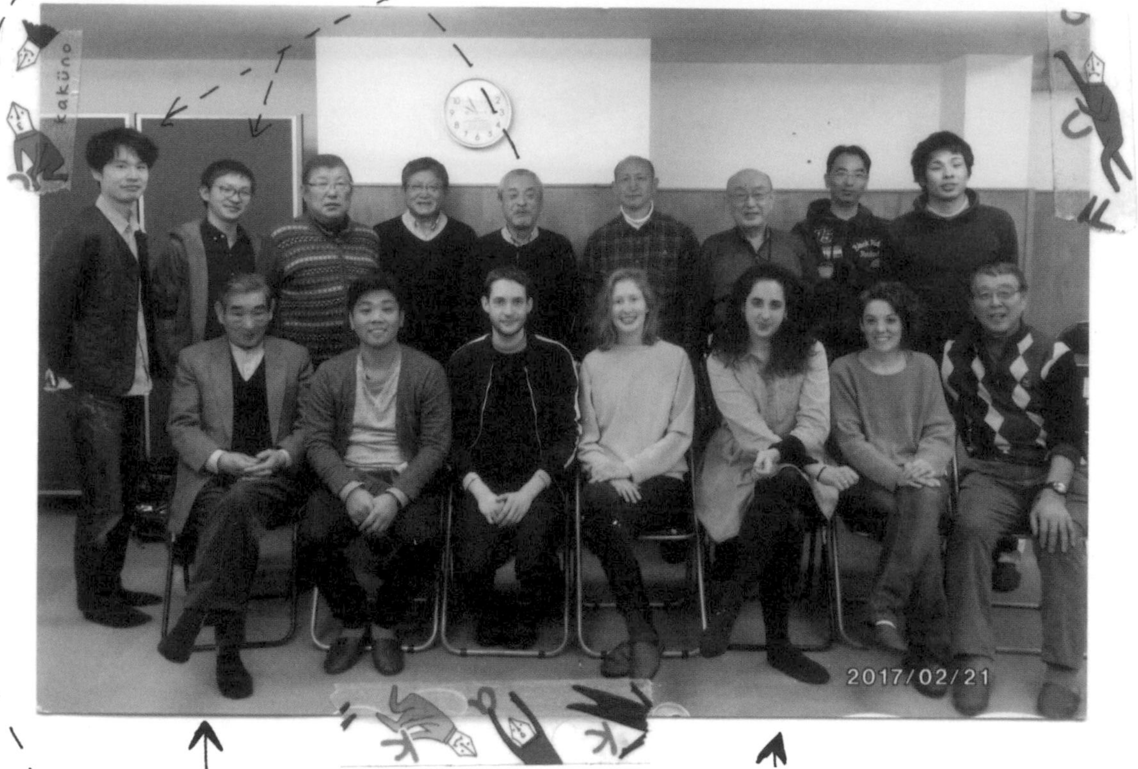
kakūno
2017/02/21

This is Makoto Horio.

I think he is also a fairly important member of the community. He told me he'd been to Italy and that he was surprised to find stone was used in building houses.

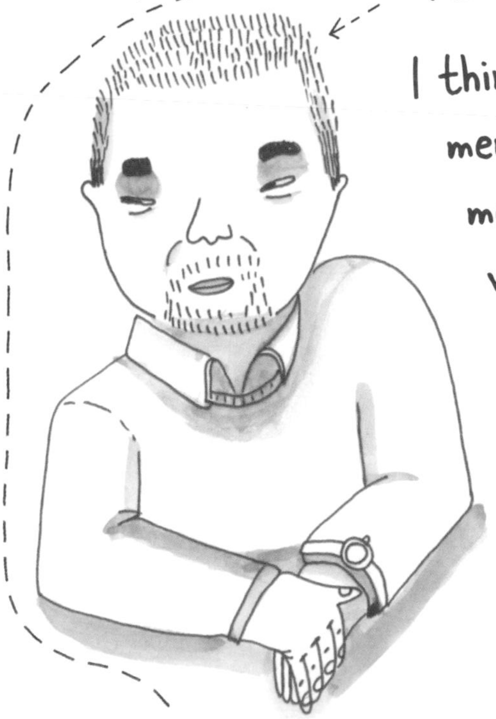

He told me he was going to die next year, but I think he was pulling my leg...

I like to look at the photo and remember that we were all in our stocking feet.

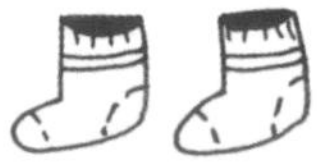

Now and then, the people behind the PARADISE AIR project and residency organize dinner parties. The excuse is to get us out into the community and learn their customs, talk a bit about the arts project... There's food and lots of alcohol: beer, wine and shōchū... When they toast they say...

Kampai!

which means something like "To your health!"

Once I told them that in Spain we say:

¡CHIN CHIN!

I didn't understand until a few days ago why they laughed so hard every time <u>I</u> said it.

In Japanese, "Chinchin" means penis.

↑

They're so polite that no one said anything to me.

Alcohol

One of the things that caught my attention is how much people drink in Japan. **THEY DRINK A LOT**. Almost all social events are alcohol related. And not just sake. There's also a lot of beer. Many drink until they're falling-down drunk. The beers I tried weren't all that strong, so you could drink a lot.

SAPPORO is the country's oldest beer. I read that it's a mild beer with a complex flavor (I've never understood these beer tasting terms very well...).

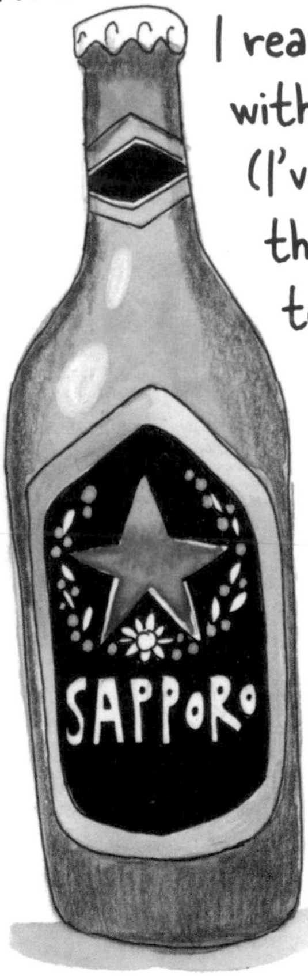

SAPPORO

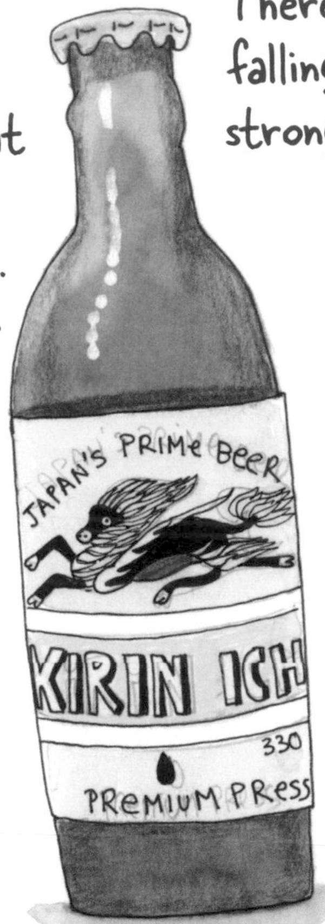

JAPAN'S PRIME BEER
KIRIN ICH
330
PREMIUM PRESS

But the story of the label is cool.

KIRIN

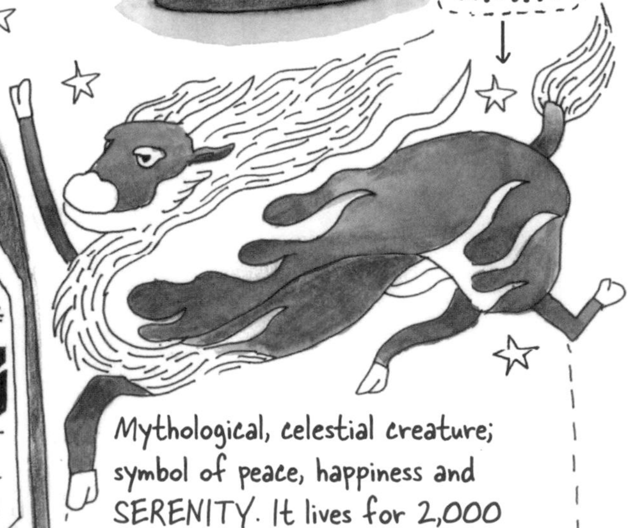

Mythological, celestial creature; symbol of peace, happiness and SERENITY. It lives for 2,000 years and comes down to earth once. They say its appearance is a sign that a GREAT LEADER will be born.

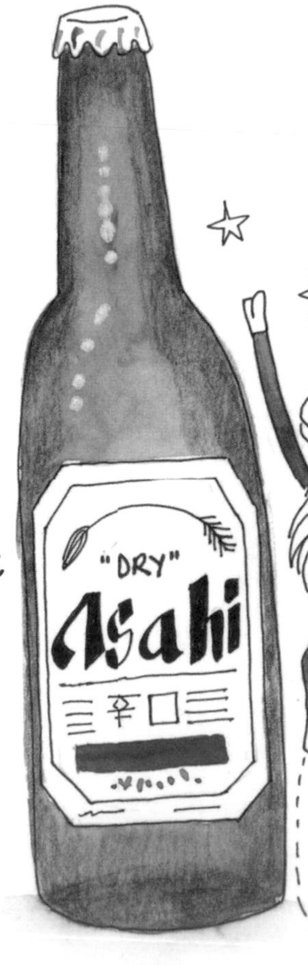

"DRY"
Asahi

ASAHI. Not all that Japanese because it's bottled in the Czech Republic... who knew?

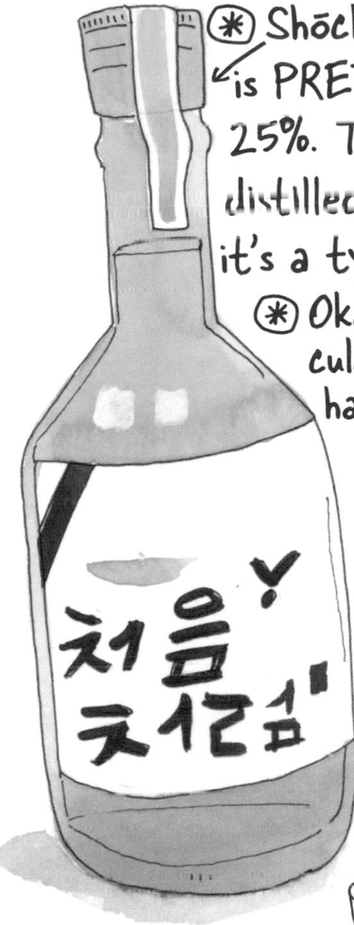

(*) Shōchū is an alcoholic drink that is PRETTY STRONG. It's about 25%. Takatashi-san told me it's distilled from potatoes and that it's a type of VODKA.

(*) Okay, so this bottle in particular is Korean. (That's what happens when you don't understand anything.)

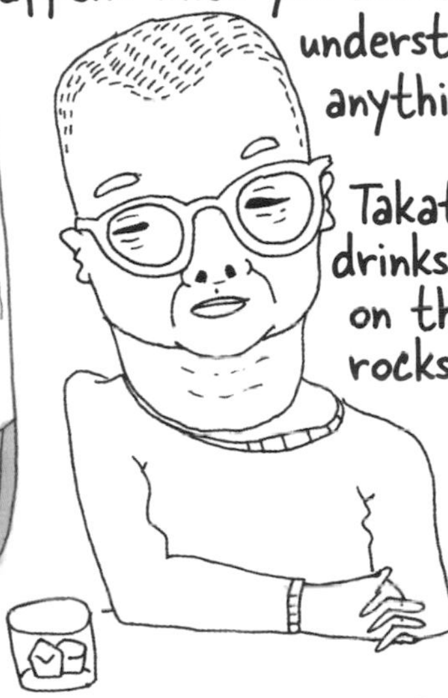

Takatashi drinks it on the rocks.

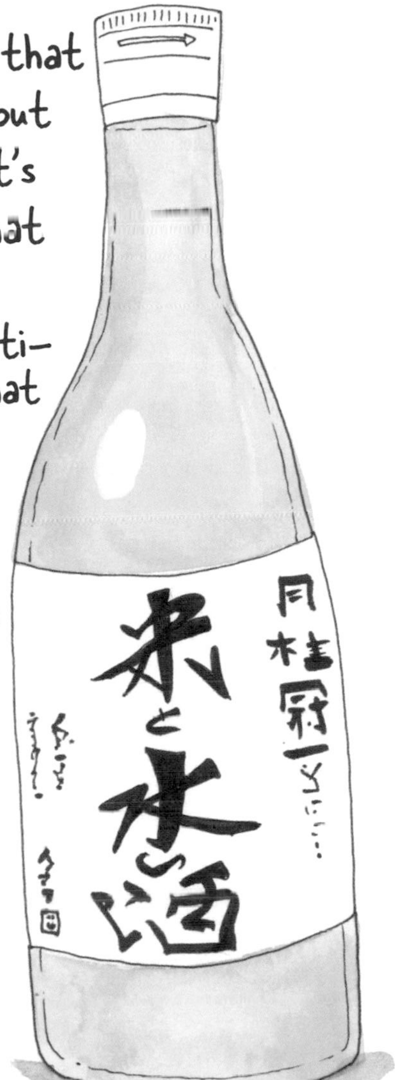

This is **SAKE** and it isn't that strong. To me it tastes like wine and literally means "alcoholic drink." It's made from rice and people drink it a lot, especially at traditional events, warm or cold, depending on the sake and its flavor.

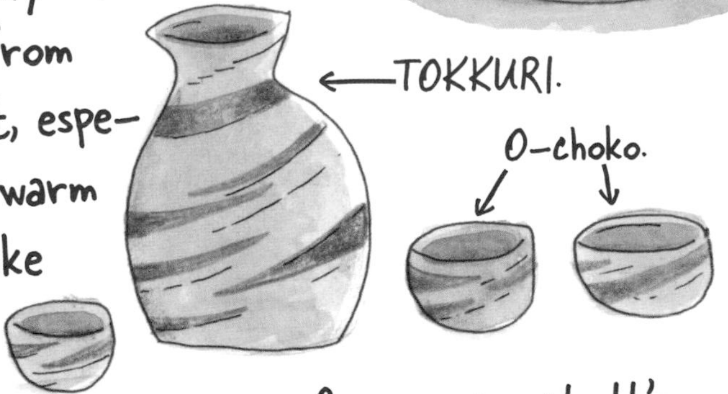
TOKKURI.
O-choko.

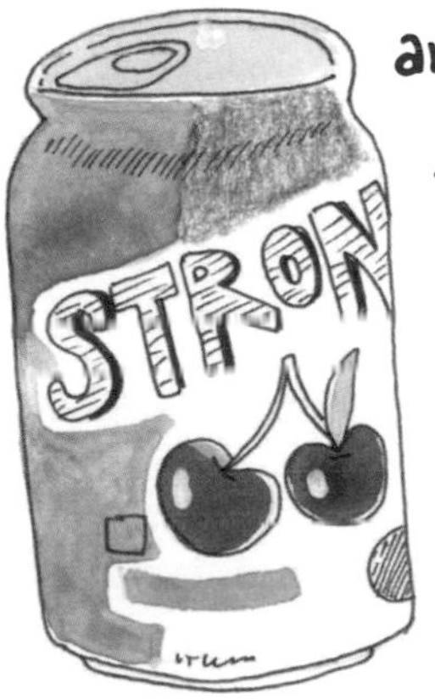
STRON

There are these ceramic jugs for serving it. It's really important to serve the other person first and then yourself. The shōchū **HIGH BALL** makes a mean little cocktail.

They mix shōchū with flavored fruit juices.

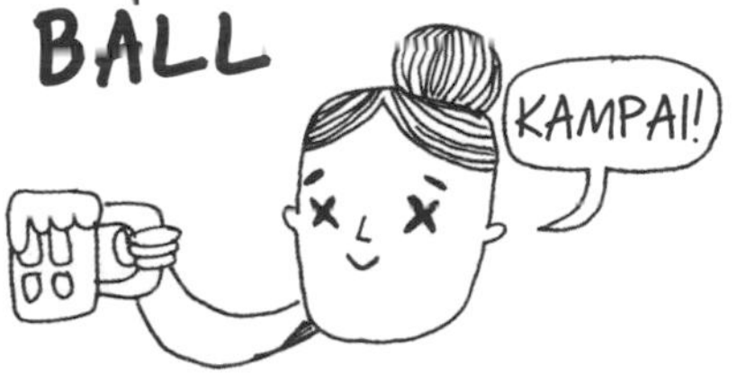
KAMPAI!

I've become aware of having gone through these three stages since I arrived. I think this could be extrapolated to other countries, but they're particularly striking in Japan.

Stage 1 : Your mind is blown. Everything amazes you, the lights, noises, sounds... You don't understand anything, but everything amuses you.
Your jaw hangs open, you don't get it, but you're bowled over by the people, the buildings, the street, the food, the way people act, even their tone of voice. Japan feels like some kind of giant amusement park to you.

Stage 2 : You begin to understand what's behind the behavior in Japanese society. You discover a "darker" part to it: the issue of work, the non-existent physical contact, the strange sexuality... Why? Where does all this come from?

Stage 3 : You get used to it. The things that enchanted you, that amazed you, stop attracting your attention. You find that you chameleonize yourself within your surroundings, you no longer stand out and you become part of the crowd, you stand in the same lines they stand in to eat ramen, you fall asleep in the subway, you don't shout, you speak quietly, you're more discreet about blowing your nose than before...

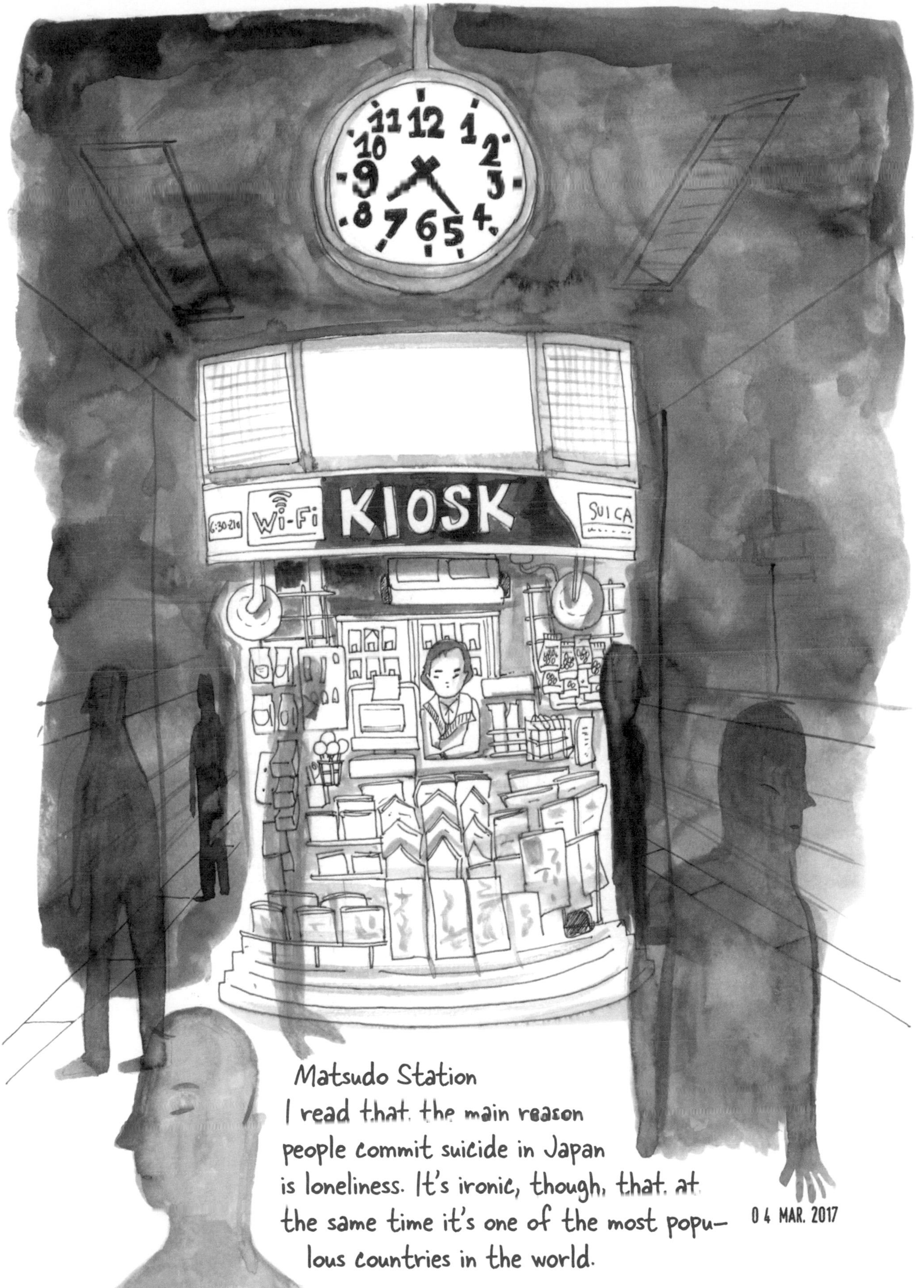
KIOSK
Wi-Fi
SUICA
Matsudo Station
I read that the main reason people commit suicide in Japan is loneliness. It's ironic, though, that at the same time it's one of the most populous countries in the world.
04 MAR. 2017

I've come to a conclusion in regard to the SURPRISING matter (because it is TRULY surprising) of alcohol consumption in Japan. They say they can't drink as much as Westerners and that they have less tolerance for alcohol, but all the same I think they drink a lot. Socially it's not only practically obligatory, but it's also not considered such a bad thing to be drunk.

It's akin to napping in public, what's called inemuri: it's a sign that you've worked a lot and you deserve a rest, a moment for relaxing with friends.

Another sign the Tokyo subway system used a few years ago to discourage a certain type of behavior on the subway. ↵

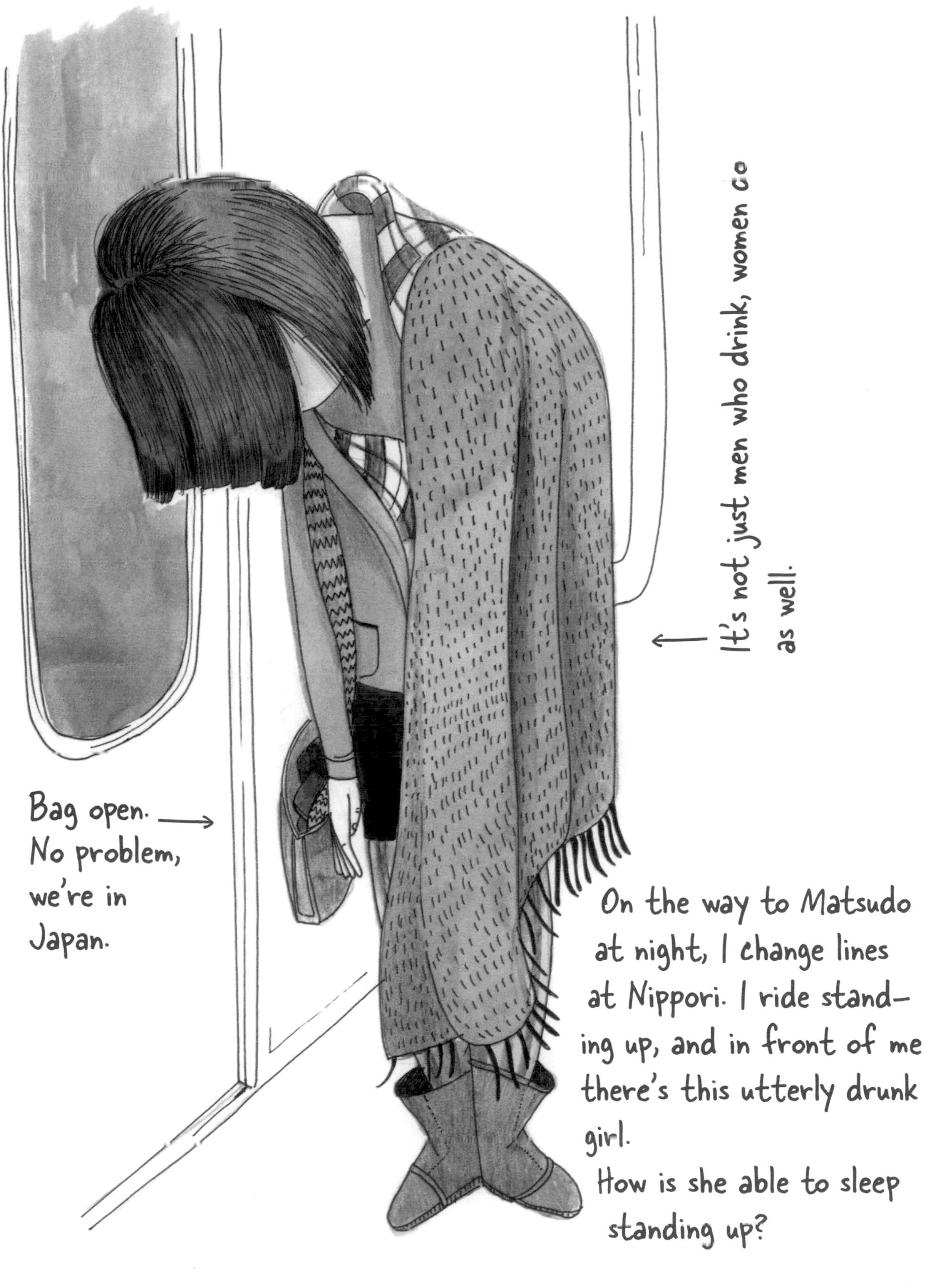
It's not just men who drink, women go as well.
Bag open. No problem, we're in Japan.
On the way to Matsudo at night, I change lines at Nippori. I ride standing up, and in front of me there's this utterly drunk girl.
How is she able to sleep standing up?

Matcha tea.

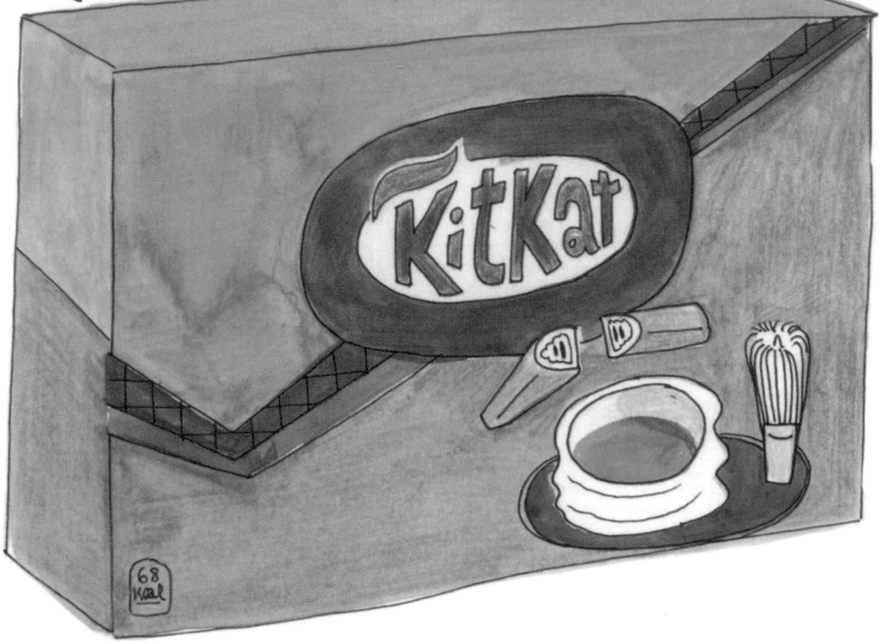
KitKat

Strawberry.

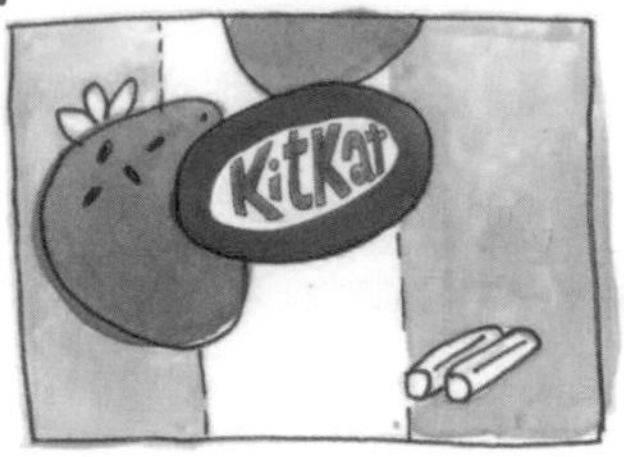
KitKat

Special Mount Fuji.

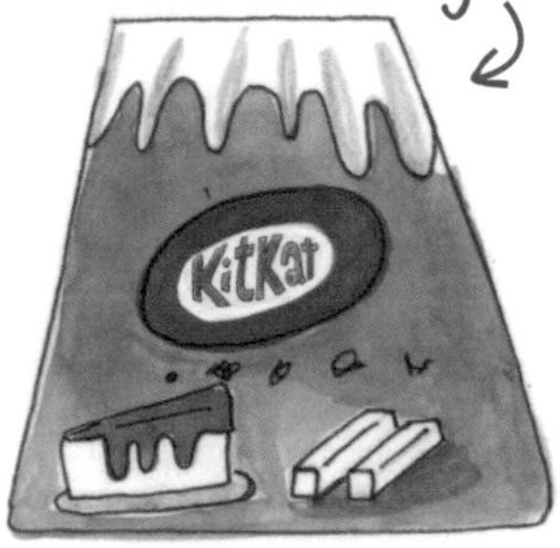
KitKat

I've seen ALL manner of Kit Kats. There are flavors associated with specific places, special editions; there's pumpkin for Halloween, green tea, sake, luxury editions for adults with dark chocolate, strawberry, melon, Hokkaidō, rum and raisin, and even strawberry cheesecake.

What is it with this Japanese Kit Kat craze?

Kit Kat sounds very similar to the Japanese

Kitto Katsu,

which means "You're sure to win!" They're given most often to students before exams to wish them LUCK. (That and the Japanese obsession with collecting does the rest.)

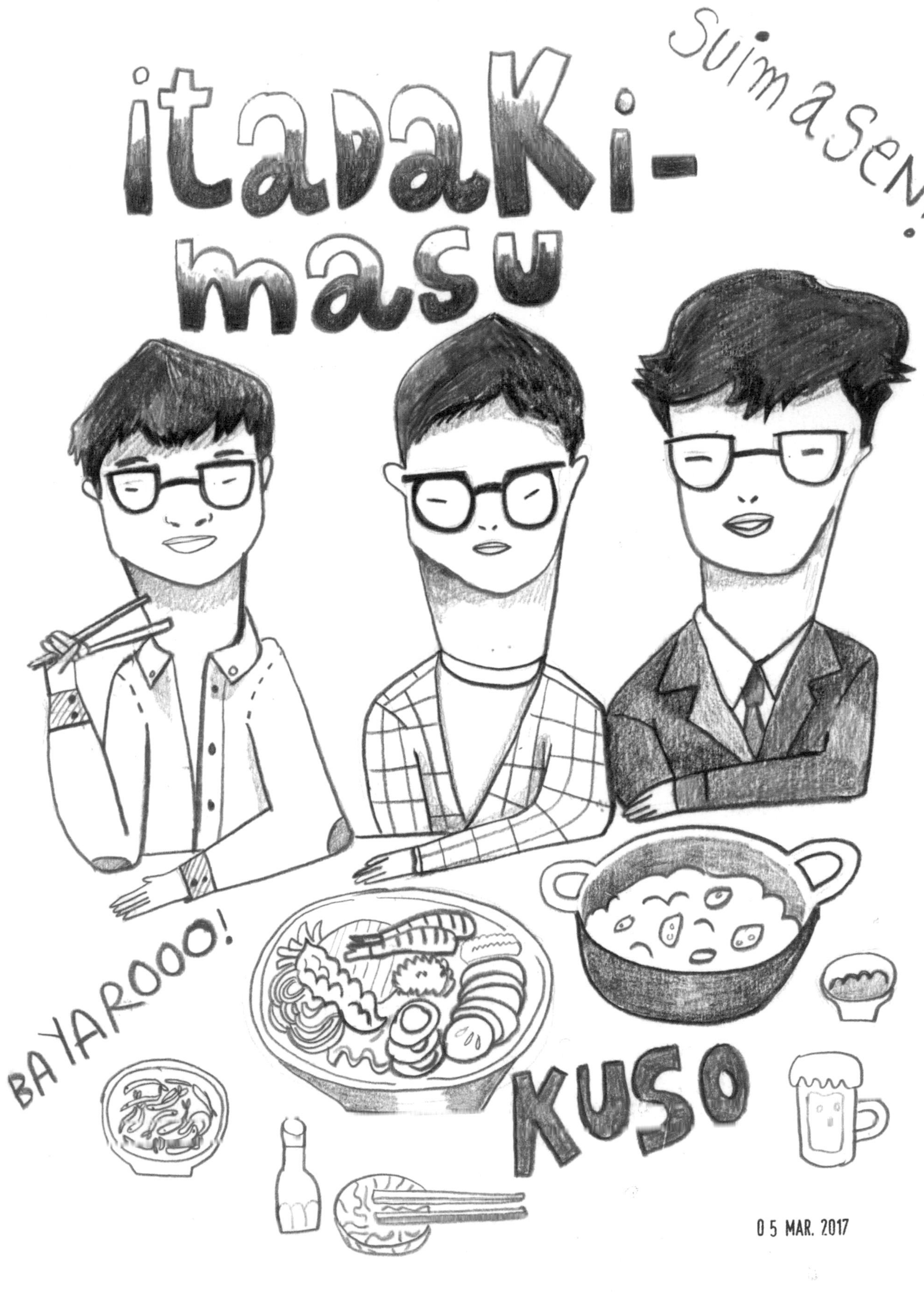

itadaki-
masu
Suimasen!
BAYAROOO!
KUSO
05 MAR. 2017

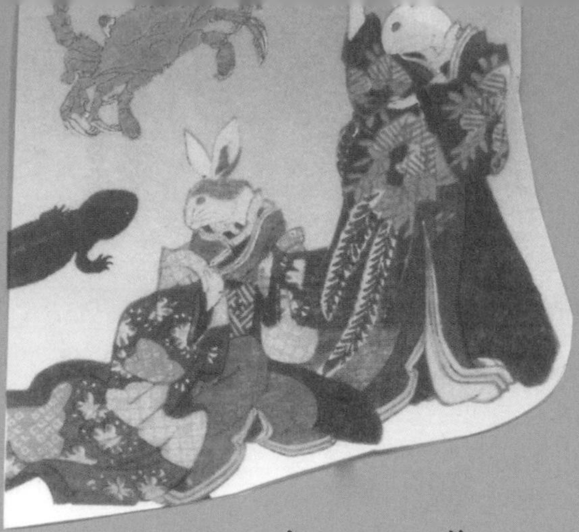

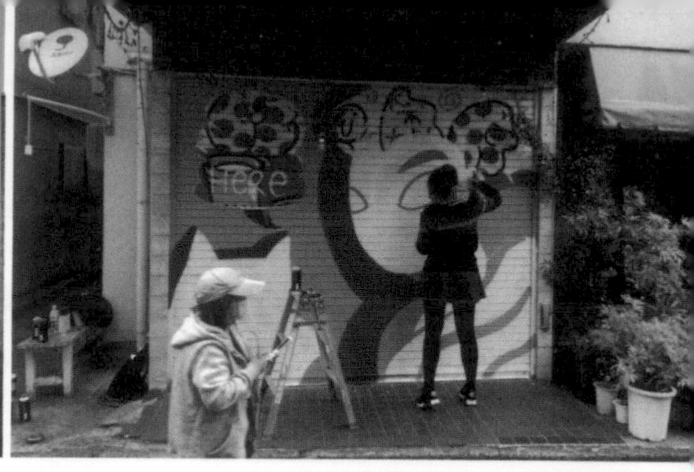
Here

Shutter I painted in the Koenji neighborhood.

A man walking a dog in a stroller.

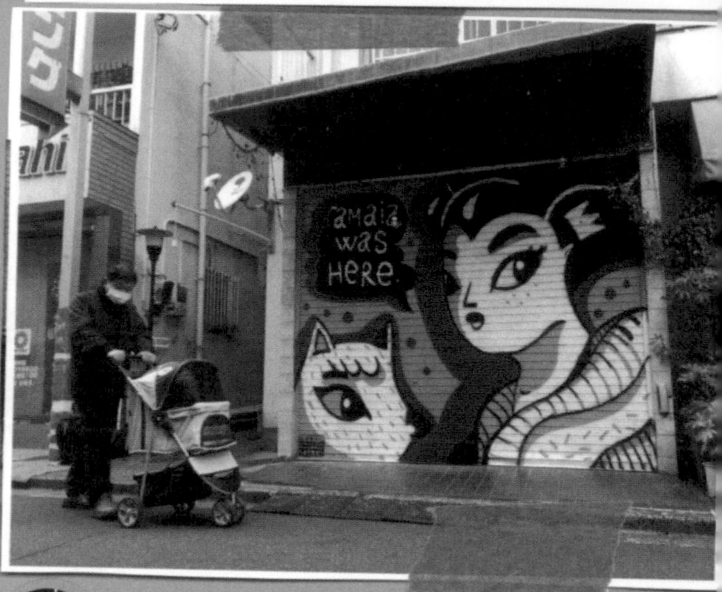
amaia
was
HERE.

PURIKURA taken in the HARAJUKU neighborhood.

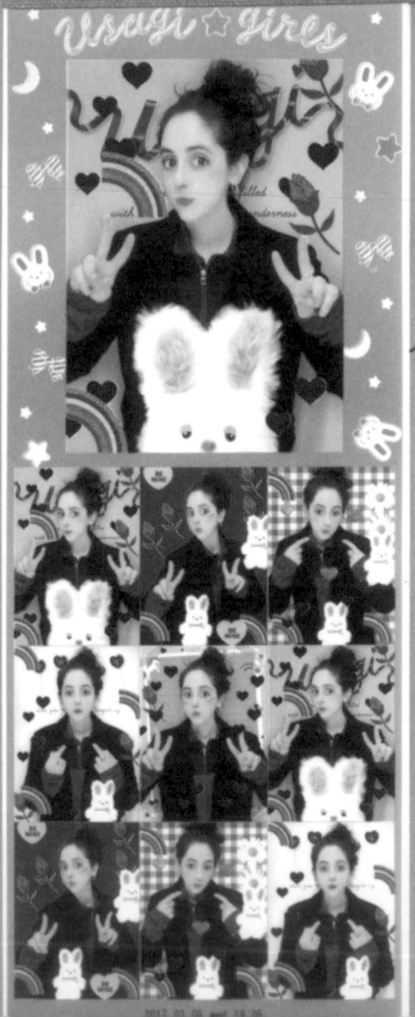
Usagi girls

In Japan WhatsApp EMOJIS EXIST for real.

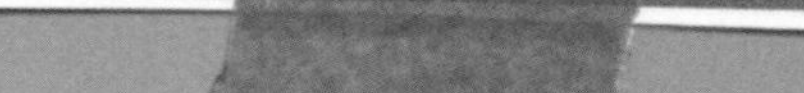
三色だんご
17. 3. 4

Week 4

 He lives in Tokyo with his wife, Yukari.

I went out to have some beers in SHINJUKU with Gerard and some friends who'd come on a trip to Tokyo.

We said goodbye at around 11:45 p.m. because I had to get back to Matsudo.

When I got to the platform on the Yamanote line where I had to catch the subway, I almost died. I'd cut it close to get on the third-to-last train, but I hadn't reckoned with the ton of people who wanted to do the same thing.

Aida and Aixa.

The feeling of being crowded in was indescribable: masses of people surrounding me, hundreds jostling me from side to side trying to get into cars that were already jam-packed.

While I tried not to lose my cool and let myself be dragged along, I couldn't help thinking of cattle headed to the slaughterhouse.

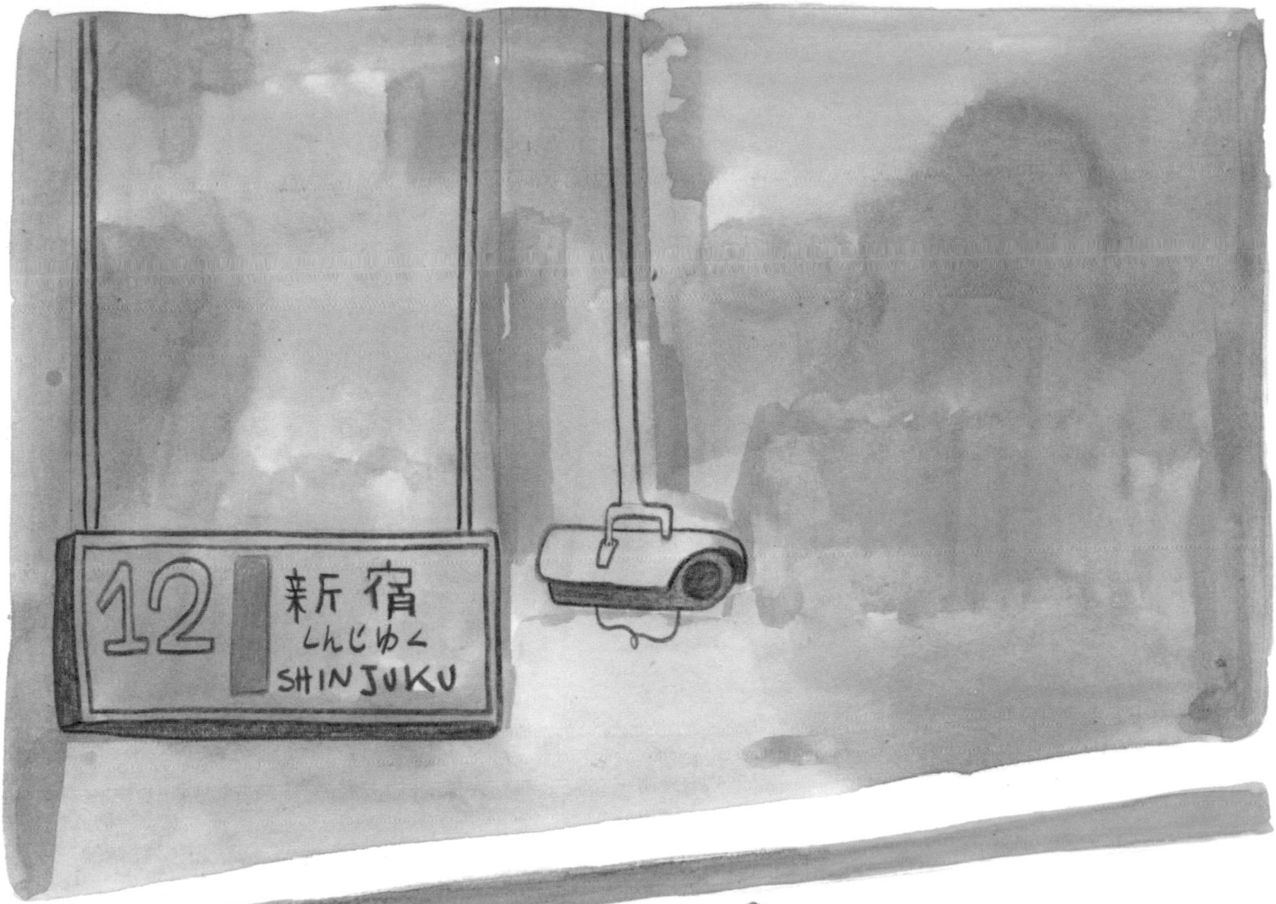
12
新宿
しんじゅく
SHINJUKU
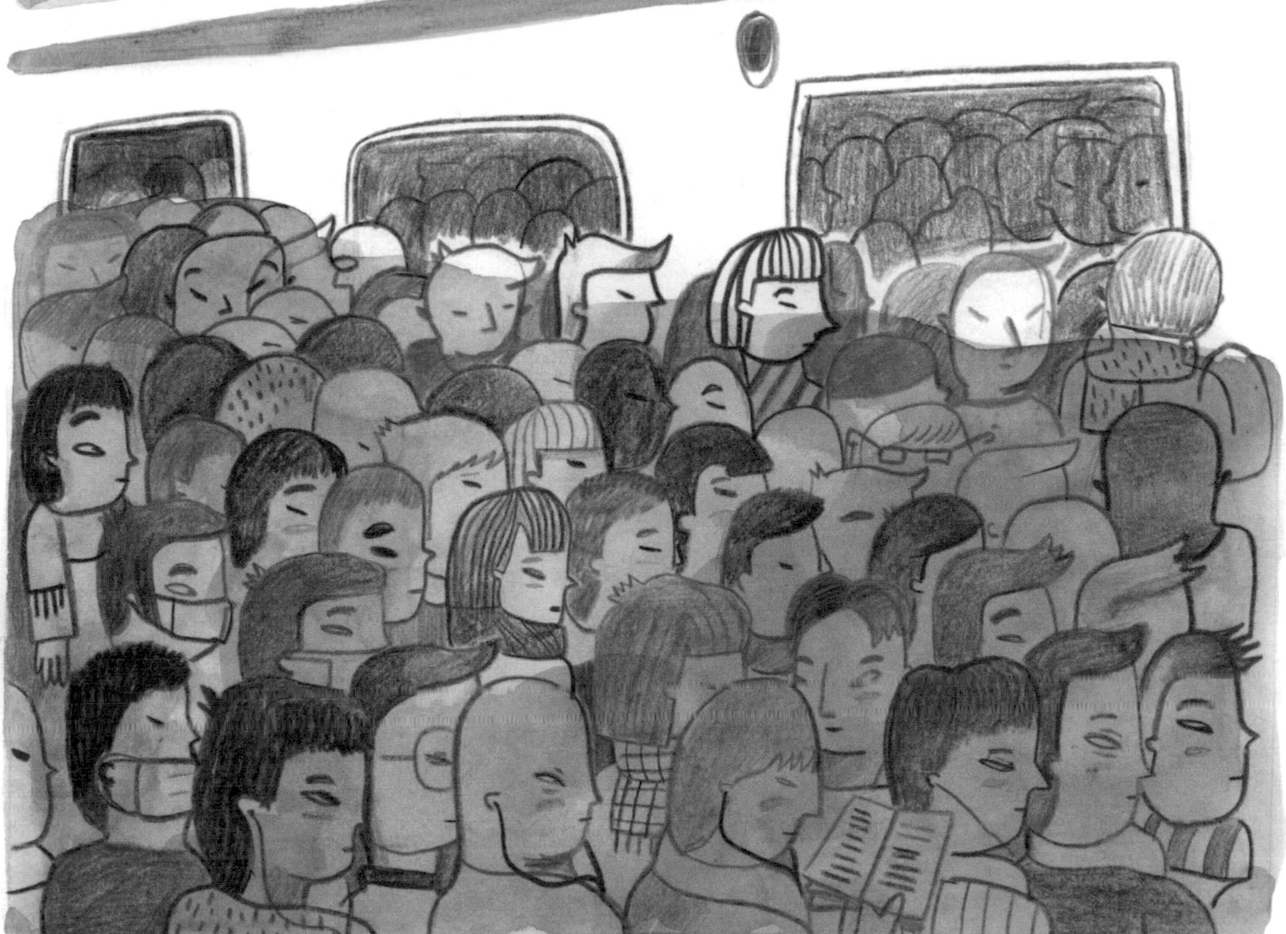

Inemuri

Falling asleep in parks, coffee shops or at work isn't frowned upon. These little catnaps are called inemuri.

Sleeping for for twenty minutes, catching forty winks, makes them think you've been working SO HARD, you've given SO MUCH to the company that you're wiped out. It's not a matter of getting into bed, but just shutting your eyes while you're sitting, on the subway or wherever you are.

Everyone does it, and if you add to that the fact that in Japan getting robbed is VERY RARE...

A Courtesan of the "Meiji Era" by Tsukioka Yoshitoshi. ⟶

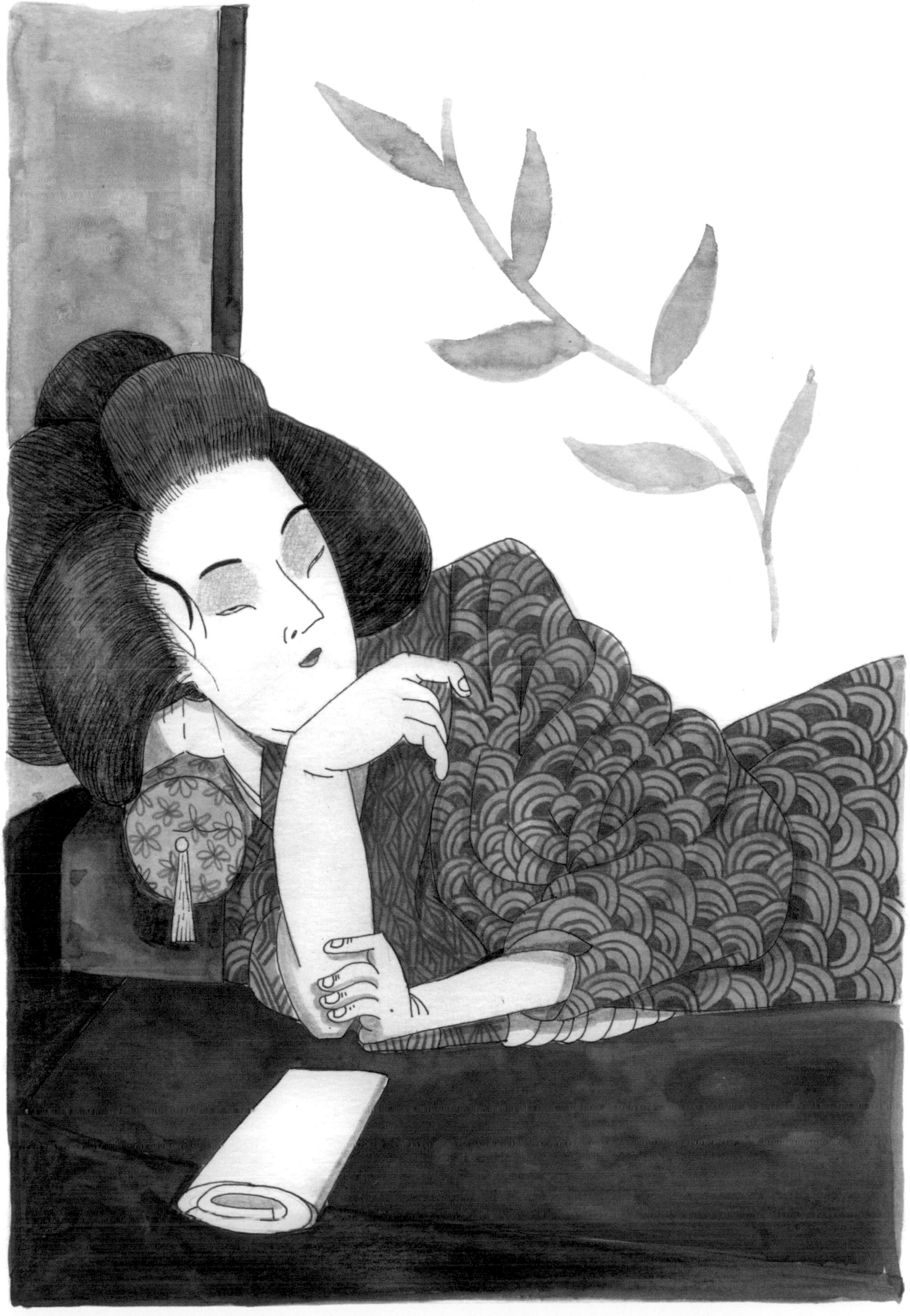

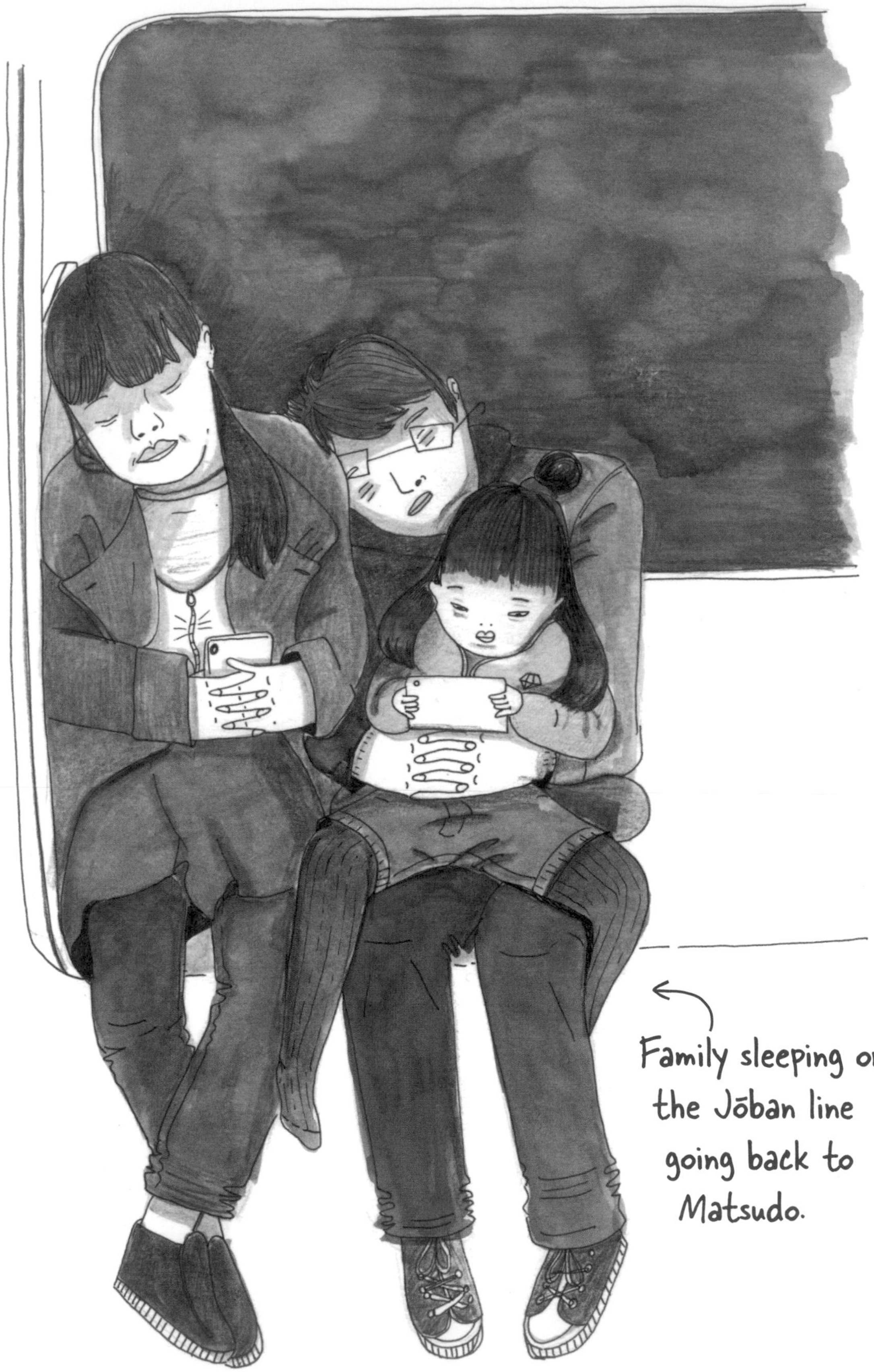

Family sleeping on the Jōban line going back to Matsudo.

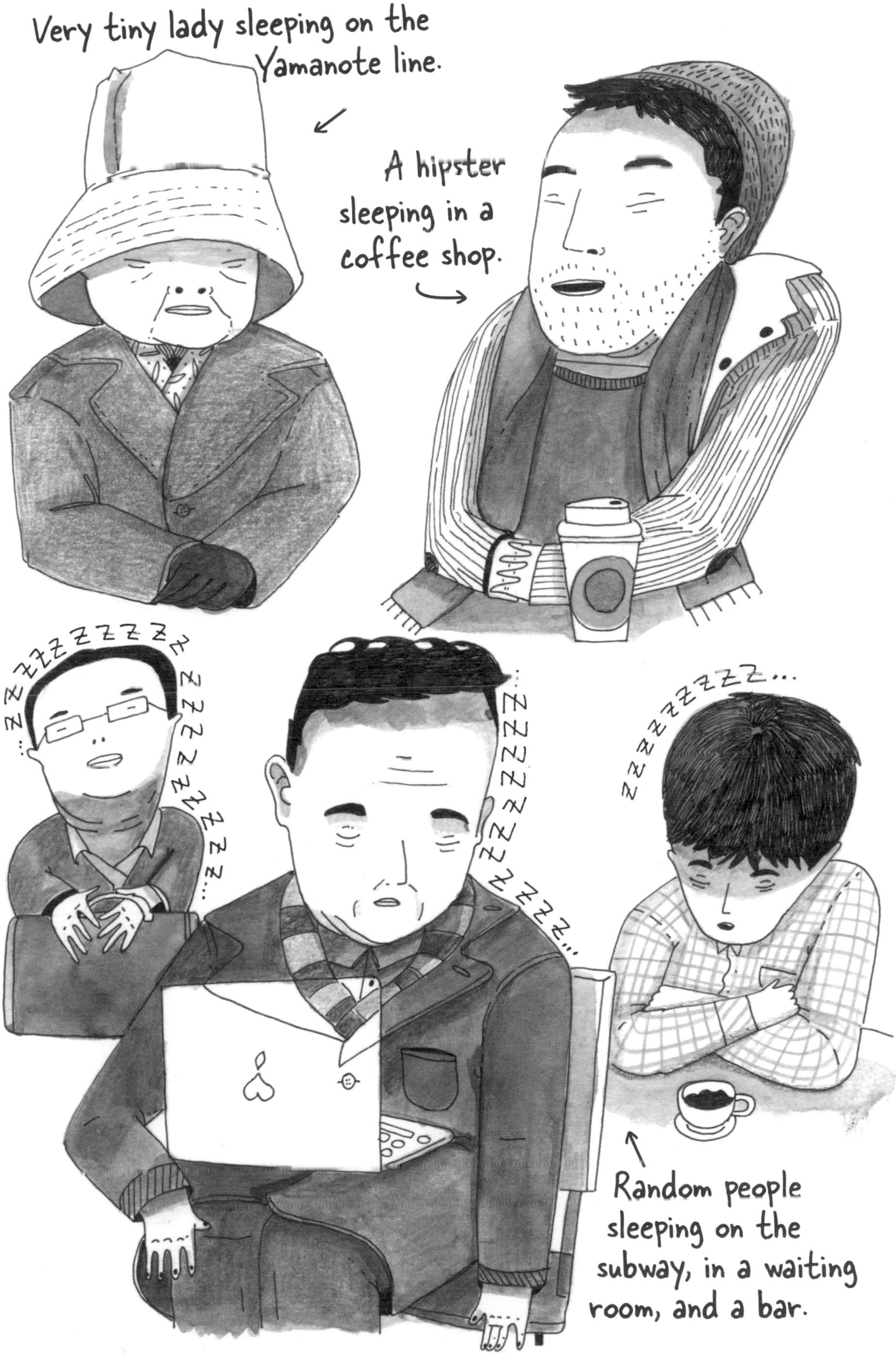
Very tiny lady sleeping on the Yamanote line.
A hipster sleeping in a coffee shop.
ZZZZZZZZZZ...
ZZZZZZZZZZZZ...
ZZZZZZZZZZZZZZ...
ZZZZZZZZZZ...
Random people sleeping on the subway, in a waiting room, and a bar.

Google him,
he's amazing. ⟶

I discovered an artist I love: HASUI KAWASE. He was a print
designer who became famous mainly for his landscapes. Having
gotten used to ukiyo-e characters in antiquated dress showing
how Japan was 500 years ago, as if they were Polaroids, I'm
taken aback by these prints of a much more modern Japan.

Print called "Zōjō-ji Temple in Shiba" ⟶
(1925).

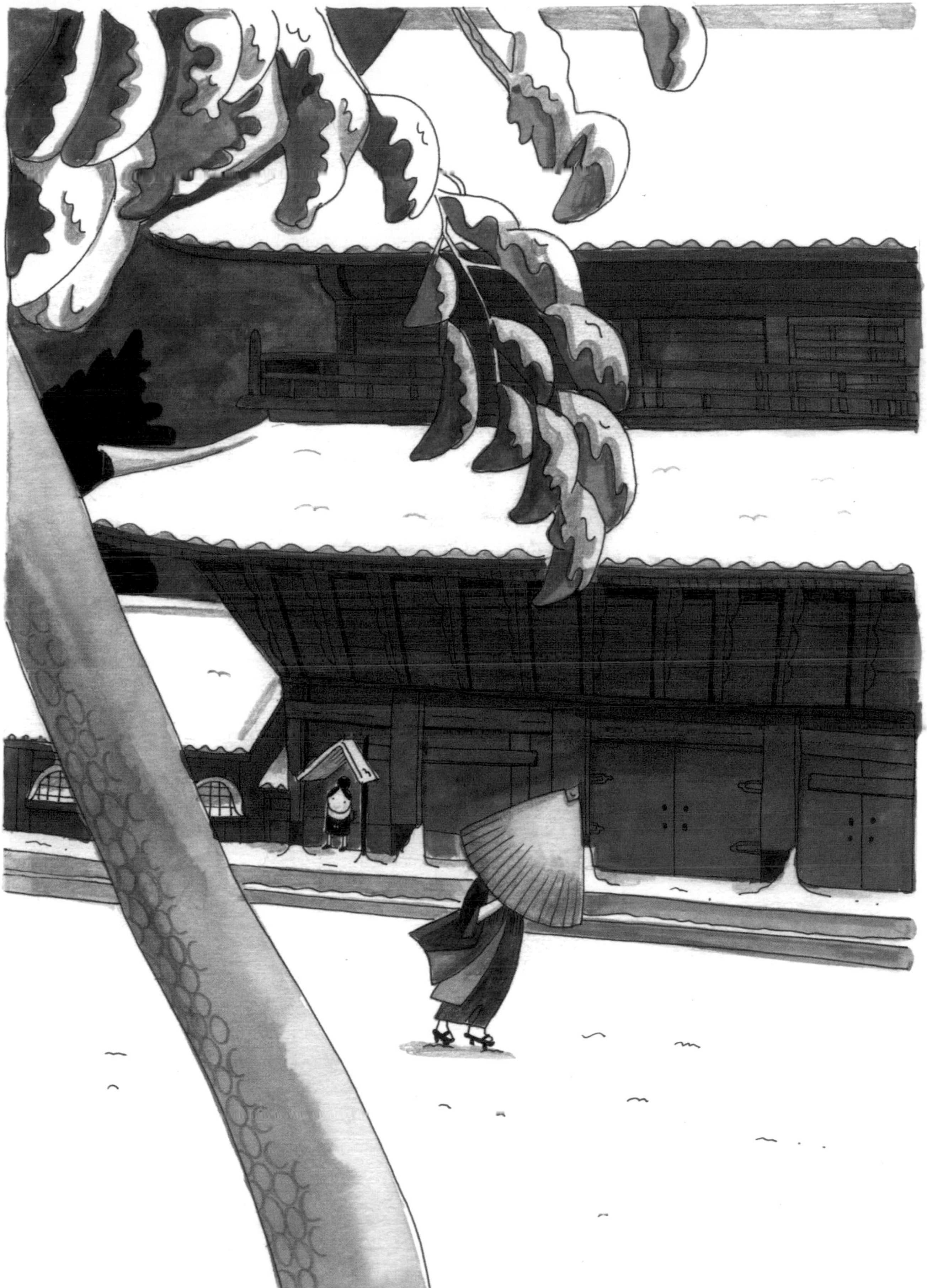

In Japan, two main religions coexist:
Shintō and Buddhism. Influence from China
also brought Confucianists, Taoists... even
Christians, although the latter make up a
very small minority.

Religion isn't a particularly defined concept
in the Japanese mentality. The Japanese
don't believe in one single religion, rather
they incorporate traits from different
beliefs into their daily lives.

Religion 1

Shintoism

or

Shintō

They say it's as old as Japan itself.

Example in Tokyo: MEIJI SHRINE

Dedicated to Emperor Meiji and his wife, Shōken.

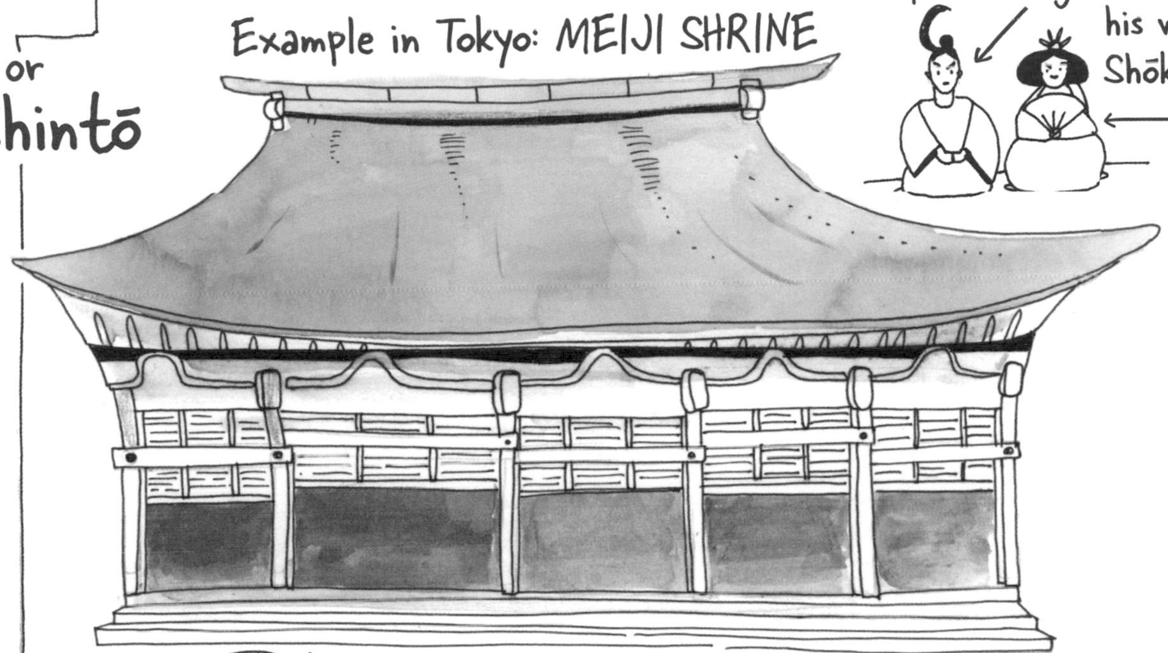

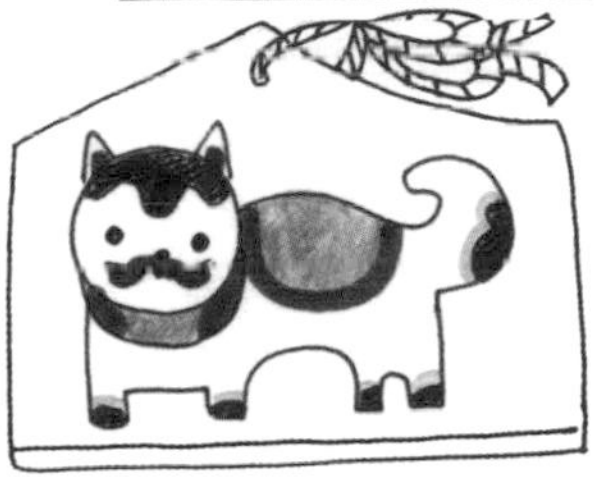

Wishes are made on these adorable plaques.

This religion is based on worshipping **KAMI**, or spirits of nature. This is a popular cult, a kind of **NATURALISTIC ANIMISM** that venerates ancestors. According to **SHINTŌ**, NOTHING IS ABSOLUTE.

These shrines often have gates called TORII,

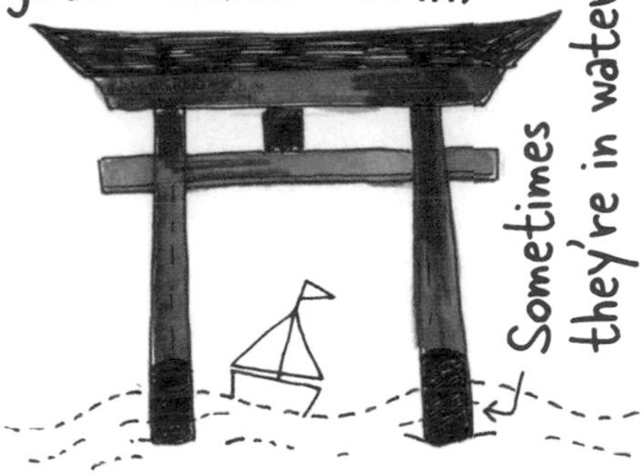

Sometimes they're in water.

which separate the SACRED space from the MUNDANE.

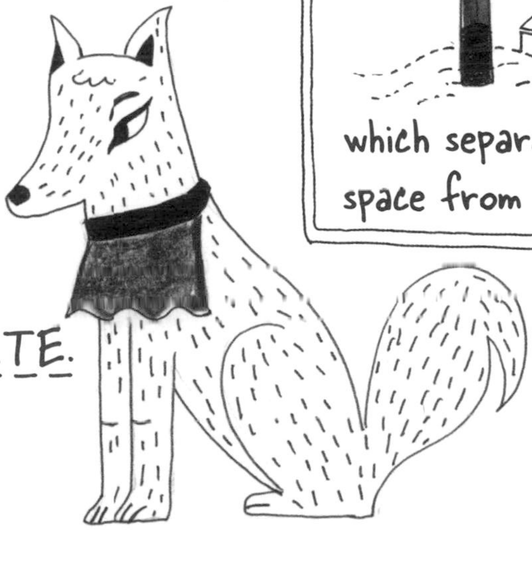

There are no sacred scriptures or founders.

AMATERASU is the SUN goddess of the Shintō religion. Supposedly an ancestor of the royal family, she is one of the most important kamis.

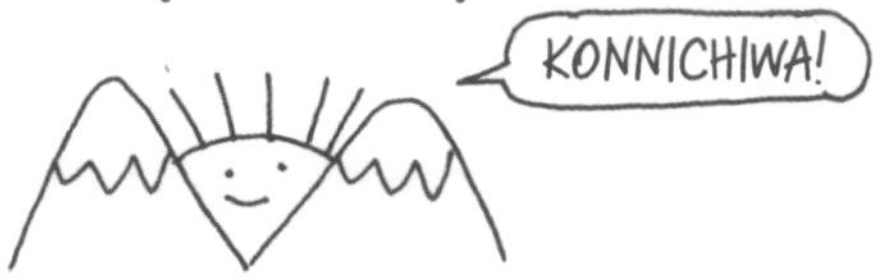
KONNICHIWA!

Legend has it that AMATERASU, angry with her brother SUSANOO*, shut herself up in a cave. Then the earth was covered in DARKNESS. The other gods had a huge party at the entrance to pique her curiosity and get her to come out.

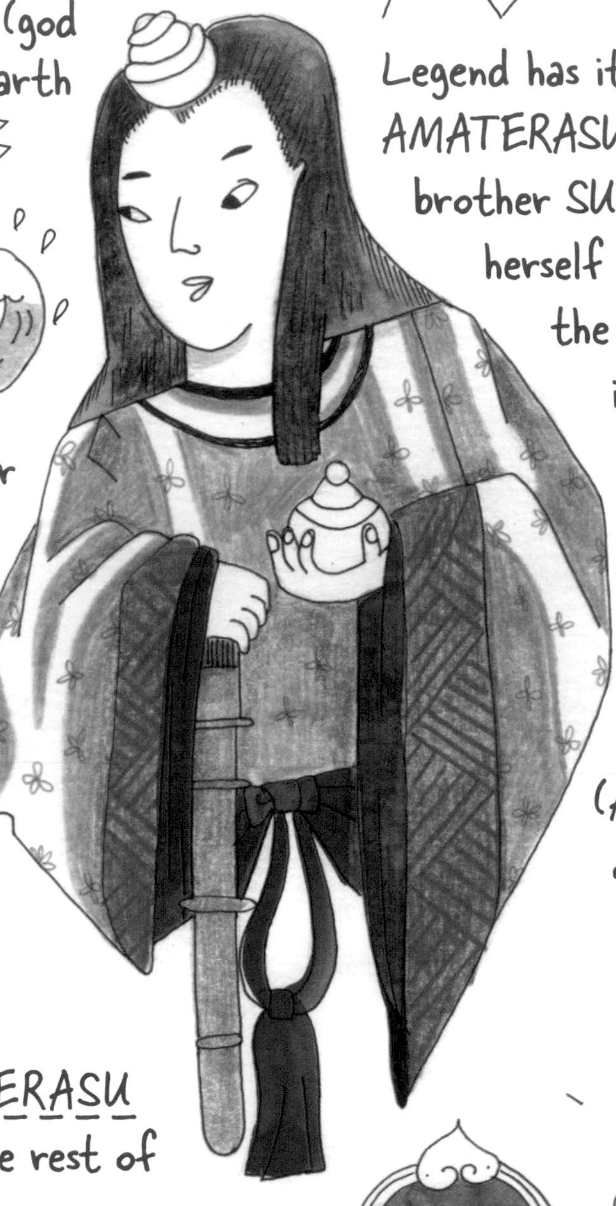

* SUSANOO (god of lightning, earth and sea).

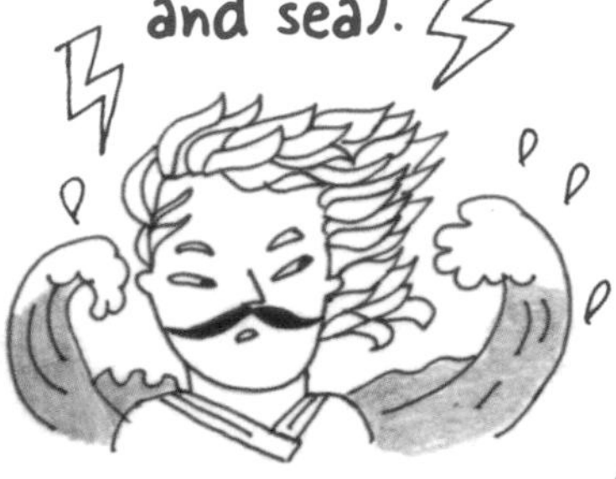

(Typical brother needling his sister.)

(Amaterasu coming out of the cave.)

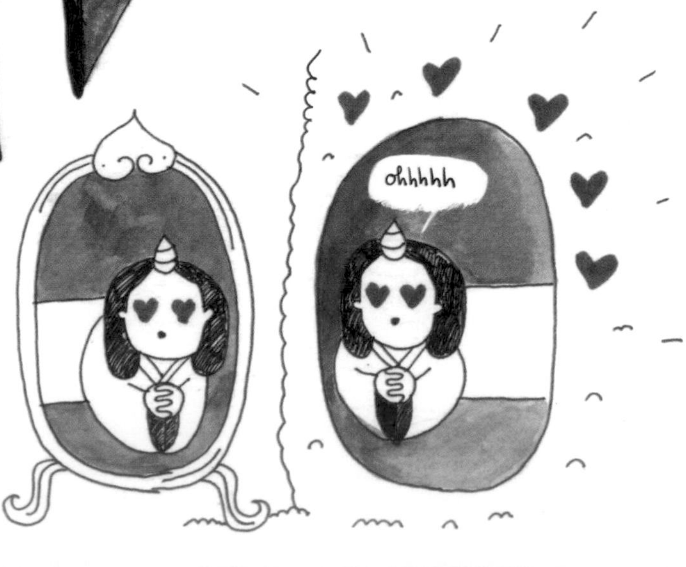
ohhhhh

When AMATERASU peeked out, the rest of the gods put up a mirror. She became so enthralled that earth regained the sun, and darkness vanished.

INARI is the deity of fertility, rice, agriculture, foxes and industry. Depicted in many different ways, including as an old man carrying rice, and as a beautiful young woman.

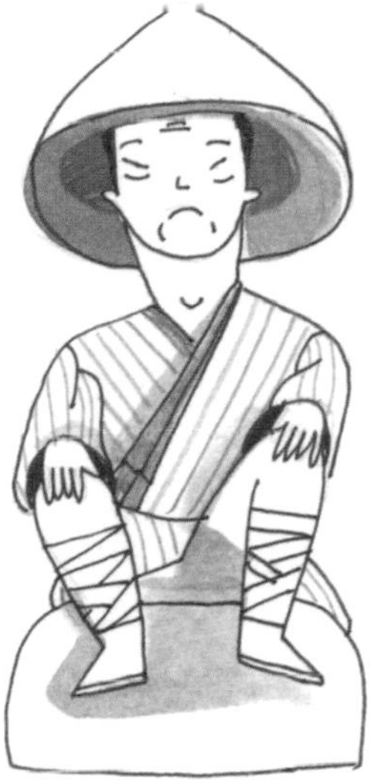

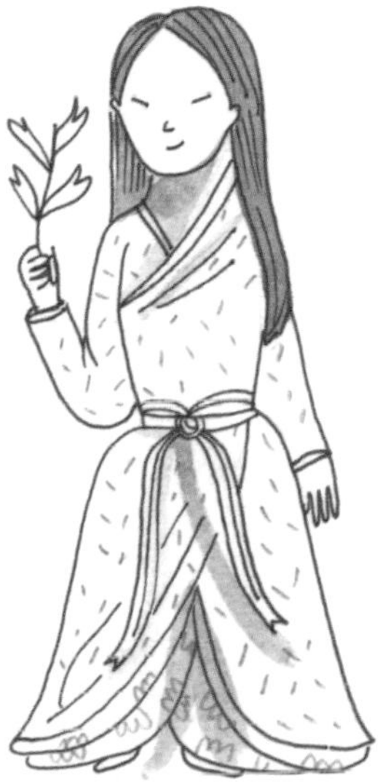

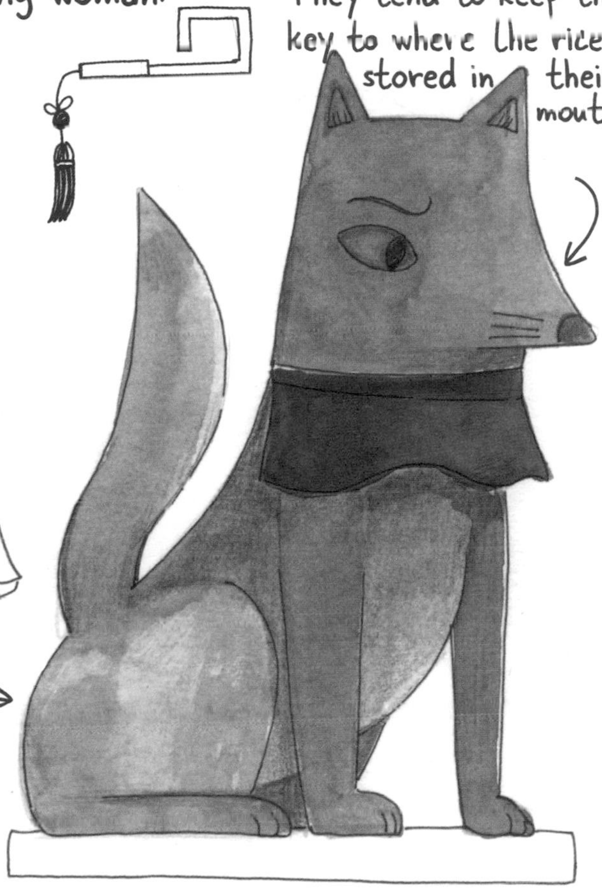
They tend to keep the key to where the rice is stored in their mouths.

Sometimes depicted as Kitsune, the fox, who is really their messenger.

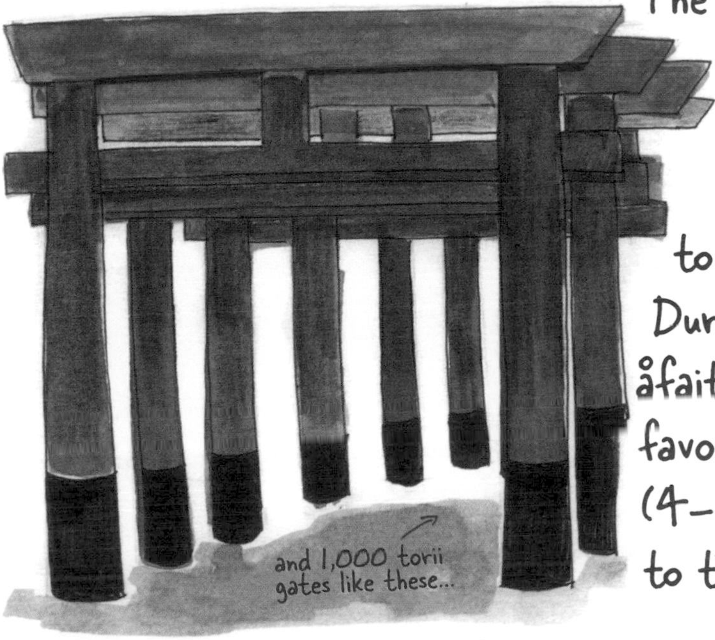
and 1,000 torii gates like these...

The FUSHIMI INARI TAISHA shrine in Kyoto is the main shrine dedicated to Inari. One of its most singular places has to be the 1,000 torii gates. During the Edo period, the faithful donated gates to request favors. They cover a 2.5-mile (4-km) path from the inner shrine to the summit of Mount INARI.

Religion 2

Buddhism

Originating in INDIA, Buddhism follows the teachings of **SIDDHARTHA GAUTAMA.** It came to Japan in the 6th century and coexists with the Shintō religion.

Example: Sensō-Ji Temple. This is the oldest Buddhist temple in Tokyo. They say it was built here when, in the 12th century, two brothers found a statue of the goddess **KANNON** in the SUMIDA River.

Hōzōmon Gate

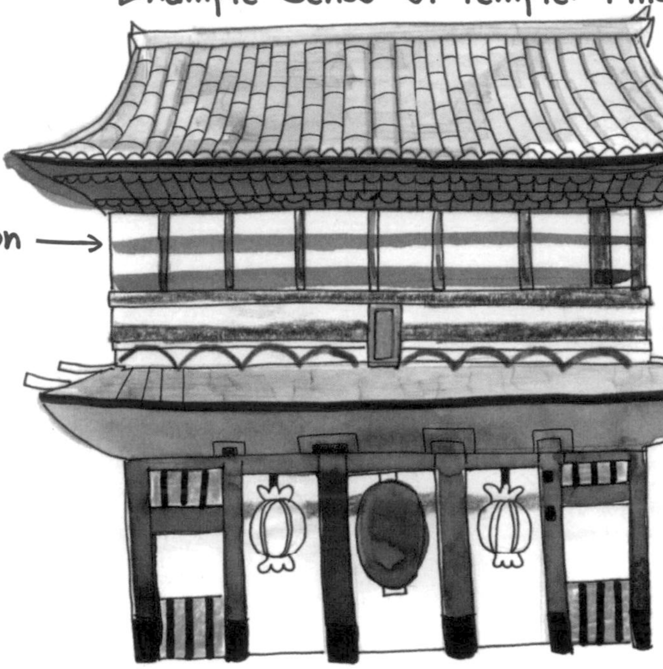

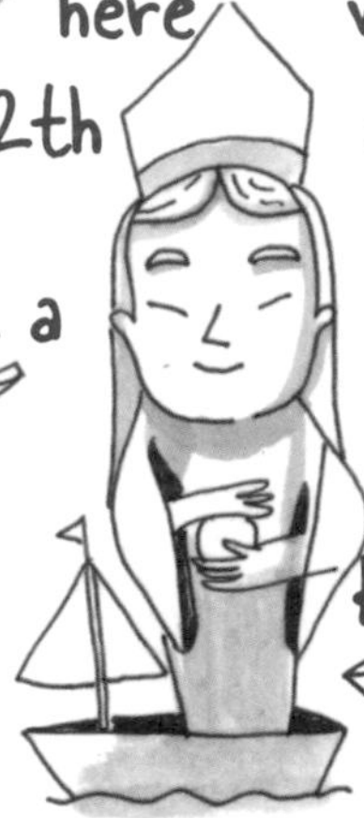

They built a small temple that developed over time to what it is now (ENOOOOORMOUS).

In **BUDDHISM** there are no gods. **BUDDHA** is more philosopher or spiritual guide. Temples have no figures to **ADORE** or to **FEAR**. There is no DIVINE punishment. The Japanese don't fear Buddha, nor do they ask him for things. They show him their RESPECT.

In Buddhism you try to reach illumination or NIRVANA by means of meditation.

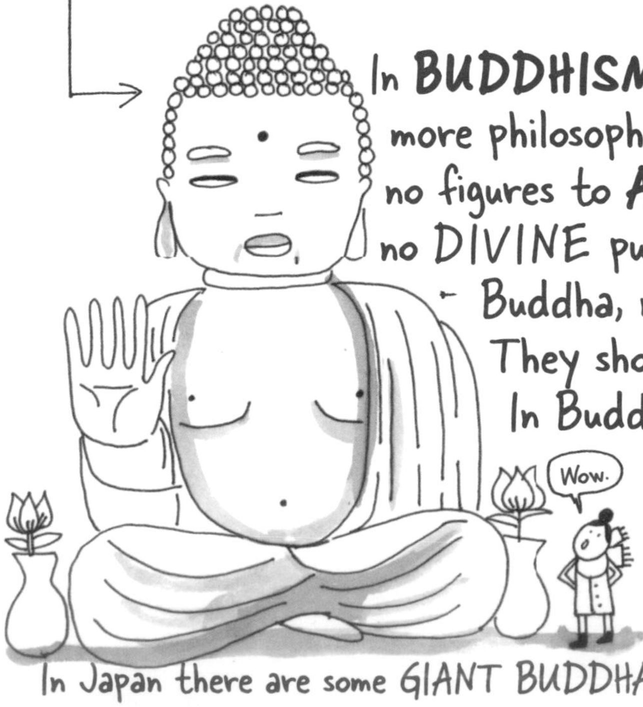
Wow.

In Japan there are some GIANT BUDDHAS.

What I like about Buddhism is the idea that no one god or SUPREME BEING will make you happy; only

YOU YOURSELF

can, through WORK, EFFORT and MEDITATION.

Although, as for NIRVANA, there's this little tray of sushi I bought for lunch...

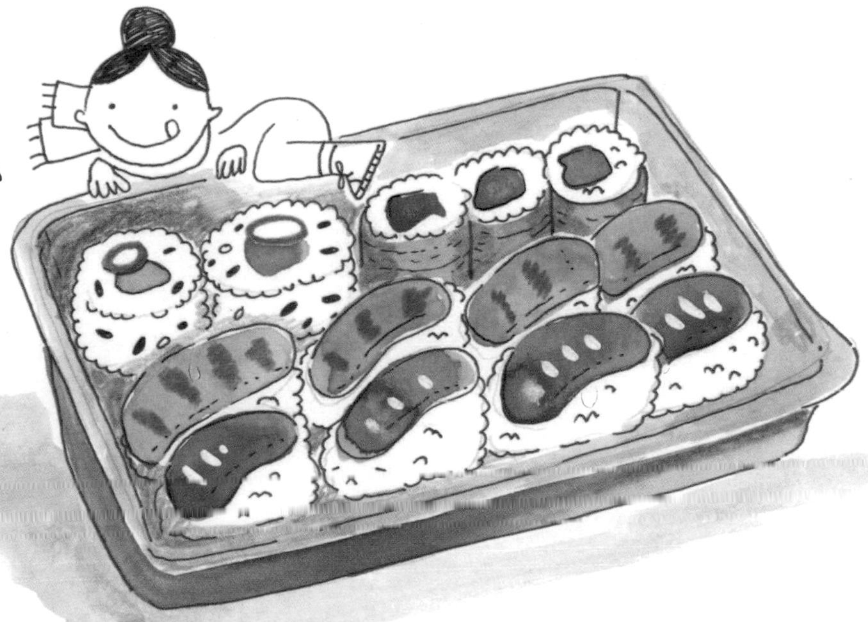

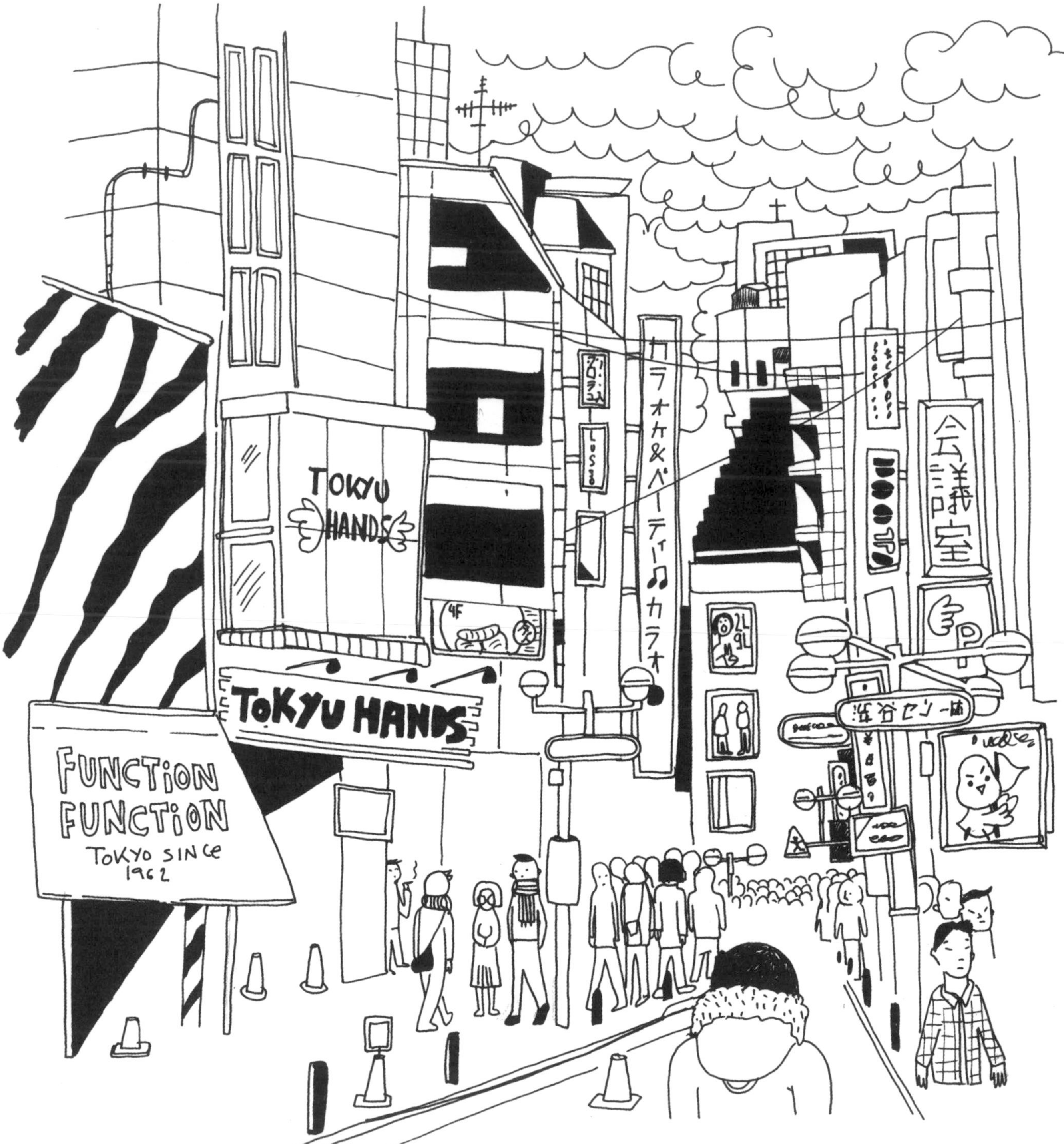
TOKYU HANDS
TOKYU HANDS
FUNCTION FUNCTION
TOKYO SINCE 1962
カラオケ&パーティー♪
カラオ
会議室

INOKASHIRA-DORI in Shibuya. 05 MAR. 2017

Wonderful things from TOKYU HANDS.

Normal, everyday objects that perfectly reflect the Japanese spirit

A heart-shaped crust remover.

Mimy

Bunny rice molds with different expressions.

m's
目玉
ピック

Googly eyes to stick on vegetables, eggs, meatballs...

バナナまもるくん

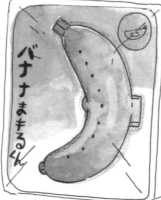

Banana-shaped food container for bananas.

Post-its in the shape of a sumo wrestler

6色
セット

Markers for coloring onigiris.

I'm impressed with the Japanese capacity for appreciating the beauty in little things, in the bare minimum. The way they care for traditions like the tea ceremony, writing haiku, or the art of calligraphy... Contact with nature, and their profound feeling of attachment to it...

IKEBANA is the Japanese art of floral arrangement. Once again, a miniscule art that pays attention to detail and unites beauty, nature and peace of mind.

There's a pattern to making these floral arrangements:

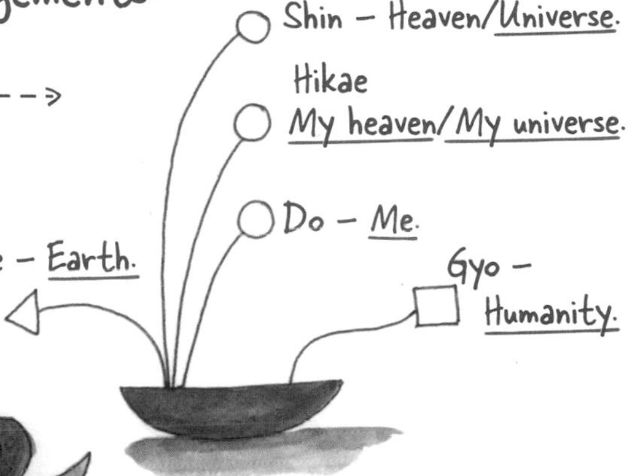

Shin – Heaven/Universe.
Hikae
My heaven/My universe.
Do – Me.
Tome – Earth.
Gyo –
Humanity.

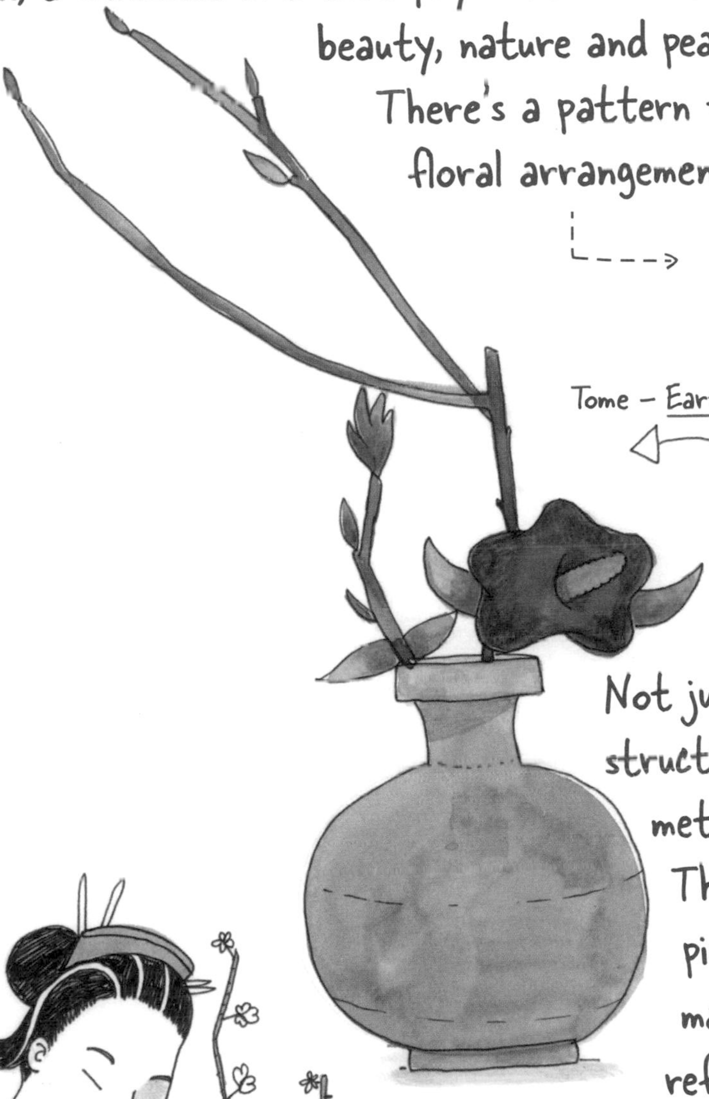

Not just a decorative construction, it's also a method of meditation. The fact that the pieces are ephemeral makes it an act of reflecting on the passage of time.

Ukiyo-e by Suzuki Harunobu

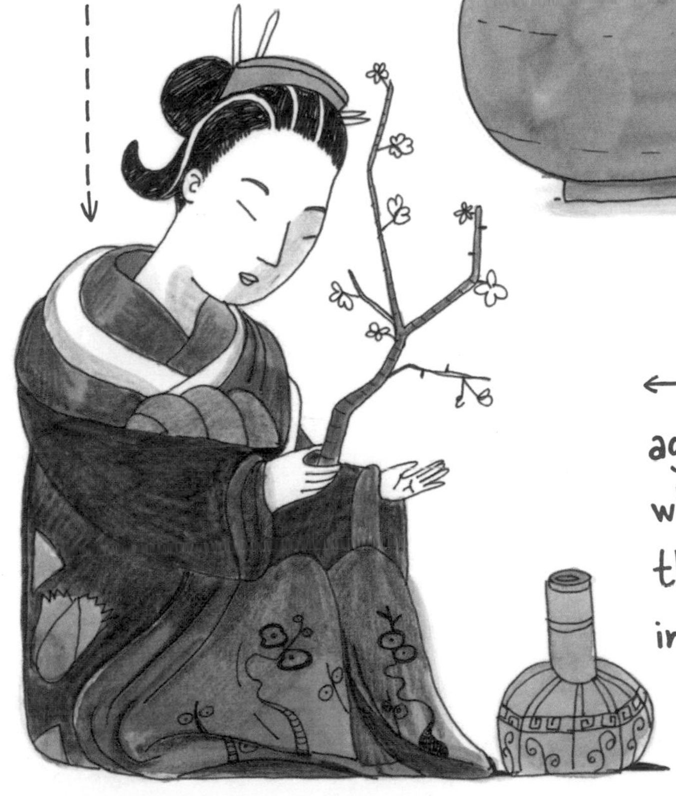

This art began 500 years ago in the bosom of religion, when a monk got FED UP with the slapdash way floral offerings were left on the Buddha's altar.

My sleepy mind
counting cherry blossoms
a rainy night

Issa Kobayashi
(dedicated to the sakura)

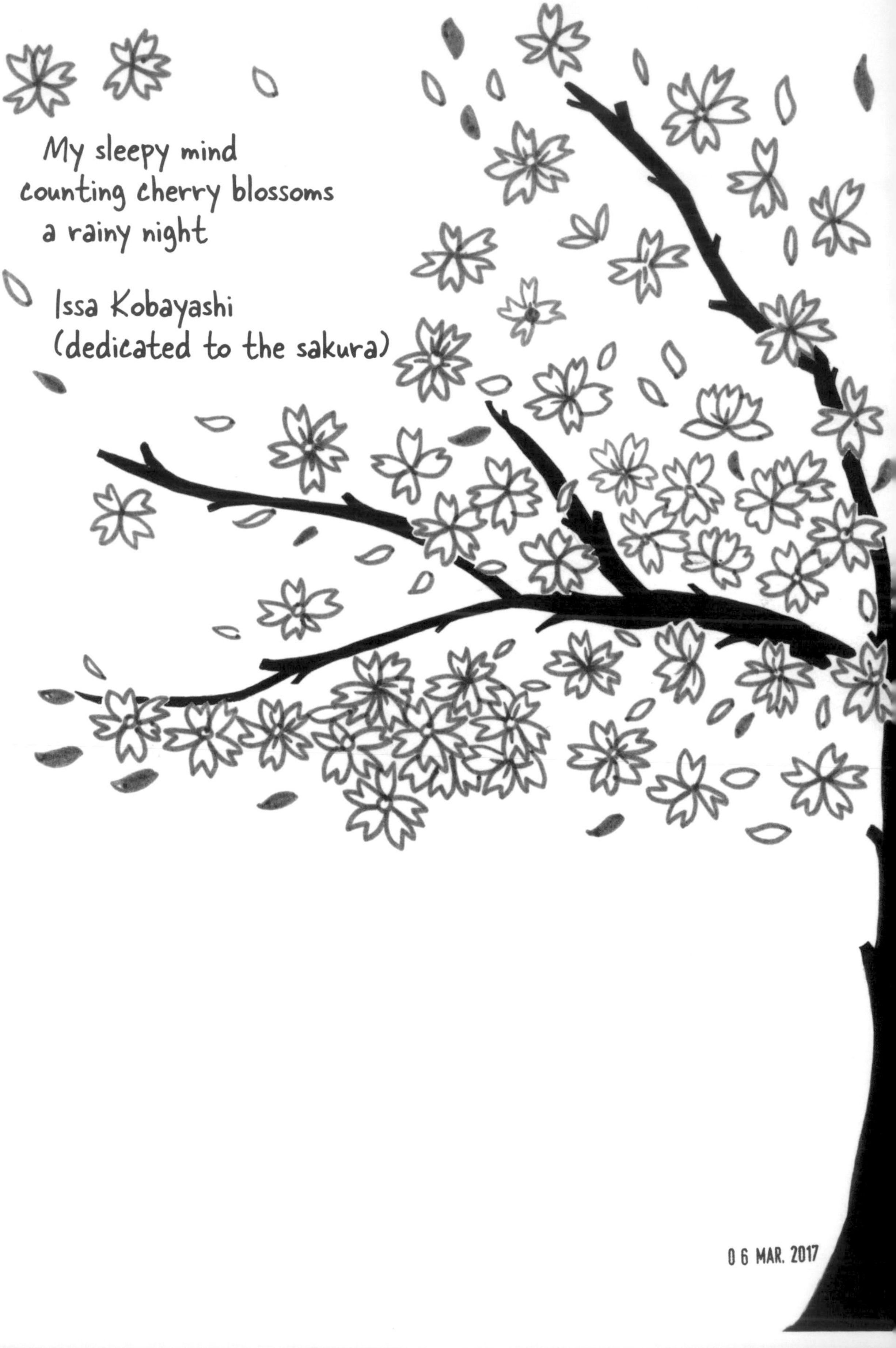

SAKURA さくら

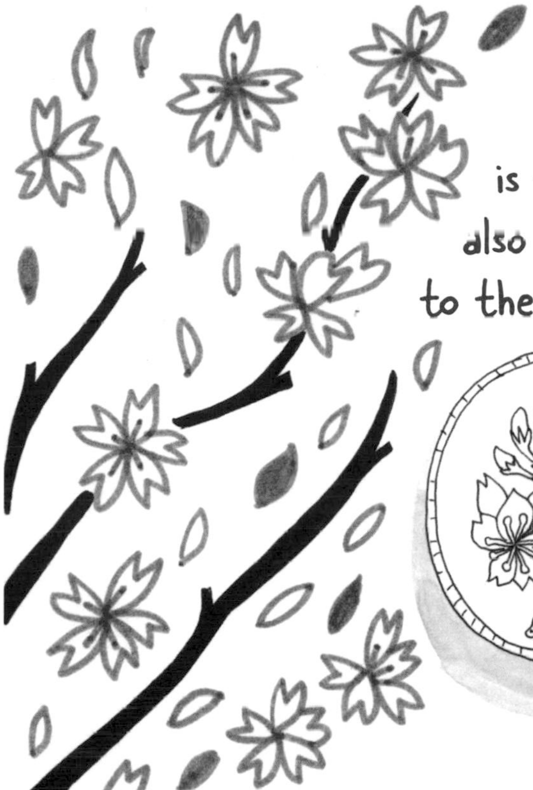

is the Japanese cherry blossom, but it's also used in a more general way in reference to the season when the cherry trees are in bloom. This event is SO IMPORTANT and they (the Japanese) go SO CRAZY that there's even a cherry blossom on the back of the 100-yen coin.

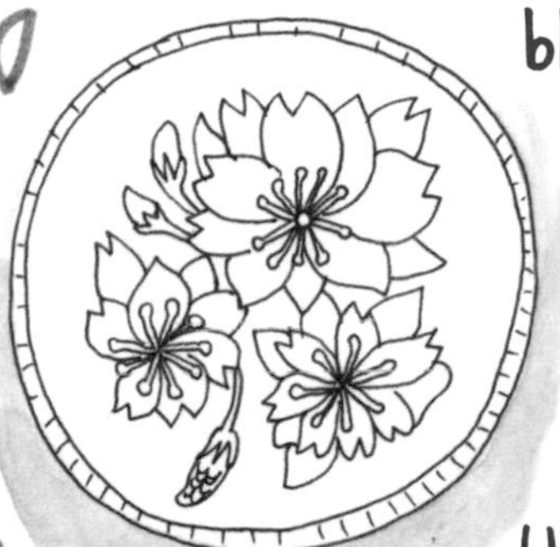

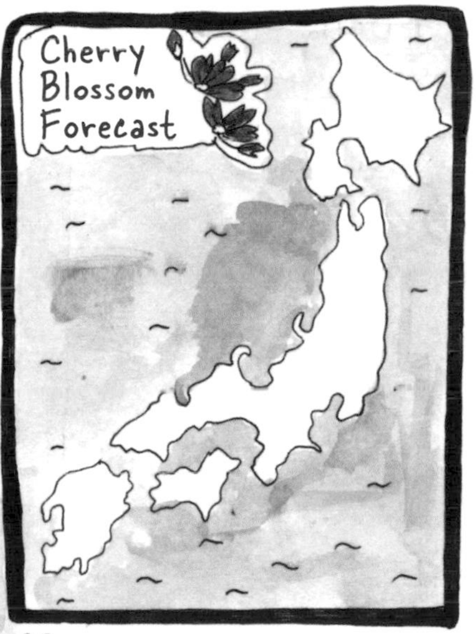
Cherry Blossom Forecast

SAKURA season is so IMPORTANT that television stations and newspapers broadcast the progression of blossoming from south (OKINAWA) to north (HOKKAIDŌ). It's so IMPORTANT that the process of admiring this phenomenon has a name: HANAMI. →

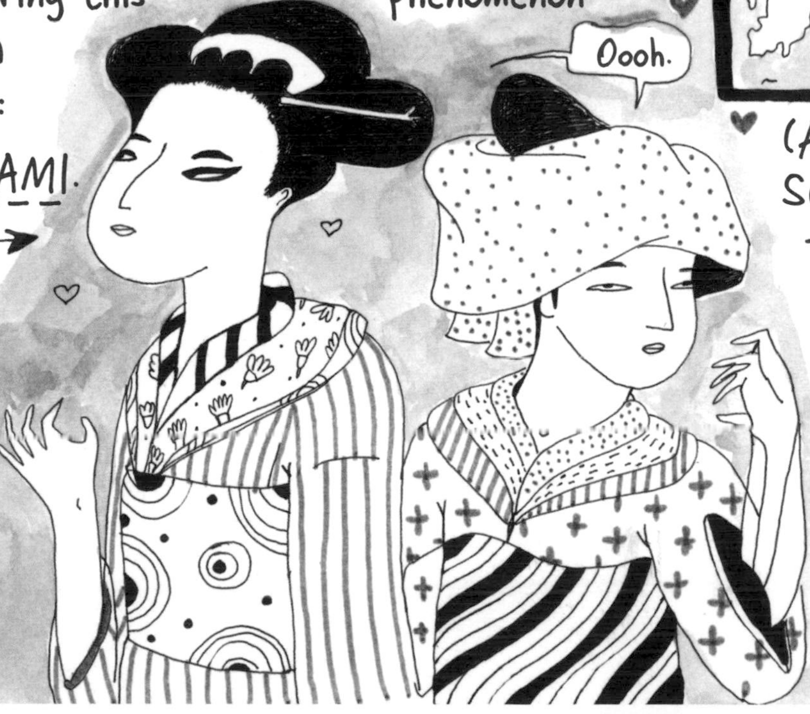
Oooh.

(And the reason it's SO IMPORTANT is that it's a metaphor for the cycle of life according to Buddhism: continual transformation for a brief period, and fleeting, EPHEMERAL beauty.)

I had a coffee and a cookie in a very minimal (and very EXPENSIVE) place.

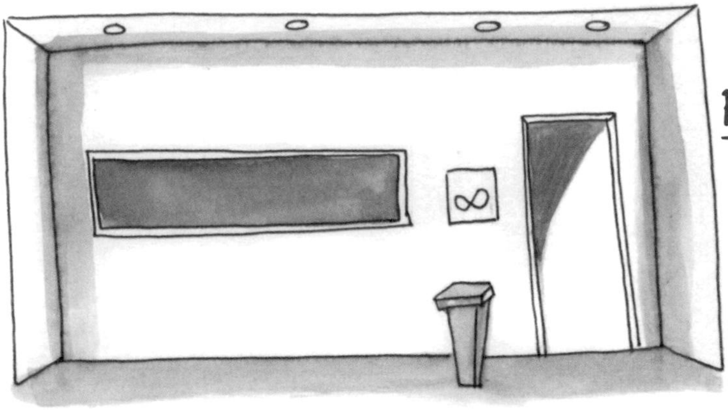

They say NAKAMEGURO is one of the best places for HANAMI. There's something like 800 cherry trees along the river, aside from it being one of those hipster neighborhoods where you can stroll around, have a coffee and window shop.

You can also buy a bonsai cactus. →

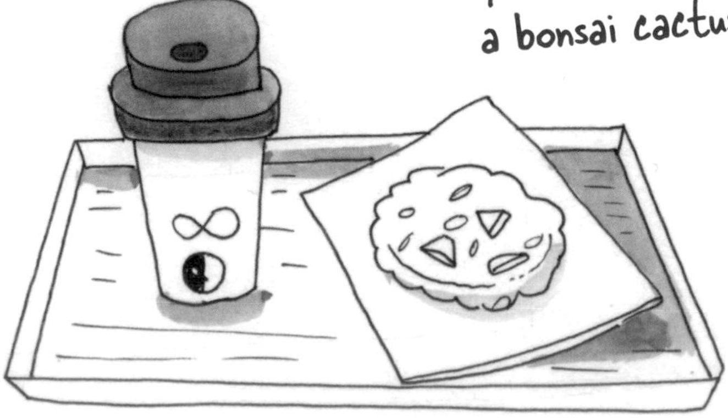

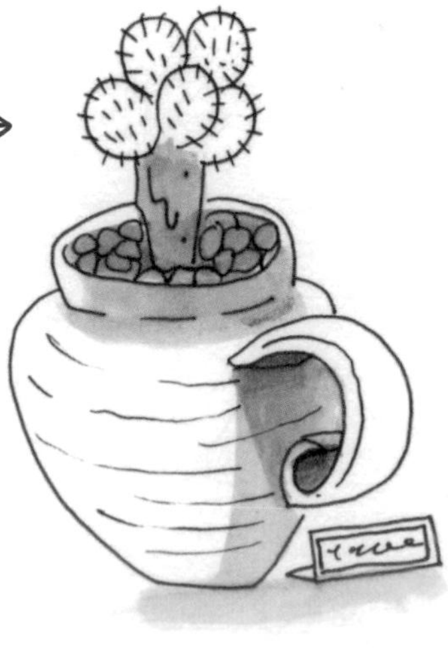

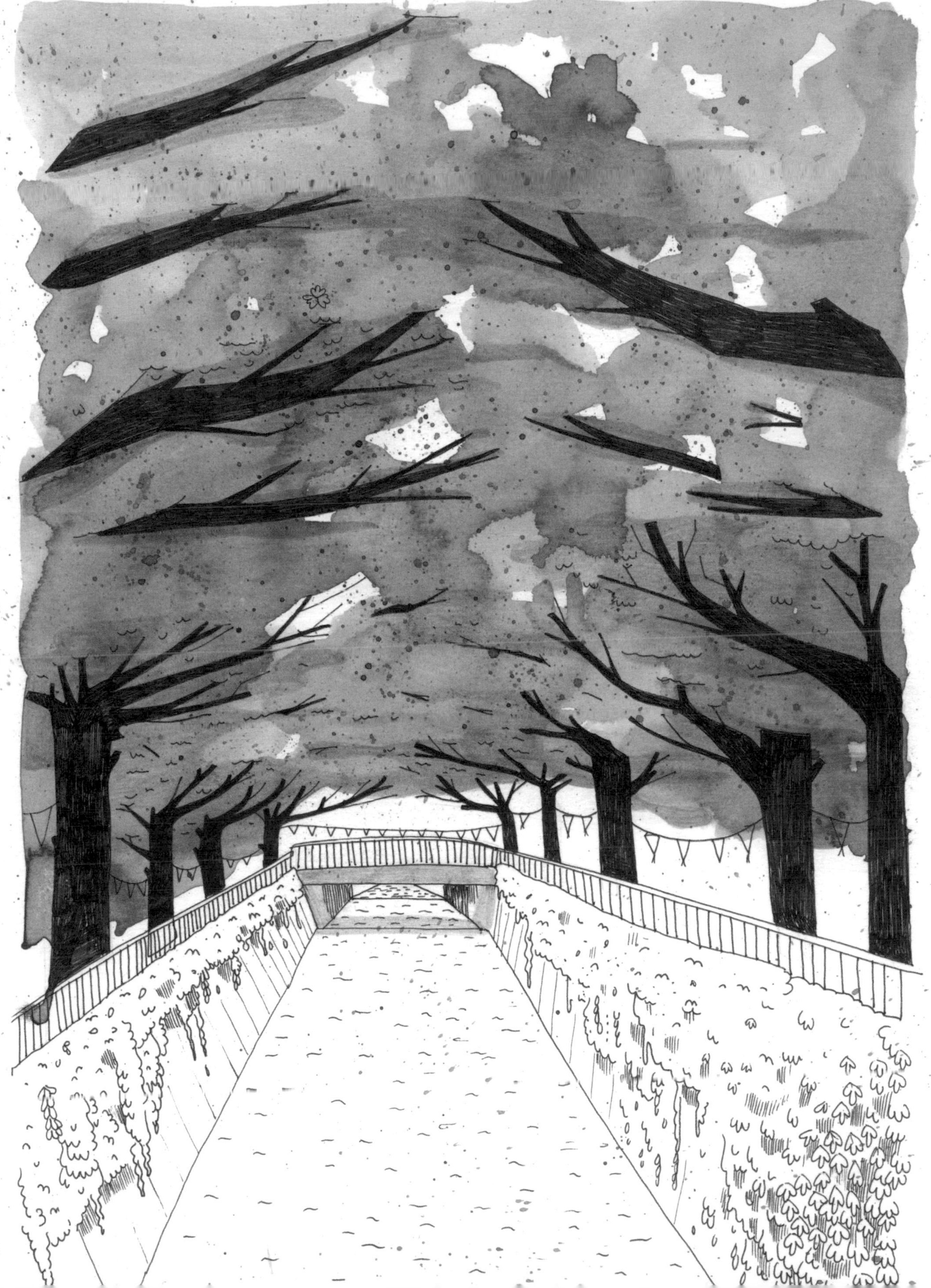

Samurai from Oda Nobunaga's army, during the Sengoku period. (Taken from a ukiyo-e by Utagawa Sadahide.)

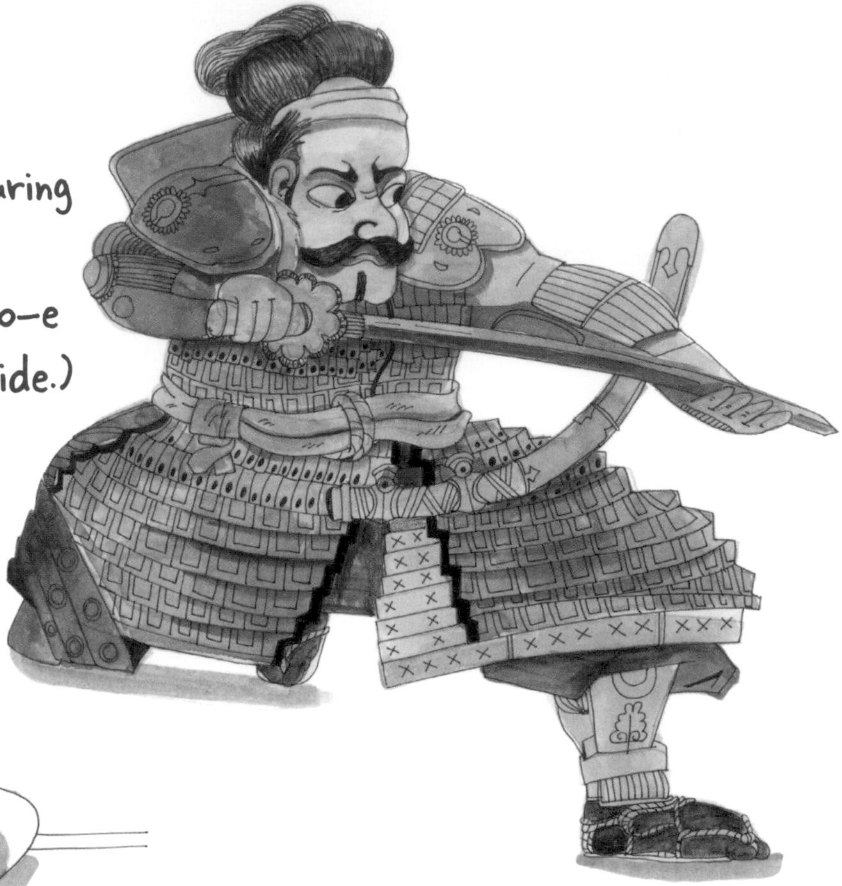

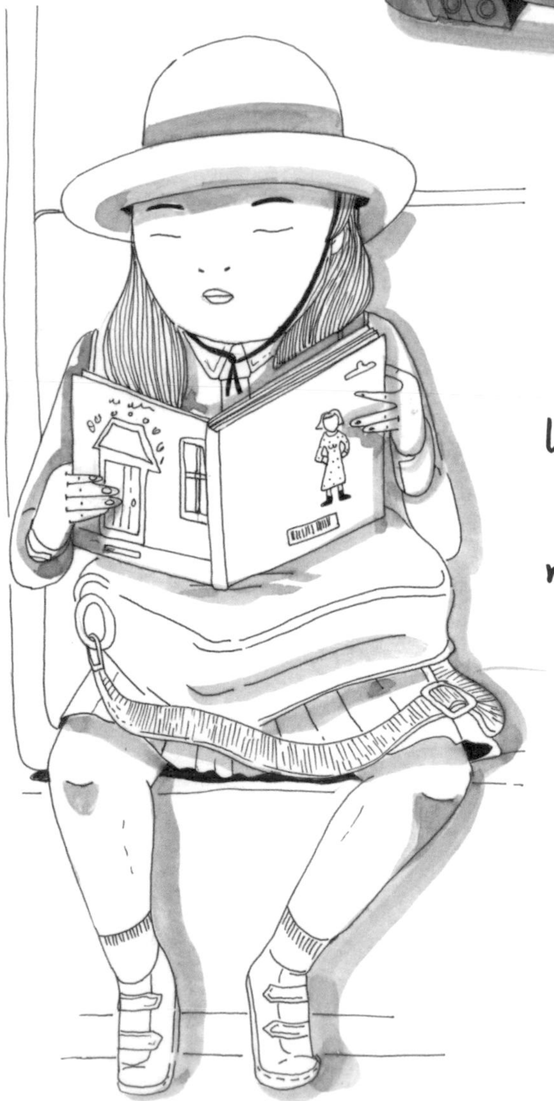

Uniformed school girl on the Hibiya line nearing Nakameguro.

0 6 MAR. 2017

Ad found in Shinjuku.

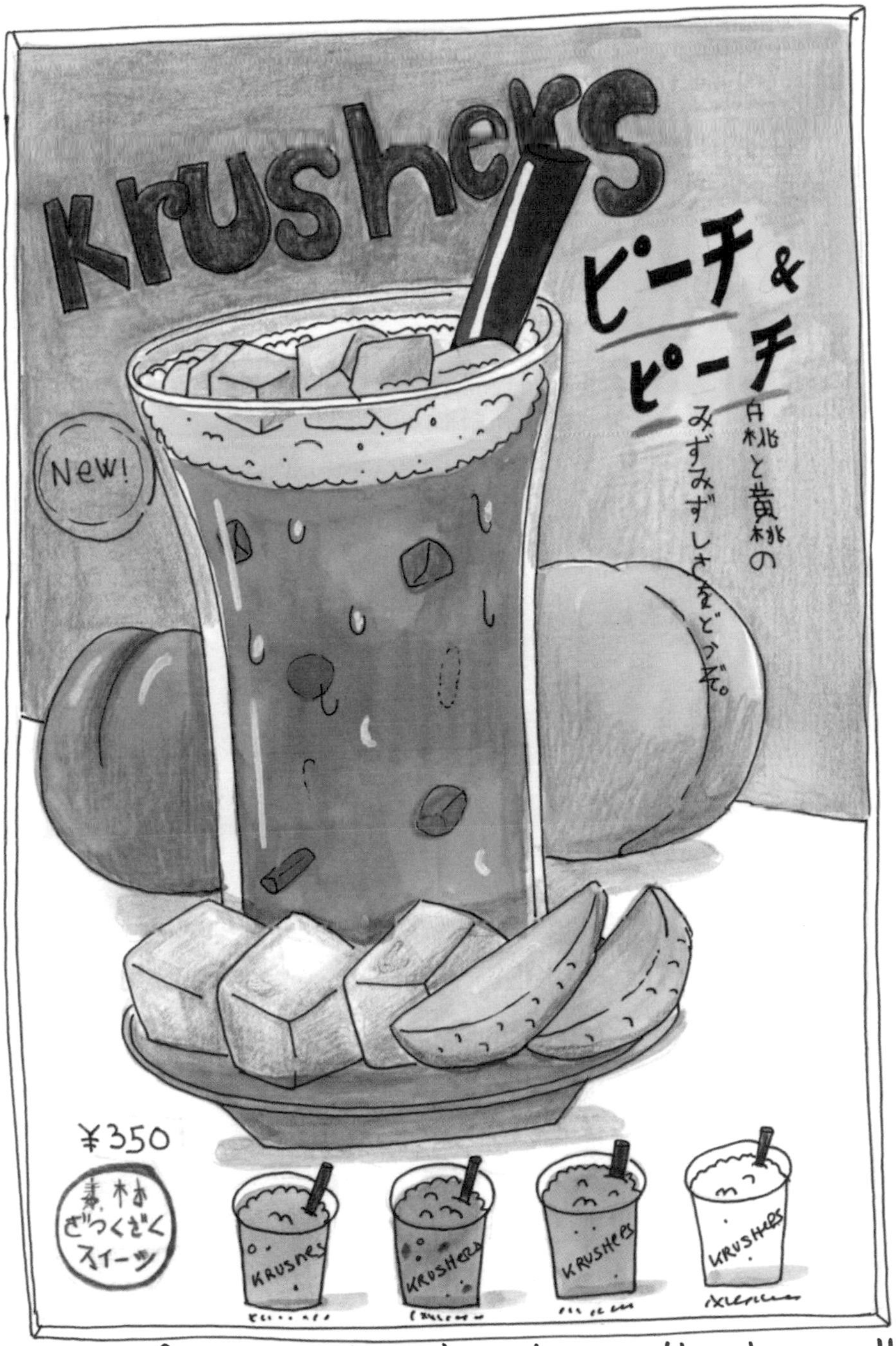
Krushers
ピーチ&ピーチ
白桃と黄桃のみずみずしさをどうぞ。
New!
¥350
KRUSHERS

The peaches look like two fannies.

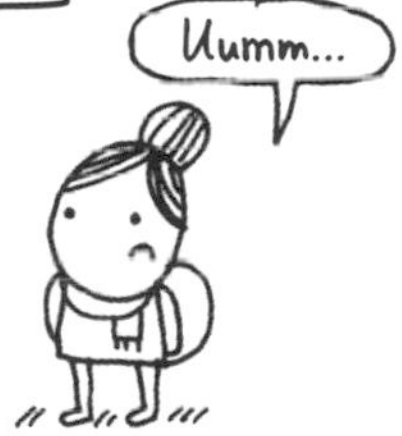
Uumm...

Speaking of peaches, there's a story with a hero called Momotaro. He was born from inside a giant peach. His parents, an elderly couple who couldn't have children, can't believe their eyes.

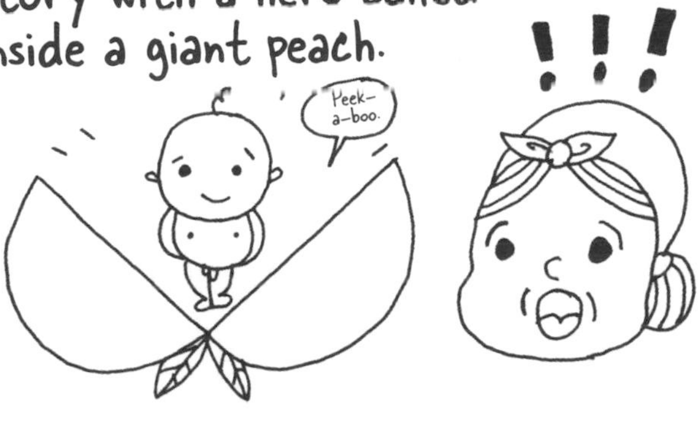
Peek-a-boo.
!!!

Ad seen on a subway car at the Kita-Senju stop.

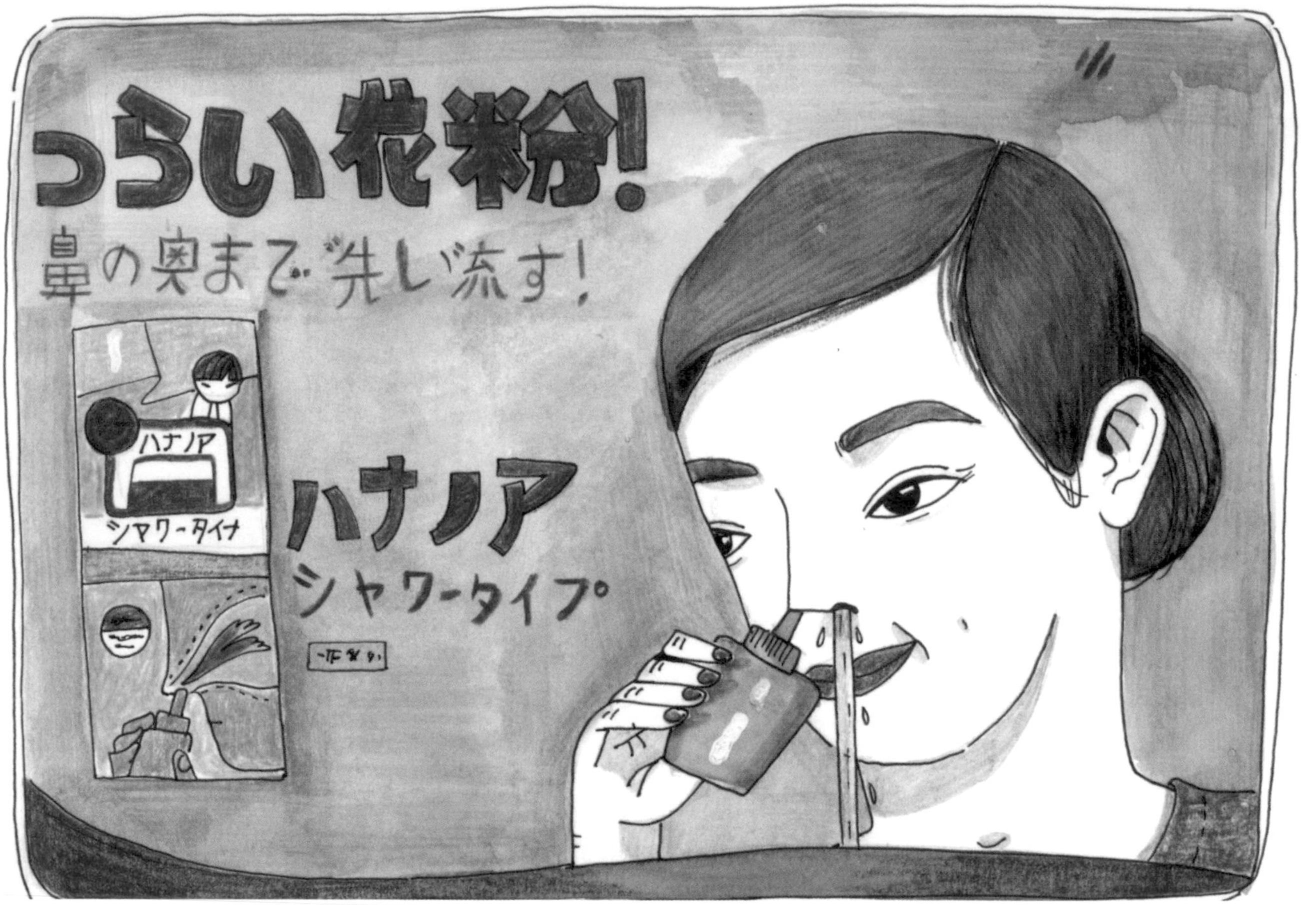
つらい花粉!
鼻の奥まで洗い流す!
ハナノア
ハナノア
シャワータイプ

I've felt more out of place in Japan than I've ever felt in my life. I understand NOTHING: not the writing, not what they say to me, not their gesturing and much less their behavior.

When I saw this ad I spent quite a bit of time analyzing it: she's very delicate, very elegant.... decontextualizing the image, I find it ridiculous: happily smiling while she cleans her nose out with a squirt of water.

I guess they must think I'm the ridiculous one, standing for 15 minutes in front of an advertisement for something as random as a nasal hygiene product.

Right before traveling, I had a little panic-attack scare. It felt like one: shortness of breath, dizziness, seeing white spots. I thought I was going to faint.

They taught me that the best way to get over something like that is to control your breathing.

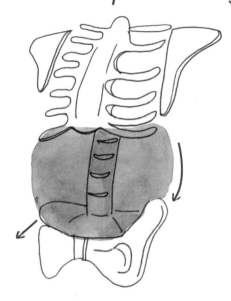

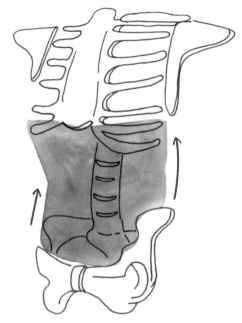

① BREATHE IN through your nose. Let the air enter and fill your abdomen. Abdominal volume should push down and out.

② BREATHE OUT through your mouth. Contract your abdominal muscles and pull your abdominal volume back and up.

Repeating these two steps makes the feeling of lack of control disappear. Oxygen is life, and if you manage to send it throughout your entire body, there's no reason to PANIC.

The first few days I had a bit of trouble with it.———>

So much breathe-in-breathe-out had me blown up like a BALLOON.

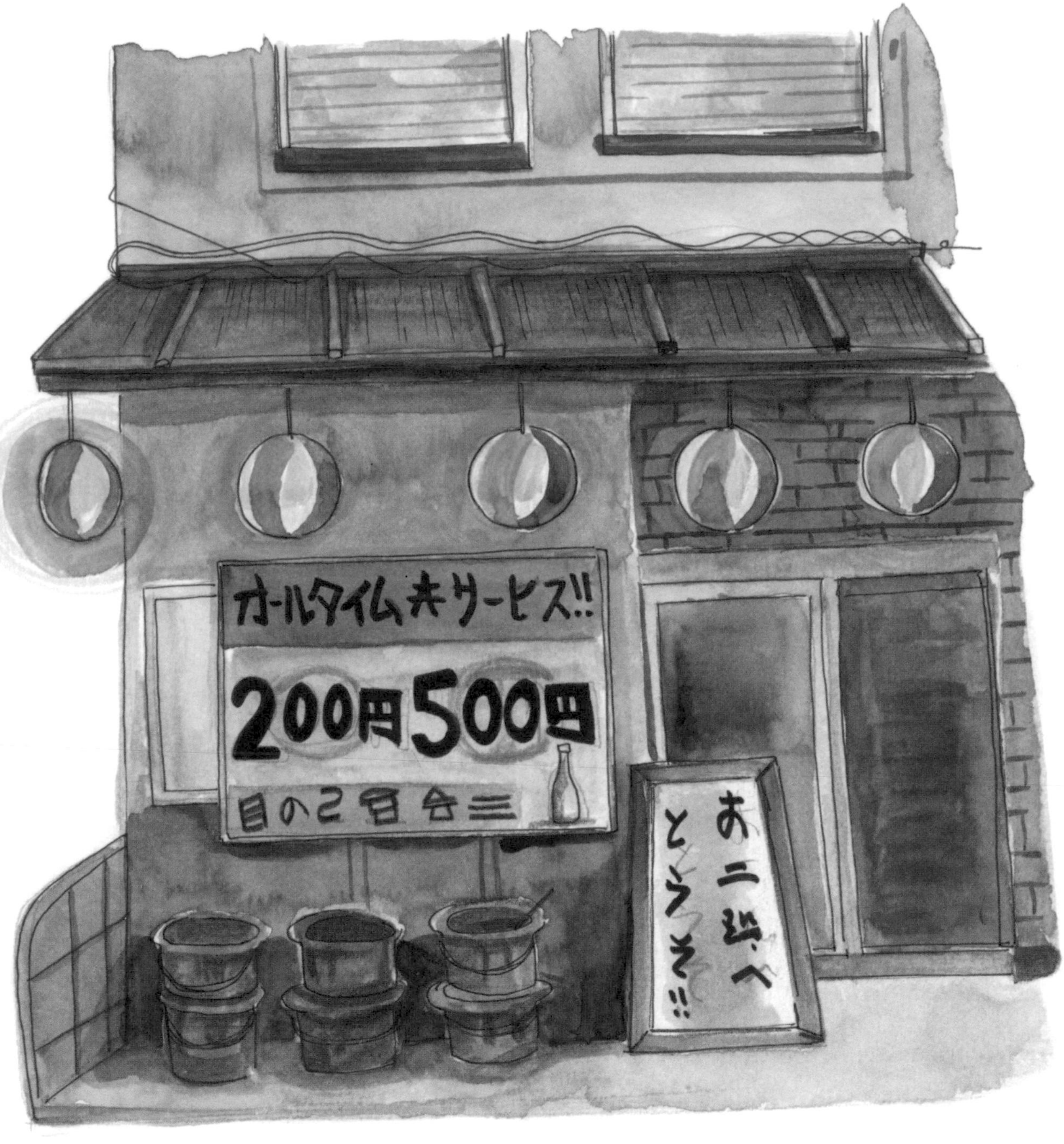
オールタイム大サービス!!
200円500円
お二階へ
どうぞ!!

07 MAR. 2017

I say all this because one of my fears when I came was that I'd <u>FREAK OUT</u> just walking along some street in Tokyo.

08 MAR. 2017

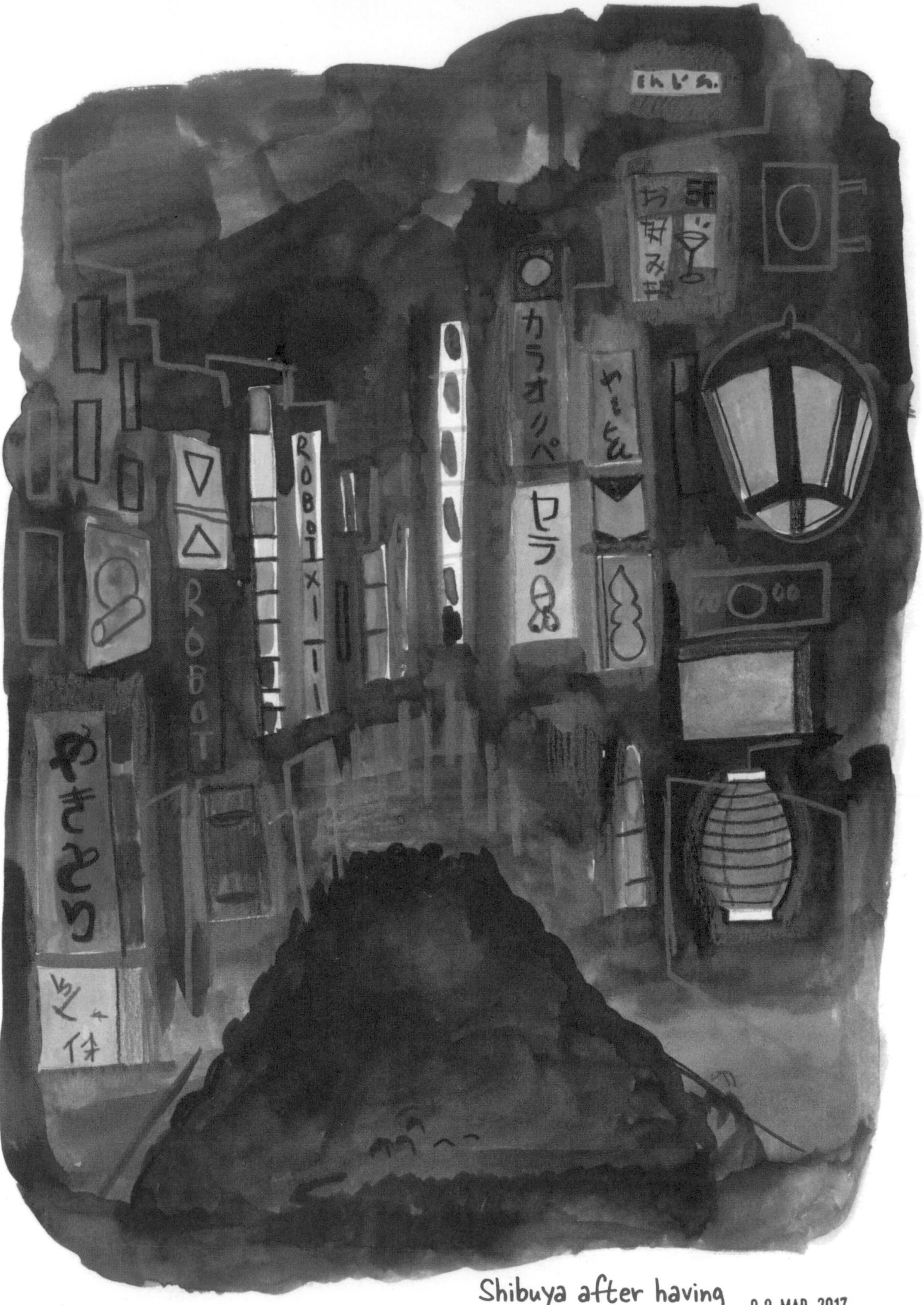
ROBOT

Shibuya after having dinner, or how to feel all alone in a place with so much light.

0 8 MAR. 2017

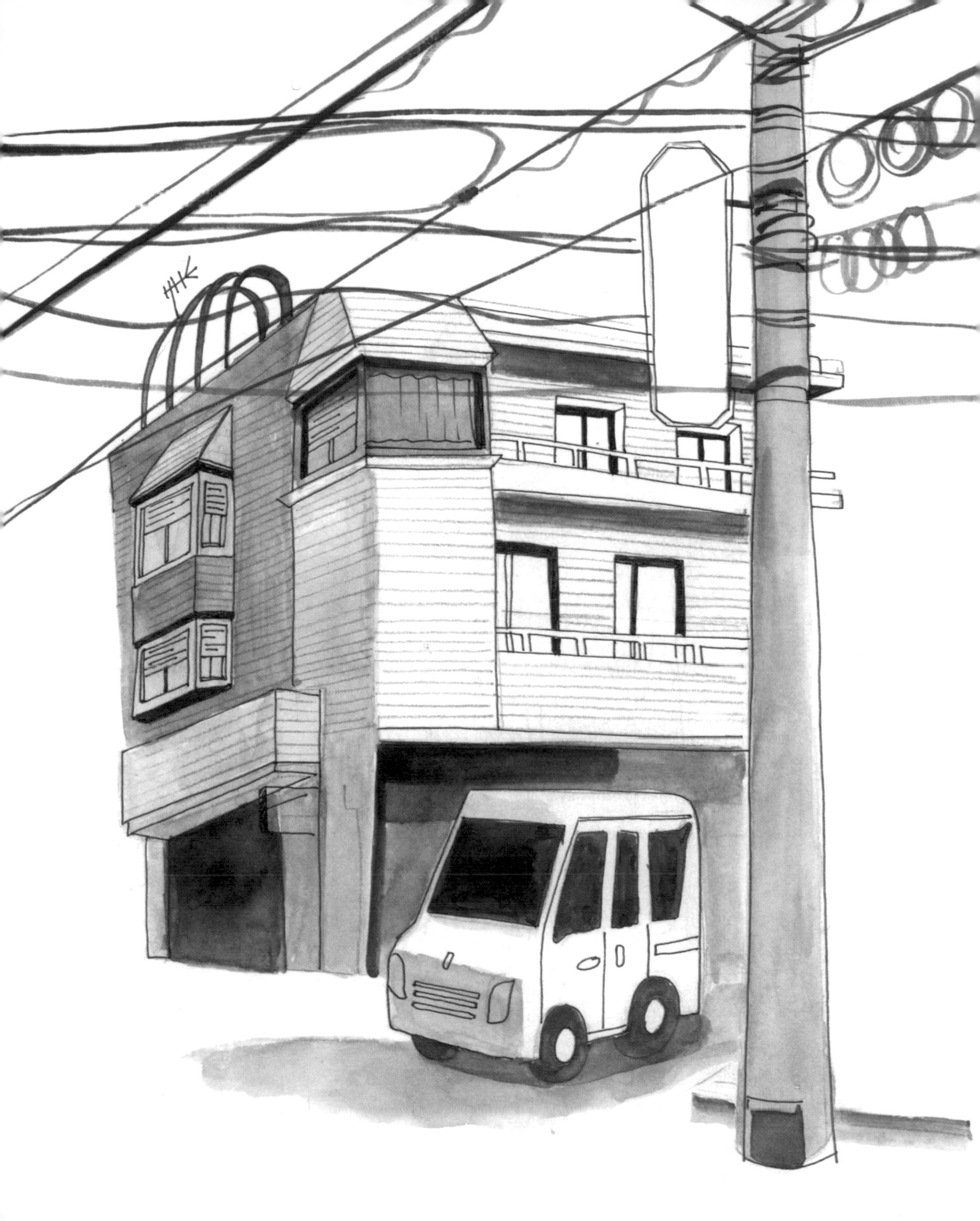

0 9 MAR. 2017

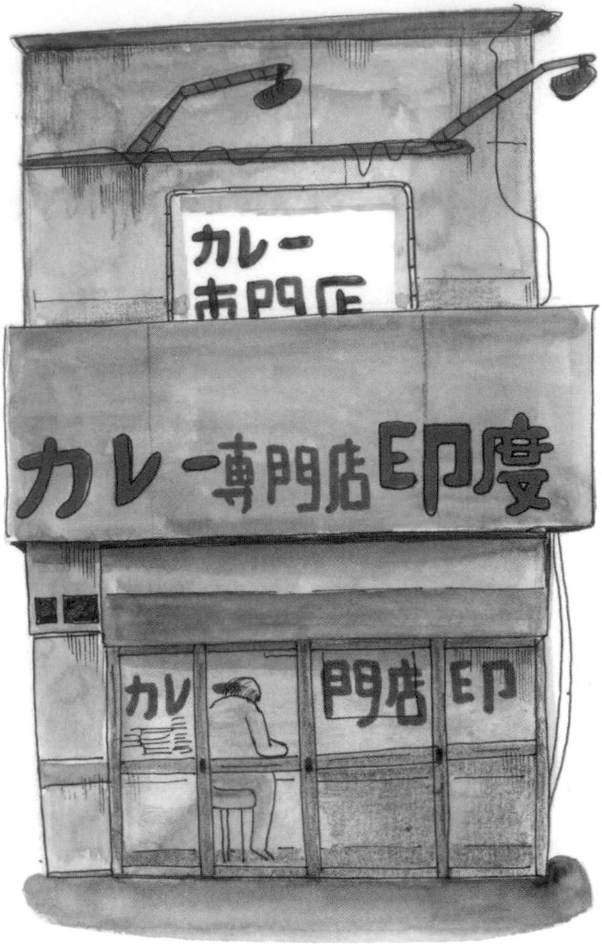
カレー
カレー専門店印度

A bar.

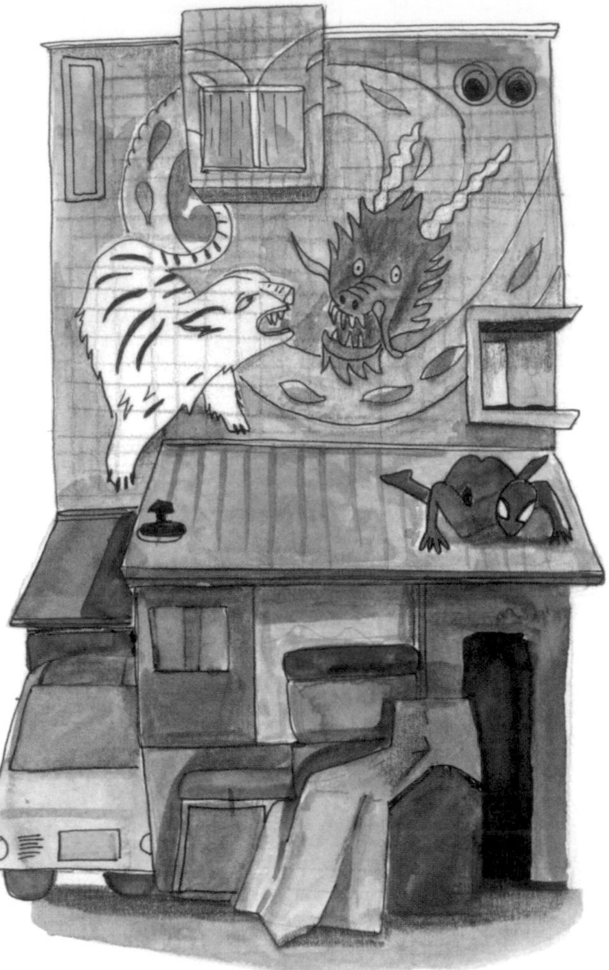

An abandoned shop with Spiderman on the roof.

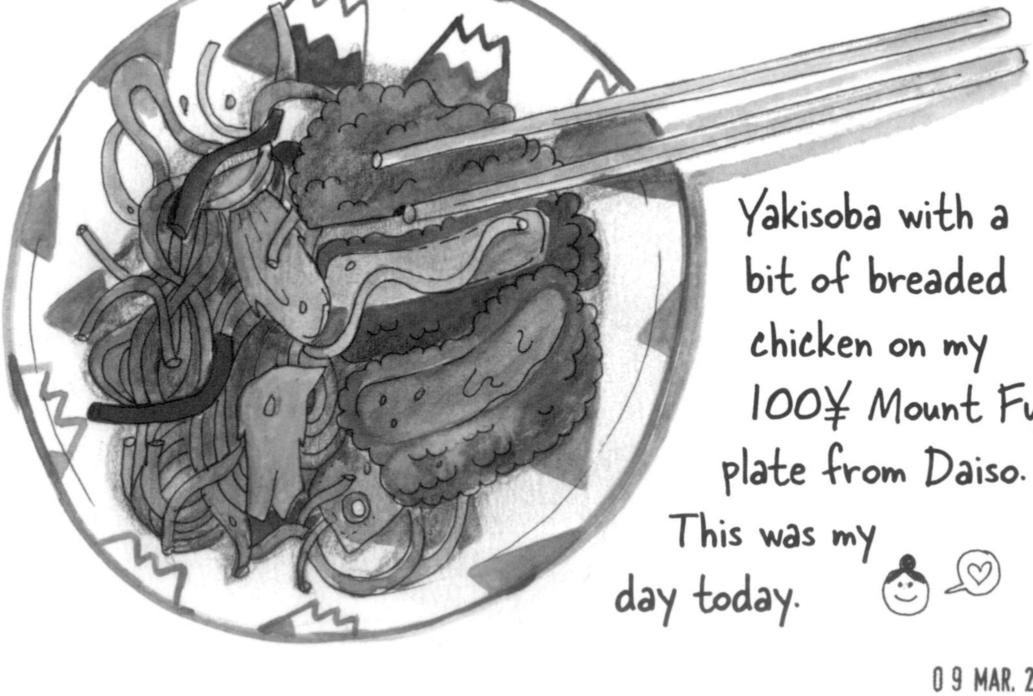

Yakisoba with a bit of breaded chicken on my 100¥ Mount Fuji plate from Daiso.

This was my day today.

0 9 MAR. 2017

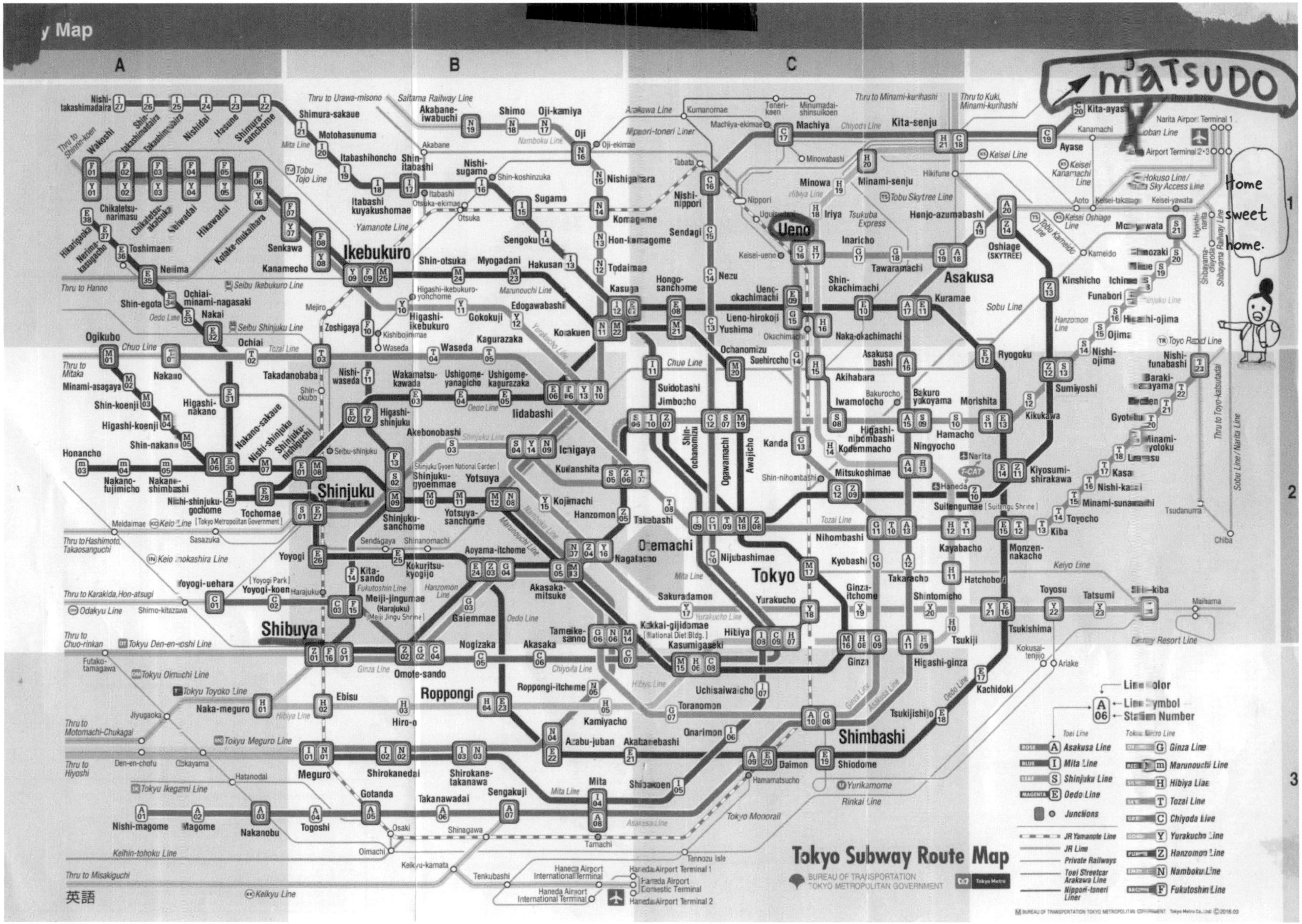

[redacted]
y Map
A
B
C
1
2
3
MATSUDO
Home sweet home.
Tokyo Subway Route Map
BUREAU OF TRANSPORTATION TOKYO METROPOLITAN GOVERNMENT
Tokyo Metro
Toei Line
Asakusa Line
Mita Line
Shinjuku Line
Oedo Line
Junctions
Ginza Line
Marunouchi Line
Hibiya Line
Tozai Line
Chiyoda Line
Yurakucho Line
Hanzomon Line
Namboku Line
Fukutoshin Line
JR Yamanote Line
JR Line
Private Railways
Toei Streetcar Arakawa Line
Nippori-toneri Liner
Ikebukuro
Shinjuku
Shibuya
Ueno
Asakusa
Tokyo
Otemachi
Shimbashi
Roppongi
Nishi-takashimadaira
Shimura-sakaue
Motohasunuma
Itabashihoncho
Akabane-iwabuchi
Shimo
Oji-kamiya
Oji
Nishigahara
Komagome
Sugamo
Sengoku
Hakusan
Kasuga
Nishi-nippori
Sendagi
Nezu
Machiya
Kita-senju
Minami-senju
Minowa
Iriya
Inaricho
Tawaramachi
Kuramae
Honjo-azumabashi
Oshiage (SKYTREE)
Kinshicho
Sumiyoshi
Ryogoku
Morishita
Kiyosumi-shirakawa
Monzen-nakacho
Kiba
Toyocho
Minami-sunamachi
Nishi-kasai
Kasai
Funabori
Ichinoe
Mizue
Shinozaki
Motoyawata
Kita-ayase
Ayase
Wakoshi
Chikatetsu-narimasu
Chikatetsu-akatsuka
Heiwadai
Hikawadai
Kotake-mukaihara
Senkawa
Kanamecho
Toshimaen
Nerima
Shin-egota
Ochiai-minami-nagasaki
Nakai
Ogikubo
Ochiai
Takadanobaba
Nakano
Higashi-nakano
Nakano-sakaue
Nishi-shinjuku
Honancho
Nakano-fujimicho
Nakano-shimbashi
Tochomae
Shinjuku-sanchome
Yotsuya
Yotsuya-sanchome
Ichigaya
Iidabashi
Kagurazaka
Waseda
Edogawabashi
Gokokuji
Myogadani
Shin-otsuka
Higashi-ikebukuro
Kojimachi
Hanzomon
Nagatacho
Akasaka-mitsuke
Aoyama-itchome
Gaiemmae
Omote-sando
Meiji-jingumae (Harajuku)
Yoyogi
Yoyogi-koen
Yoyogi-uehara
Ebisu
Hiro-o
Naka-meguro
Meguro
Shirokanedai
Shirokane-takanawa
Azabu-juban
Kamiyacho
Toranomon
Kasumigaseki
Hibiya
Ginza
Yurakucho
Kyobashi
Nihombashi
Kayabacho
Hatchobori
Tsukiji
Higashi-ginza
Shiodome
Daimon
Mita
Shibakoen
Sengakuji
Gotanda
Togoshi
Nakanobu
Magome
Nishi-magome
Akihabara
Ochanomizu
Suehirocho
Ueno-hirokoji
Ueno-okachimachi
Naka-okachimachi
Shin-okachimachi
Kanda
Mitsukoshimae
Ningyocho
Hamacho
Suitengumae
Kodemmacho
Jimbocho
Suidobashi
Kudanshita
Takebashi
Tsukishima
Toyosu
Tatsumi
Shin-kiba
Kachidoki
Tsukishijo
Haneda Airport
Narita Airport Terminal 1
英語

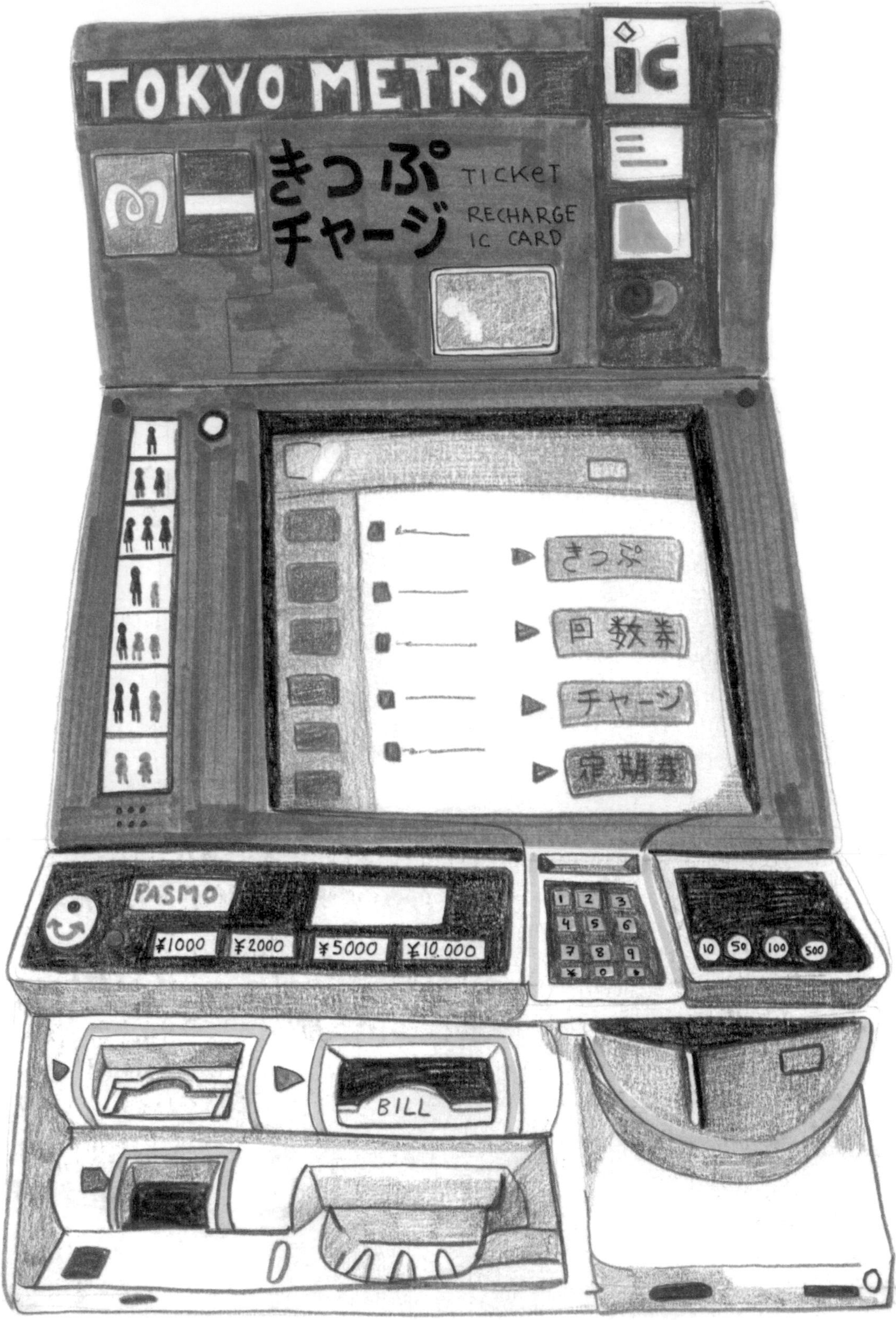
TOKYO METRO
IC
きっぷ
チャージ
TICKET
RECHARGE
IC CARD
きっぷ
回数券
チャージ
定期券
PASMO
¥1000
¥2000
¥5000
¥10.000
1
2
3
4
5
6
7
8
9
0
10
50
100
500
BILL

My battles with the transit card recharging machine have been epic.

11 MAR. 2017

One of the creatures from Japanese folklore I MOST ADORE is this raccoon dog, a talisman for fortune and wealth.

TANUKI

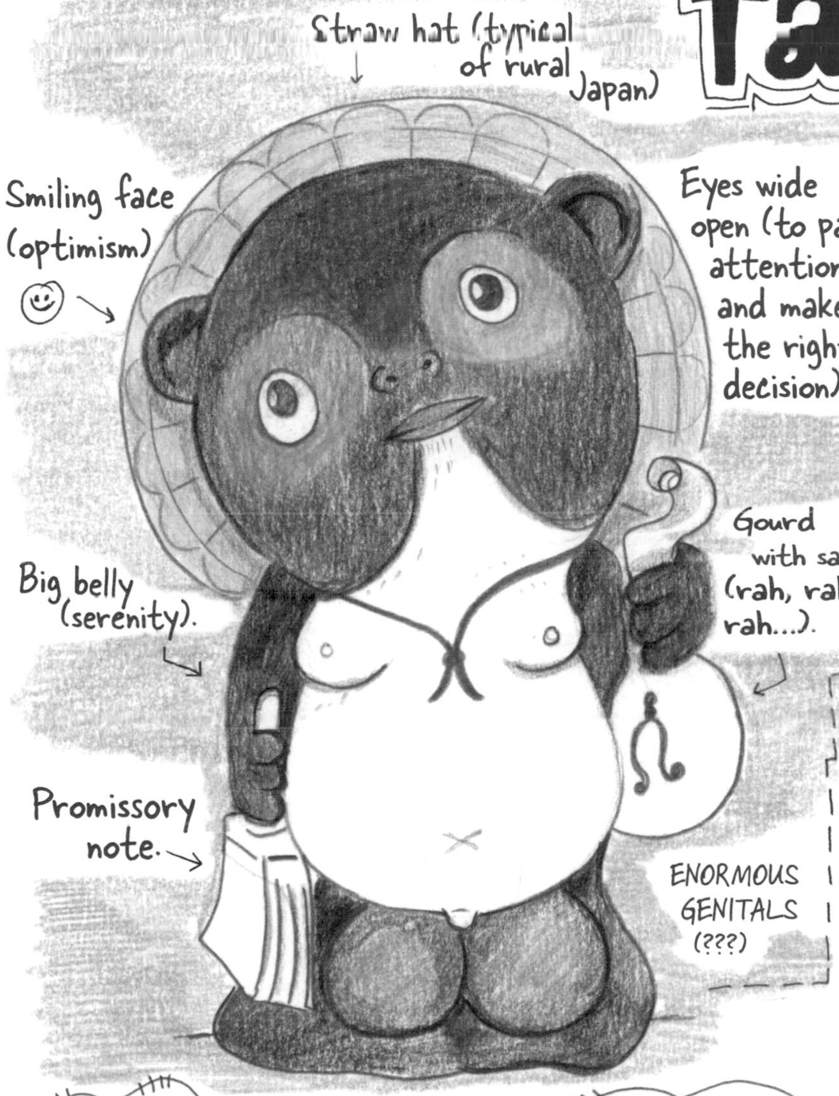

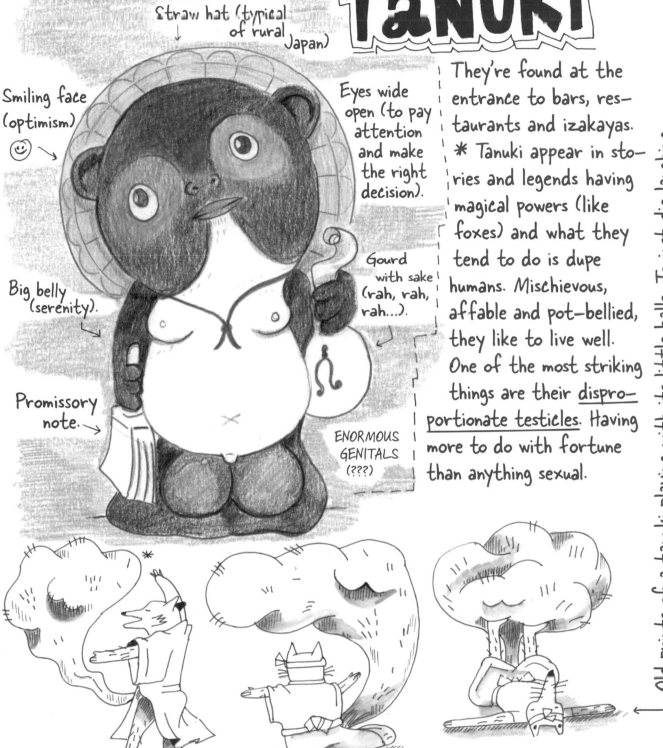

Straw hat (typical of rural Japan)
Smiling face (optimism)
Eyes wide open (to pay attention and make the right decision).
Gourd with sake (rah, rah, rah...).
Big belly (serenity).
Promissory note.
ENORMOUS GENITALS (???)

They're found at the entrance to bars, restaurants and izakayas. * Tanuki appear in stories and legends having magical powers (like foxes) and what they tend to do is dupe humans. Mischievous, affable and pot-bellied, they like to live well. One of the most striking things are their <u>disproportionate testicles</u>. Having more to do with fortune than anything sexual.

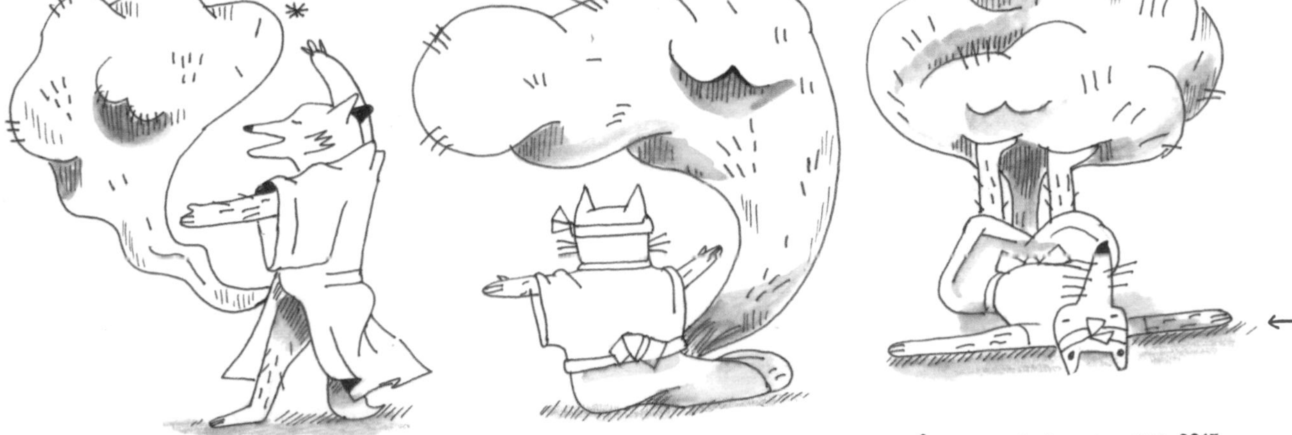

Old prints of a tanuki playing with its little balls. To just die laughing...

In fact, in Japan testicles are called kintama (BALLS of GOLD). 12 MAR. 2017

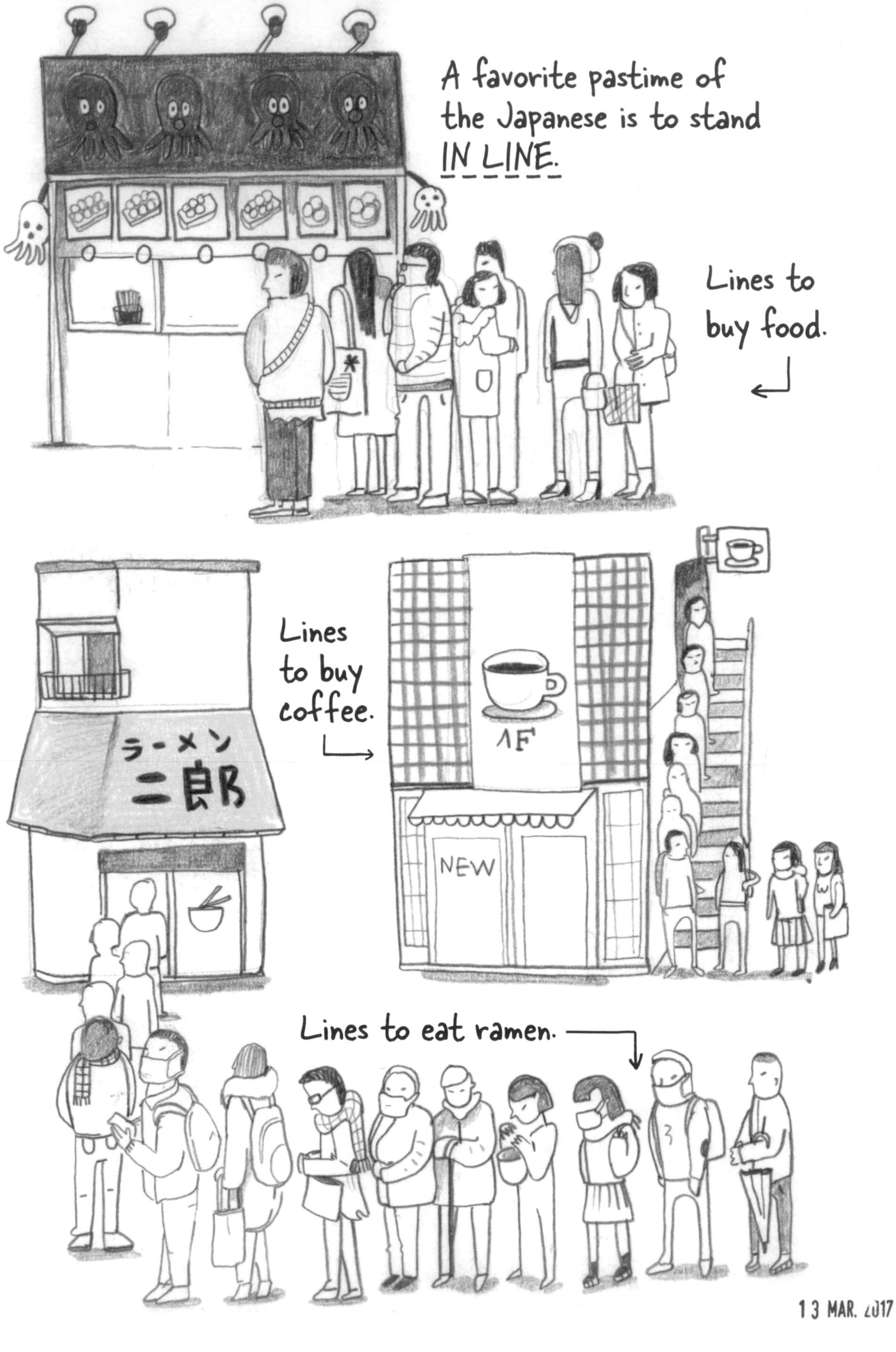
A favorite pastime of the Japanese is to stand IN LINE.
Lines to buy food.
Lines to buy coffee.
ラーメン
二郎
1F
NEW
Lines to eat ramen.
13 MAR. 2017

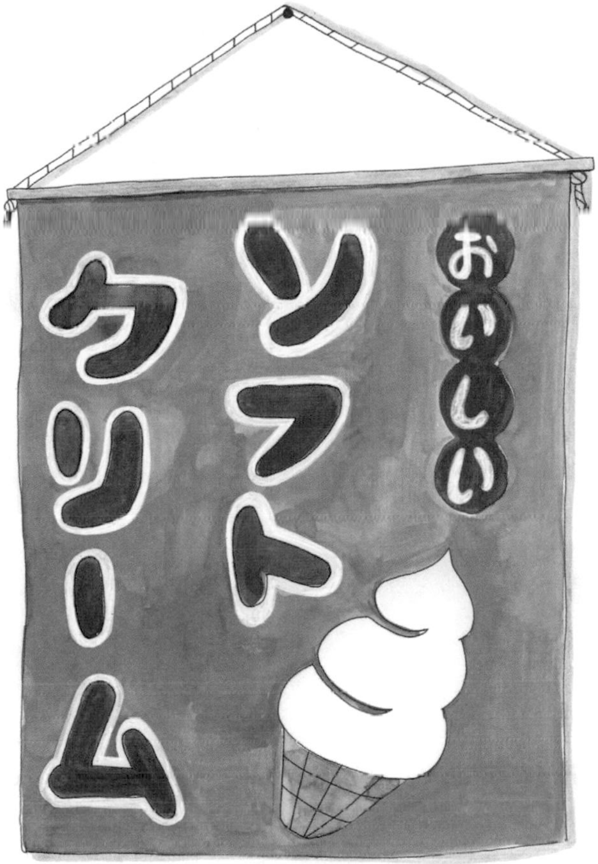
おいしい
ソフトクリーム

I bought these banners for 100 yen in Daiso. I'm not sure what they say, but that's O.K.: in Japan I never understand 100% of what anything says.

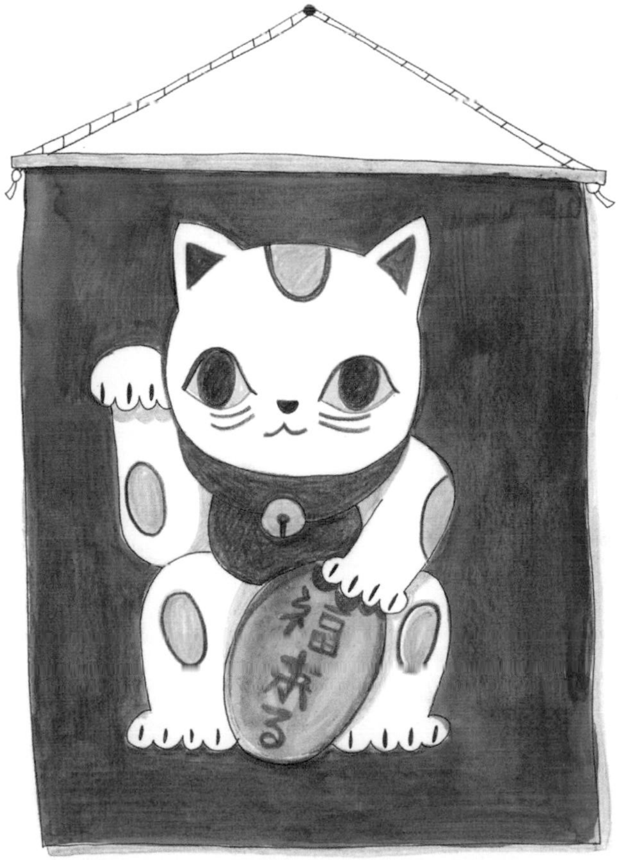
福来る

I've learned to appreciate objects without knowing their context, what they're for... I like them for their simple designs and their colors.

A month drinking this milk without knowing if it was low-fat, whole, skim, soy, rice...

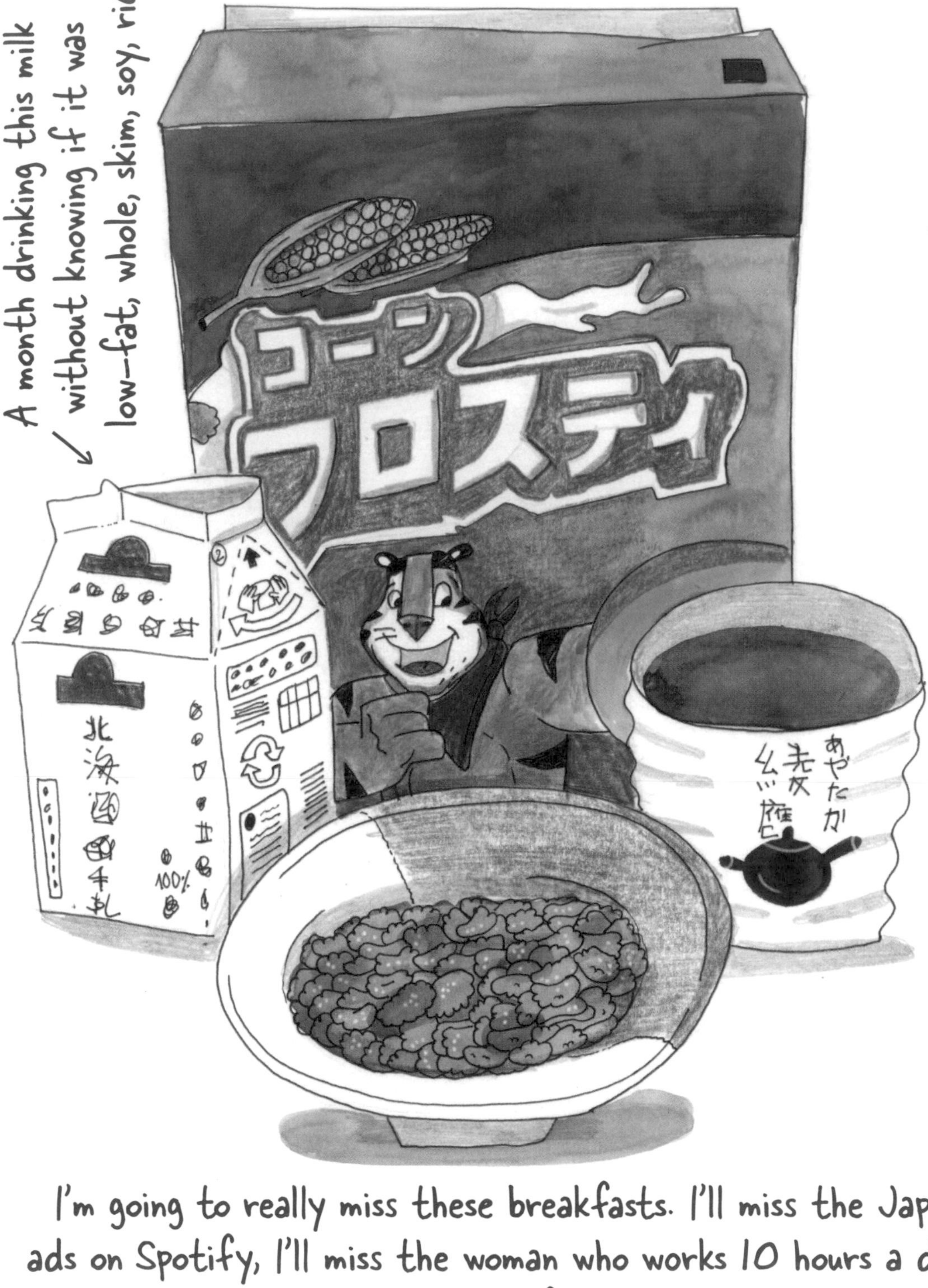
コーン
フロスティ
100%
あやたか

This cup is coming with me. I'll fill it with pencils, and when I look at it I'll remember my solitary breakfasts.

I'm going to really miss these breakfasts. I'll miss the Japanese ads on Spotify, I'll miss the woman who works 10 hours a day opposite my window, but most of all I'll miss the strange mix of <u>loneliness and freedom</u>.

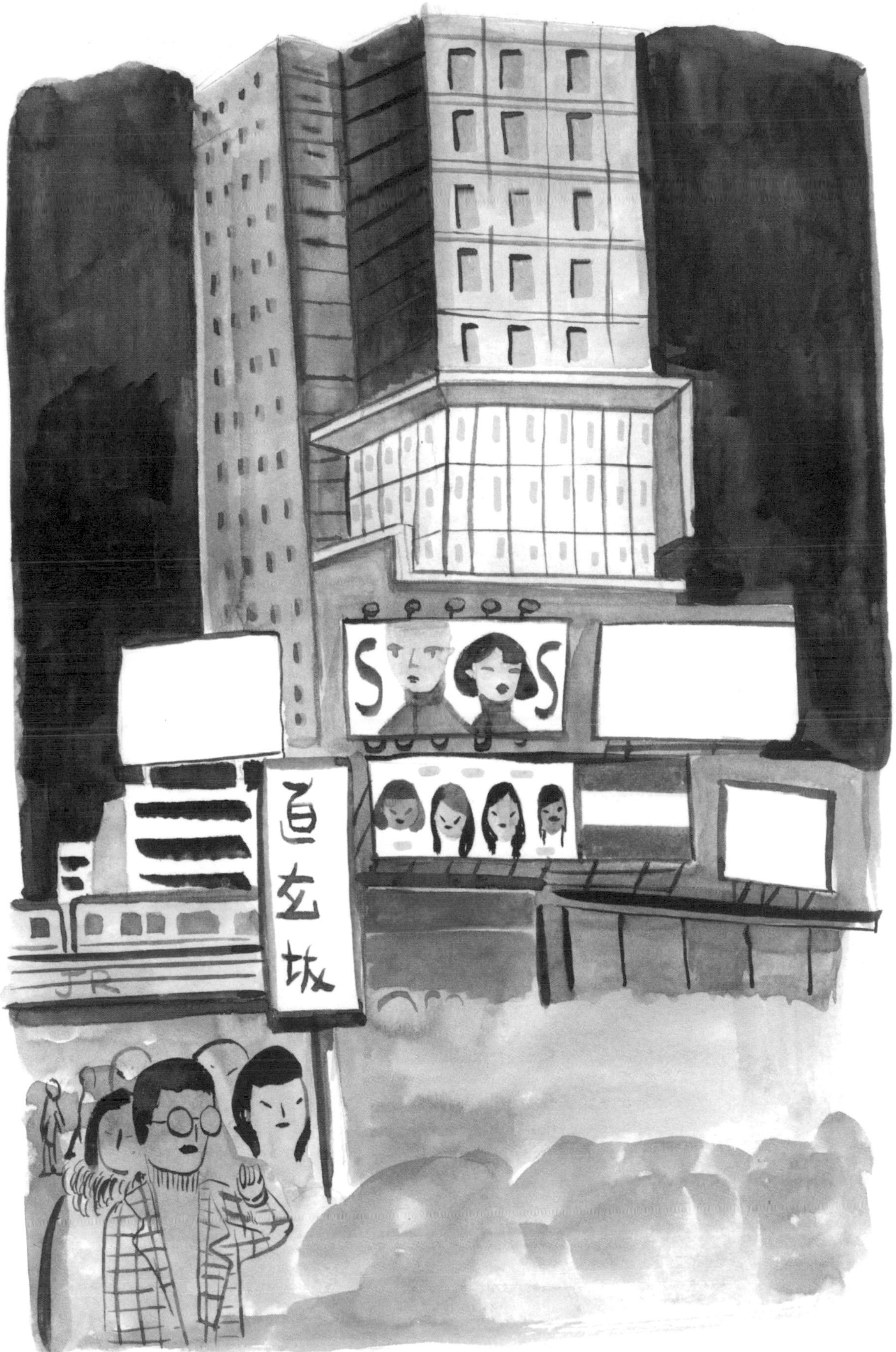
S
S
道玄坂
JR

14 ~~FEB.~~ 2017
MARCH!!

KINTSUGI is an artisanal technique using lacquer mixed with gold to repair cracks in ceramics. The golden seams made (and make) evident the passage of time. As if to display the scars with pride, demonstrating how much stronger they are now.

↙ The gold cracks make the piece prettier and more valuable than when it was intact.

This technique is the perfect metaphor for a certain philosophy of life: Resist.
Take the blows and face adversity by becoming stronger.
SHOW OFF whatever kind of SCARS you have, and accept that time passes.

Love your imperfections.

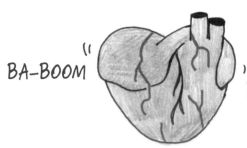

BA-BOOM " " BA-BOOM

One more reason why Japan is incredible.

Life is what causes us to crack little by little. We shouldn't just live with our scars; we need to be aware that they've led us to where we are.

There isn't just one path, there are many. Full of potholes, falls taken, blows that leave bruises.

The KINTSUGI technique falls within the WABI SABI aesthetic/philosophy.

♡

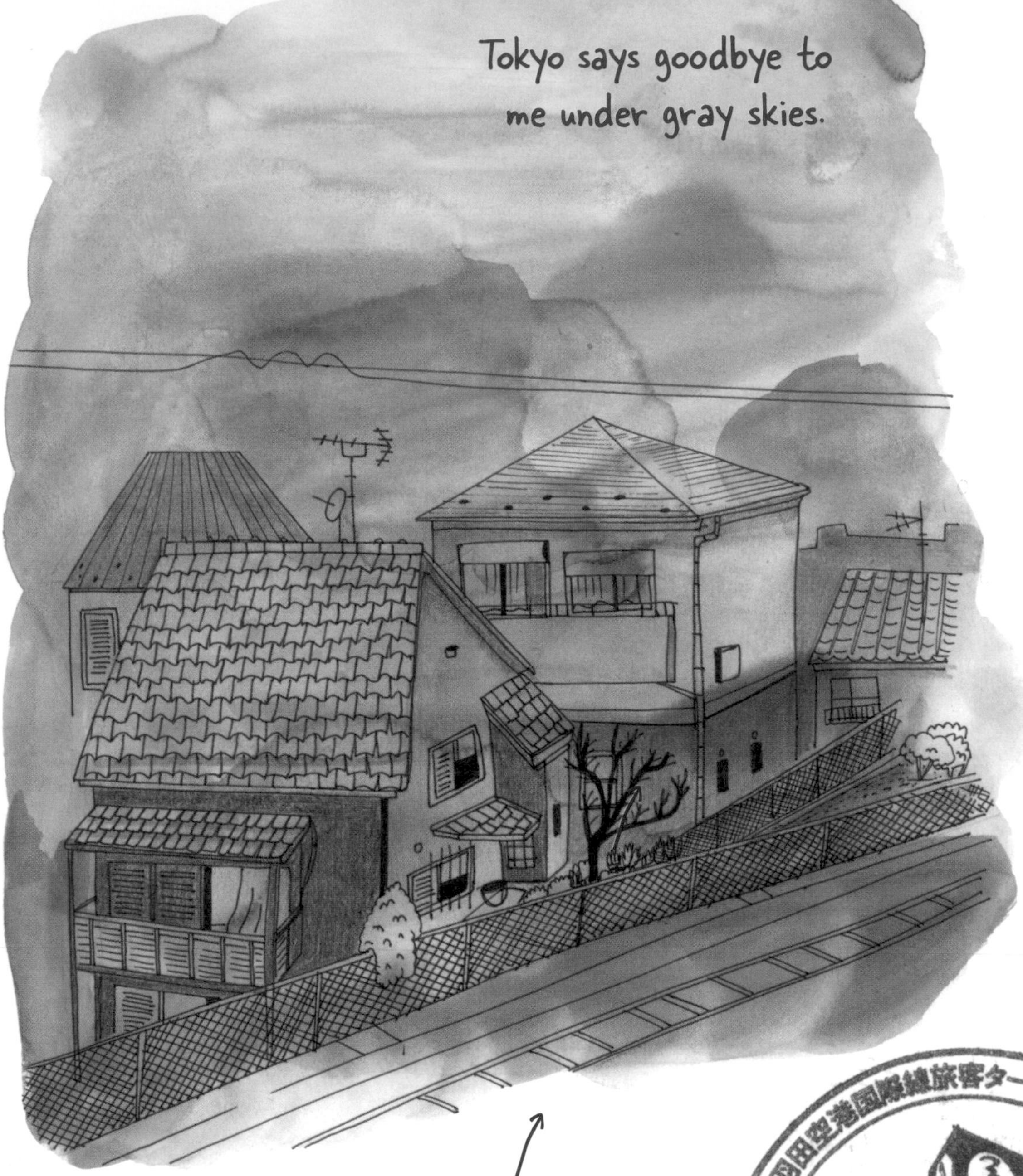
Tokyo says goodbye to
me under gray skies.

Residential neighborhood between Matsudo and Tokyo on the Jōban line, 6:15 a.m.

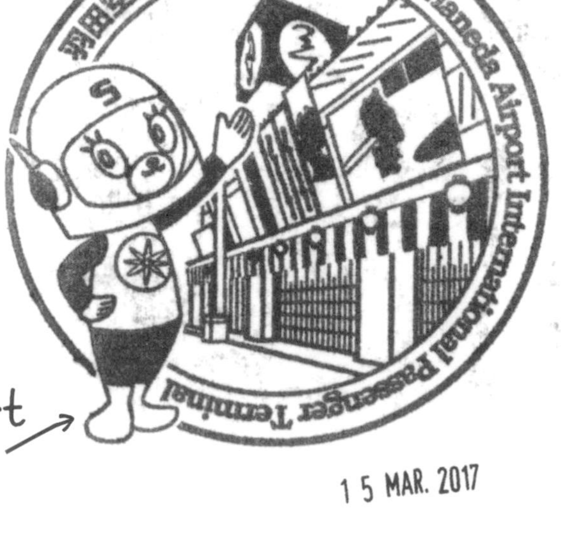
羽田空港国際線旅客ターミナル Haneda Airport International Passenger Terminal

Haneda Airport eki stamp.

1 5 MAR. 2017

ABOUT TUTTLE
"Books to Span the East and West"

Our core mission at Tuttle Publishing is to create books that bring people together one page at a time. Tuttle was founded in 1832 in the small New England town of Rutland, Vermont (U.S.A.) Our fundamental values remain as strong today as they were then—to publish best-in-class books informing the English-speaking world about the countries and peoples of Asia. The world has become a smaller place today and Asia's economic, cultural and political influence has expanded, yet the need for meaningful dialogue and information about this diverse region has never been greater. Since 1948, Tuttle has been a leader in publishing books on the cultures, arts, cuisines, languages and literatures of Asia. Our authors and photographers have won numerous awards and Tuttle has published thousands of books on subjects ranging from martial arts to paper crafts. We welcome you to explore the wealth of information available on Asia at www.tuttlepublishing.com.

Published by Tuttle Publishing, an imprint of Periplus Editions (HK) Ltd.
www.tuttlepublishing.com

First edition published as *Wabi Sabi: Un mes en Japón*, by Editorial Planeta, S.A.
Copyright © 2018, Amaia Arrazola
www.amaiaarrazola.com
Lunwerg is an imprint of Editorial Planeta, S A
Avenida Diagonal, 662–664–08034 / Calle Josefa Valcárcel, 42–28027 Madrid
lunwerg@lunwerg.com / www.lunwerg.com

Library of Congress Cataloging-in-Publication Data in Process

ISBN 978-4-8053-1536-1

Distributed by

North America, Latin America & Europe
Tuttle Publishing
364 Innovation Drive
North Clarendon, VT 05759-9436 U.S.A.
Tel: 1 (802) 773-8930
Fax: 1 (802) 773-6993
info@tuttlepublishing.com
www.tuttlepublishing.com

Japan
Tuttle Publishing
Yaekari Building, 3rd Floor
5-4-12 Osaki
Shinagawa-ku
Tokyo 141 0032
Tel: (81) 3 5437-0171
Fax: (81) 3 5437-0755
tuttle-sales@gol.com

Asia Pacific
Berkeley Books Pte. Ltd.
3 Kallang Sector #04-01
Singapore 349278
Tel: (65) 6741 2178
Fax: (65) 6741 2179
inquiries@periplus.com.sg
www.periplus.com

First edition
22 21 20 19   10 9 8 7 6 5 4 3 2 1   1404EP

Printed in Hong Kong

For Colmillo, the monster killer

Thank you to the Paradise AIR people for awarding me the residency.
Thanks to all of you who have put up with me while this book was being put together.
   (To you, Flinks.)
Special thanks to Itzi for her company, and to my mother for the watercolors.

I went to Japan on February 15, 2017. The Spanish edition of this book was printed on February 14, 2018.
   One year. A closed cycle.
I guess I can paint in the eye of my daruma now.